On Creative Writing

On Creative Writing

edited by PAUL ENGLE

 E. P. DUTTON & CO., INC.
New York ~ 1964

"The Writer on Writing" by Paul Engle appeared under the title "Salt Crystals, Spider Webs, and Words" in the *Saturday Review* (March 21, 1964). "The Novelist as Meddler" by George P. Elliott appeared in the *Virginia Quarterly Review* (Winter 1964).

COPYRIGHTS FROM WHICH PERMISSION TO QUOTE
HAS BEEN GRANTED:

"Musée des Beaux Arts" from *The Collected Poetry of W. H. Auden*. Reprinted by permission of Random House, Inc. Copyright 1940 by W. H. Auden.

"Lauds" from *The Shield of Achilles* by W. H. Auden. Reprinted by permission of Random House, Inc. Copyright © 1955 by W. H. Auden.

"Equal in Paris" from *Notes of a Native Son* by James Baldwin. Reprinted by permission of the Beacon Press. Copyright © 1955 by James Baldwin.

"All That Fall" from *Krapp's Last Tape and Other Dramatic Pieces* by Samuel Beckett. Reprinted by permission of Grove Press, Inc. Copyright © 1957 by Samuel Beckett and copyright © 1958, 1959, 1960 by Grove Press, Inc.

"Sorrow Rides a Fast Horse" by Dorothy Gilman Butters. Reprinted by permission of Brandt & Brandt. Copyright © 1962 by The Curtis Publishing Company.

Art and Reality by Joyce Cary. Reprinted by permission of Harper & Row, Publishers. Copyright © 1958 by Arthur Lucius Michael Cary and David Alexander Ogilvie, executors of Joyce Cary's estate.

"The Wine Menagerie" from *The Collected Poems of Hart Crane*. Reprinted by permission of Liveright, Publishers, N.Y. Copyright © 1961 by Liveright Publishing Corp.

"Missing Dates" from *Collected Poems of William Empson*. Reprinted by permission of Harcourt, Brace & World, Inc. Copyright 1935, 1940, 1949 by William Empson.

"The Goddess" by Thom Gunn. Reprinted by permission of the author.

DEDICATION

One of the powerful themes of literature in the twentieth century has been the alienation of the writer from his times and his country because he felt that he had no home there.

This book is dedicated to a heartening variety of individuals, foundations, and corporations who have refused to believe that this must be true. In recent years they have given funds to the Program in Creative Writing at the University of Iowa, so that young writers from all regions of the USA and many areas of the earth could come here and make an international community of the imagination. In this congenial place they have worked with established writers at the problems described in this book. Such generosity has an imaginativeness similar to that of the talents it has helped.

With the aid of such funds, these young writers have been recognized by objective judgments far out of Iowa City: The Pulitzer Prize for Poetry, The National Book Award for Poetry, The National Book Award for Fiction, the Lamont Award of the Academy of American Poets (twice), The Yale Series of Younger Poets (twice), The Literary Guild, The Atlantic Monthly "First" Short Story Award, the annual prizes for writing in the Philippines, The Newdigate Poetry Prize at Oxford University.

This suggests that writing talent can be found, and that it can be helped to help itself, which is the purpose of this book. It also suggests that, in an open society such as ours, writer, businessman, and university can join to make an environment which is useful to the writer, friendly for the businessman, and healthy for the university. The following believed this:

Northern Natural Gas Company of Omaha; Reader's Digest
Foundation; The Fisher Foundation of Mashalltown, Iowa; W.
Averell Harriman of Washington, D.C.; The Maytag Co. Founda-
tion, Newton, Iowa; U.S. Steel Foundation; the John D. Rocke-
feller III Fund; Time Inc.; The Louis W. and Maud Hill Family
Foundation of St. Paul; The Cowles Charitable Trust; The New
York Foundation; The Fred Maytag Family Foundation; Quaker
Oats Co.; Amana Refrigeration; Gardner Cowles, Jr.; Miss Lillian
Gish; H. J. Sobiloff, New York; Mrs. John P. Marquand; *Esquire*;
J. Patrick Lannan, Chicago; The Robert R. McCormick Founda-
tion; Mrs. Loyal L. Minor, Mason City, Iowa; Mr. Joseph Rosen-
field, Mr. Ed Burchette, and Iowa Power and Light Co., all of Des
Moines; WMT-TV and Radio, Iowa Electric Light and Power Co.,
Iowa Manufacturing Co., Merchants National Bank, Iowa Steel and
Iron Works, May Drug Co., John B. Turner and Sons, and Iowa
National Mutual Insurance Co., all of Cedar Rapids, Iowa, that
remarkable city.

CONTENTS

A WARNING TO THE READER

Do not read this book if you believe that writing is fun, fun, fun, or if you have a deeper interest in making a career as a writer than you do in the turmoil of the curious, doomed, and lovely human race, or if you think that writing is a butterfly which, if you merely lift up your hand, will float down and settle on a finger.

But do read this book if you believe in the beauties of the often-used wastebasket, in the use of the intelligence as well as of the intuition, and in the painfully acquired experience of writers who have proved that they know how to arrange those puzzling words on a page to make a form.

Every chapter of this volume was written by a practicing writer who is in the midst of solving the same problems which he discusses for your sake. He has tried to look at the literary form which he uses every day, examine its teeth to see what gives it bite, its legs to see what makes it run, and its eyes to see what life there is in it. He has, in brief, tried to be very practical about the imagination.

This book should be read along with your own writing. Read the chapter on whichever of the various forms interests you most, then read your own manuscript to see whether any of the advice could be immediately applied to you; next, read the examples at the end of each chapter to see how the writer applied his chapter to them. Remember, criticism is not simply a fiendish attack on a book, but a constant part of the writer's job, beginning with his rejection of one concept in favor of another, one image, one phrase, rather than others.

In some places, "creative writing" is a dirty expression. This book believes that it is a decent phrase, meaning, quite simply, writing to which something new has been added. It tries to tell you ways of finding and saying the new. Use it to touch the stone of your talent.

PAUL ENGLE

On Creative Writing

The Writer on Writing

PAUL ENGLE

Writing is like making love—it is astonishing how far pure instinct (if it really is pure) will carry you. It is also true of both these lyrical forms of expression that a few things consciously learned will push toward perfection what might otherwise be an ordinary act.

It is the purpose of this book to recognize that truth.

And yet can writing actually be taught? Is there much more you can give to a beginner beyond Flaubert's no-nonsense advice of a kiss on the brow and a kick on the behind?

In pointing out that a writer crystallizes a concept, as when he endows a woman with qualities she simply does not have, Stendahl produced an image which, however little it flatters the ladies, does dramatize the process by which persuasive words can turn a dull object into something glittering and gay. He observes that a dead branch, dark and ugly, if left overnight in the salt mines of Salzburg, will be covered with crystals and next day will glitter in the sunlight. (Did Stendhal have in mind a few ladies of doubtful feature whom he would have liked to put away in salt mines?)

This image of the salt crystals on the branch wisely and attractively illustrates what the writer does with that curious and secret substance called his "material." What writer has not been stopped by an eager-eyed and bushy-tailed person who cries out despairingly, "I've got the greatest material for a book, if I could just *write!*"

The first and most important point about writing is that there is no such thing as material by itself, apart from the way in which a person sees it, feels toward it, and is able to give it organized form and an expression in words. For a writer, the form is a part of the content, affecting it, realizing it. A man may go through the most dramatic and horrible experiences in war, but actually draw out of them less "material" for writing than shy Emily Dickinson in the second-floor room of an Amherst house lowering notes in baskets out the window and thinking gently of death, or even (biographers speculate) of a man she knew but little, whom she might never see again.

Henry James wrote of experience that it is "an immense sensibility, a kind of huge spider-web of the finest silken threads suspended in the chamber of consciousness, and catching every airborne particle in its tissue. It is the very atmosphere of the mind." This is crucial, for it is not what happens in the outside world which is of absolute significance, but what happens to the external event when it is discovered, and then ordered, by the internal power of mind. James goes on to speak then of the creative aspect: "and when the mind is imaginative ... it takes to itself the faintest hints of life, it converts the very pulses of the air into revelations."

By experience, then, being a writer does not mean having adventures. In answering a critic who had complained about the novel that it is impossible to have one without bold action, James protested, "Why without adventure, more than without matrimony, or celibacy, or parturition, or cholera ... ?"

Anything is suitable for fiction, which is not a record of incidents happening *to* men and women, but of the response they make within themselves to the incidents. This is because fiction deals with character, which determines action, and thus actions illustrate character. The conduct of a man in a shouting ring, fighting an enraged bull, and the soft wave of a woman's hand are equally moving and suitable.

Experience is not fixed, but varies with the power of perception in the man or woman participating in it. During World War II, experiments at Ohio State University proved that air force applicants were using their eyes normally at around twenty per cent of their real capacity. Heightening the ability to perceive could be, for a pilot in war, a matter of life and death, as he had to discriminate rapidly the shape and identity of an object moving at great speed through the sky.

It is necessary for anyone wanting to be a writer to develop just that sort of intensified perception about human life. Once again, Henry James made the great remark. Recognizing that a young writer should always base his work on his own proved experience, but that before he could do this he must learn to bring into his consciousness as much and as heightened experience as possible, James advised: "Try to be one of the people on whom nothing is lost!"

To demonstrate what he meant by not losing any part of any experience, James cited an example of an English woman novelist who had been praised for writing in such an insightful way about young Protestants in France. On being asked how she had learned so much about these rather scarce people, she replied that only once had she even seen Protestants in France, and then she had not spoken to them. Walking up a staircase in Paris, she passed an open door and saw inside a room the family of a pastor sitting around a table just after dinner.

James then writes: "The glimpse made a picture; it lasted only a moment, but that moment was experience. She had got her direct personal impression, and she turned out her type. She knew what youth was, and what Protestantism; she also had the advantage of having seen what it was to be French, so that she converted these ideas into a concrete image and produced a reality. Above all, however, she was blessed with the faculty which when you give it an inch takes an ell, and which for the artist is a much greater source of strength than any accident of residence or of place in the social scale."

A million Frenchmen may walk down a Paris street (it might be only ten thousand, but being French they would *seem* like a million) and, turning a corner, forget the place, but Toulouse-Lautrec walking down the same street would see, with his shrewd eye, and remember, with his artist's force of retention, not bricks but visions. It is in this way that the imagination works not only on the stuff which is stored in the mind, but also on the very act of experiencing. Like the pilot, the writer must see faster and more completely than the ordinary viewer of life.

Out of his practical skills in the writing of fiction, James described the process of the writer using his experience. "The power to guess the unseen from the seen," he said, "to trace the implication of things, to judge the whole piece by the pattern, the condition of feeling life in general so completely that you are well on your way to knowing any particular corner of it—this cluster of gifts may almost be said to constitute experience, and they occur in country and in town, and in the most differing stages of education. If experience consists of impressions, it may be said that impressions *are* experience, just as (have we not seen it?) they are the very air we breathe."

This is final wisdom about writing. The writer, when given an inch, takes an ell. Remember that an ell is forty-five inches. If that is the degree of heightening, then the eye of the writer must look at life with forty-five times as much perception. That is a marvelous degree of intensity, and in particular when it comes from the author of *Portrait of a Lady*—a book in which, although it concerns the relationship between a man and a woman, it has been remarked that there is only one kiss, and the heroine, poor thing, did not enjoy it.

But some will argue: writing, like all art, is intuitive, and any intrusion of the reason will destroy the lovely, natural thing. This is dead wrong. It reduces writing to the level of a child babbling without regard to the shape of what he is saying. It would be, indeed, so much like the uninhibited confessions from the psychiatrist's couch, sodium amytal cheerfully flowing through the veins and breaking down shyness, that it would seem proper to give inhibition-removing drugs to the writer. He could sit there gaily listening to the rustlings of his unconscious. And of course the hallucinatory state would be the most creative of all.

It is quite possible that some good things could be thus spontaneously created. I met in India people who could induce visions. Yet surely the great and structured works of writing are done with the intelligence playing over against the intuition, each bracing the other, the mind giving form and sense, the intuition giving immediacy of impression, the stored-up memory, the deeply instinctive phrase.

To say that writing comes only from the intuition is to belittle it as coming from one narrow aspect of our lives alone. The opposite is true. The total life of the writer is the source of his work. All of these go into his writing, in varying quantities: the senses, as of taste and touch, the rate of metabolism, the blood pressure, the digestion, the body temperature, the memory of things past, perhaps going back to the childhood not only of the writer but of the race itself, the liveliness and alertness of the brain, previous reading of books, shrewdness of insight into human character, the libido, the ear for the sound of language.

The writer, therefore, must not only have a more than ordinary capacity for life, and the power to retain what he experiences in a readily available memory, he must also have an astonishing degree of self-knowledge. Unless he is aware of his material, he cannot use it, save for the always present quantity which flows up from the deep well of the unconscious recollection. Without access to knowledge of self, the writer can make dreams but not art. As Dr. Lawrence S. Kubie says, without self-knowledge, "We can have the neurotic raw material of literature, but not mature literature. We can have no adults, but only aging children who are armed with words."

By self-knowledge I do not mean self-expression. Although all good writing always bears the individual mark, sound, motion of the writer, he is not trying to put his own self into words, but to create a piece of writing. Often, the less of his own self involved or expressed, the better. His own personality ought to be dissolved into the images or characters of his book. The writer is offering us not reality, but his reaction to whatever reality he has experienced.

Yet the ego is important. It must be that within the creative person there is a constant tension between an awareness of the reality around him, a thrusting up of the unconscious life and its memory, and the drive of the ego toward controlling these in a form which also heightens them. These are crude terms to describe subtle conditions, but the creation of any art is one of the most complex of human activities, involving every animal and human quality. The ego must shape the mortal impulses. It is here that something can indeed be taught about writing, for it is in this shaping that the individual's private events are turned into public forms. It is here that writing becomes an art, and not merely a report on experience, and this is true of the best reporting.

The ego is individual. A thousand men looking at the same object will see a thousand different objects. How many people in 1827 knew about the action brought in the Criminal Court of Grenoble against a young man named Antoine Berthet, accused of murder and pleading guilty, with the accused himself writing to the Public Prosecutor, "my wish is that I may be condemned tomorrow, and be led out to execution on the day following. . . . I have already found life so hateful, that you, by your prolonged proceedings, can make it no more odious. Let me no longer be compelled to breathe the air of corruption." This took place in the Department of Isère. A writer of the time, not very well known, using the name of Stendhal, was a native of Isère. His real name was Henri Beyle; he had fought with Napoleon in Italy, Germany, France, Russia. His usefulness here is that, of all the citizens of France in the dark and cheapened years of the Restoration of a monarchy which had all the characteristics of a vulgar regime and few of an authentic kingliness, he alone wrote a novel based on the life of that pathetic Antoine Berthet. Why? And in what way is Stendhal's novel *The Red and the Black* a piece of literature and not simply an account of a man murdering a woman who had been his lover?

Antoine Berthet was the son of a blacksmith in a small village. A bright young man, he had been instructed by the local priest, who had found him, when he was nineteen, a position as tutor in the family of an industrialist named Michoud. It seems certain that he made love to Mme. Michoud, and was later fired by M. Michoud. After an unsuccessful attempt to become a student for the priesthood, Berthet again took a job as tutor in a family, and was again fired, on the ground that he had made passionate advances to a daughter of the family. His frustration turned into a conviction that Mme. Michoud was to blame. One Sunday in the village church, while Mme. Michoud had her head bowed during the celebration of the Mass, Berthet shot her in the back, and then tried to commit suicide. Neither died. During the trial, Berthet's head was wrapped in bandages. He begged not for forgiveness but for death.

From this pathetic event the villagers made gossip, but Stendhal made a novel, yet he shared with them an identical knowledge of the incidents, the place, the men and women involved. It seems obvious to us, in another century and with the lapse of many disenchanting years, that Stendhal must have seen in Berthet an image of his own youth, struggling to enter a world more romantic and grander than the one into which he was born, and suffering for a sad and ironic reason: the very intelligence which gave him access to that world also gave him a terrible resentment at not being wholly accepted by it. The intensity of his bitterness came naturally from the intensity of his mind and emotions, and led to the violent action of an attempted murder and suicide.

Reading about this miserable sequence of events was an experience shared by a good many Frenchmen in 1827, but only Stendhal made great literature from it. His creative imagination experienced that story as well as his eyes. He shaped his own work of art out of a newspaper reporter's work. What mattered was not the dreary recital of a provincial crime, but the imaginative energies which the events released in a man of high verbal talent, who saw through them to the essential scene as it related to his own life, and gave to that human turbulence a form more living than the men and women who endured it.

It may well be that the substance of a writer's work comes from whatever in his observation he recognizes (perhaps without knowing the recognition) as a shred, an image, a mockery, a vision, of his own life. Myriads of men have almost identical experiences, and have very similar emotional reactions to them. It is the peculiar power of writing that it can shape those feelings into a form which will, in turn, produce the most moving feelings in other men. How many boys have played around greenhouses? Swarms. But how many, on growing up, have put their feelings about that place into powerful poetry? Only Theodore Roethke (died, 1963). His account is proof.

Roethke asks what does it matter that he grew up in and around a beautiful greenhouse, hated school, worked in a pickle factory, lived sometimes quietly and sometimes foolishly and violently, and meant almost nothing to the people of his own state, the man in the street, but passionately desired their regard.

"All such details, and others like them," Roethke comments, "seem particularly trivial and vulgar in my case because I have tried to put down in poems, as barely and honestly as possible, symbolically, what few nuggets of observation and, let us hope, spiritual wisdom I have managed to seize upon in the course of a conventional albeit sometimes disordered existence. I have tried to transmute and purify my 'life,' the sense of being defiled by it in both small and formal and somewhat blunt short poems, and, latterly, in longer poems which try in their rhythms to catch the very movement of the mind itself, to trace the spiritual history of a protagonist (not 'I' personally) of all haunted and harried men; to make in this series (now probably finished) a true and not arbitrary order which will permit many ranges of feeling, including humor. . . ."

And then he says in verse:

> My heart sways with the world.
> I am that final thing,
> A man learning to sing.

Although this may suggest a self-consciousness not shared by all poets, it is further evidence of that deep need for self-knowledge which is a strength and a source. Roethke knew *what* he was trying to do in those moving and often tortured poems, and this awareness, far from inhibiting the imaginative freedom of the verse, enriched it. The cool mind, curiously enough, it seems, really can express a warm feeling.

Once the writer has a sense of his experience, and of his own self, and this must be disenchanted, without illusion, tough-minded about his own weakness and vulgarity, what else can he possibly learn? What can he *do* to make his writing better, assuming that he is not trapped in the conviction that writing is a wholly automatic outburst from underground?

He can examine the knowledge of their own writing habits as great men have made it available. It is odd the things writers have done. The German poet Schiller used to keep rotting apples under the lid of his desk because their smell helped him write. Pilots on the river at Rouen would see the light in Flaubert's study very late at night as he utterly shut himself away from the world to worry two pages of prose a week into the ruthlessly purified and perfected shape he demanded. Why this enormous care? The old wisecrack says that a physician who fails can always bury his patient out of sight. Frank Lloyd Wright remarked that an architect who fails can at least urge his client to plant vines. The writer, however, once his work is in print, can do nothing. There the text is, black on the page, and any errors and any ugliness will be there forever. There are rare exceptions, of course, like William Butler Yeats, who in his old age, with that marvelous lyrical mind hardened by the criticism of others, went back to the poems of his youth and cut out much of the sentimentality, the soft, vague language.

Reticent as always, William Faulkner said that the tools of the writer's trade are paper, tobacco, food, and whiskey. Of these, the most dangerous is not tobacco or whiskey (and writers are famous for abusing them) but paper. One of the most terrifying sights is that waiting, threatening, blank sheet. Its force is proved by the Japanese writer who, after much success, could not, for a long time, push ahead with his writing. One autumn (this is a true story) he disappeared. The next spring his body was found, after the snow had melted, high up in the mountains. Pinned to his jacket was a note only the suffering writer could have written: "I have done this because I could no longer endure the sight of the empty page."

All those writers who have commented on their craft agree that a work of art is work. How could the joining of passion and idea in slippery words be anything but a labor? That first really modern novel, *Madame Bovary,* was composed by Gustave Flaubert with the deliberation of a medieval monk cutting the Lord's Prayer on the head of a pin. The French novelist could write quickly and fluently, as his early books and his lively letters show, but he would never give up a sentence until it was beyond improving. To get his description of the landscape correct, he sat all day on a balcony looking through pieces of different colored glass in order to note the changes in shape of fields and roads and trees hour by hour.

Never was a writer more emotionally involved with what he was writing than Flaubert. When he described Emma Bovary poisoning herself, he was so moved that he could taste arsenic on his own tongue and felt so poisoned himself that he vomited his dinner. And yet when he finally finished that scene, he had engineered it onto the page with an almost fanatical control. Once again, the writer's talent had produced an immortal passage out of a passionate deliberation.

Flaubert would begin a single paragraph by setting down its general idea, with perhaps a few images (a risk always, for he had a brilliant image-making faculty; he wrote that he was devoured by metaphors as by vermin and spent his time crushing them). Then he wrote a first draft, reading it aloud for sound and sense (always read any sort of text out loud: the surest way to catch the feeble phrase, the trite adjective, the outworn image, the dull rhythm, the phony speech). Then he would rewrite, again and again, as a fine craftsman polishes over and over the same increasingly brilliant piece of maple or mahogany. Every word which did not act with energy was thrown away, until the paragraph was lean, tough, expressive. *Madame Bovary's* final version was written on 1,788 pages, but these were only the latest of many times that number of pages actually written. At times, fifteen or twenty pages would be reduced to four. Thus, when Flaubert said that he spent a week over two pages, he meant over the two finally perfected pages out of many more.

Flaubert may be the only man in history who told his girl friend, "You should write more coldly." This was a part of his advice that "We must be on our guard against that kind of intellectual overheating called inspiration, which often consists more largely of nervous emotion than of muscular strength . . . my brow is burning, sentences keep rushing into my head. . . . Instead of one idea I have six, and where the most simple type of exposition is called for I find myself writing similes and metaphors. I could keep going until tomorrow noon without fatigue." And yet he could follow such an outburst with the blunt advice, brief, wise, but taking most writers a lifetime to learn: "Everything should be done coldly, with poise." When putting down the word "hysterics" one day he was so carried away that he bellowed loudly, and felt so sharply what Emma Bovary was going through that he was afraid of having hysterics himself.

Can it be that the French, more than any other people, are able to balance heat and cold, desire and deliberation, and make a single intense but controlled utterance? The modern poet Paul Valéry wrote that poetry must be a holiday of the mind, and then said, with greater calm, that when he writes, "I proceed like a surgeon who sterilizes his hands and prepares the area to be operated on . . . clearing up the verbal situation."

The English seem more practical, if a little less dedicated to perfection. The novelist Joyce Cary described his process thus: "A finished book of mine starts usually perhaps ten years before as a character sketch and a bit of description; it goes on to an incident or so, it gathers subsidiary characters, and then perhaps I grow interested in it, and set out to give it form as a book. I sketch a plan; I may write the end, the middle and the beginning and very often just in this order. That is, I decide how and where the book shall end, which is just as important to a book as to a play, and then I ask myself where are the most difficult turns in the book. Then I may write one of these difficult passages to see if it is viable . . . . I may stop there. But if it does work, then I may devise a beginning and finish the book."

How contrary to the old notion of inspiration to find Cary devising a beginning of a novel of which he has written bits in various parts and without order. This is evidence that what the writer is really doing is not so much writing a poem or play or story which he has firmly in mind, but rather is using his writing to discover what it truly is he is trying to say. Often he will not know until the final revision of the last page what he had been trying to do from the start.

One would hardly guess the zest and liveliness of Chekhov's mind if he had seen only a moody performance of *The Sea Gull*. Commenting on the new "decadent" writers, Chekhov noted, "they're a lot of strong, healthy young men: what they need is to be sentenced to a few months hard labor! This new-art business is just a pack of nonsense. . . . There's nothing new in art except talent." Chekhov constantly wrote subjects for stories in moments taken from his medical practice. ("Medicine is my lawful wife, literature my mistress. When I am tired of the one, I spend a night with the other.") One notebook contained a hundred entries. Some of these are diverting: A building contractor of great frugality loathed paying repair bills. When he married, he chose an exceptionally healthy woman so that he would have no repair bills with her.

A writer should be as objective as a chemist, he commented, and have nothing to do with the subjective approach which most of us make in our everyday lives. And when he wrote that the writer should never sit down to his work until he felt cold as ice, he was remarkably like Flaubert. Any reader of Chekhov's short stories will be amazed to find how very simple were the original notes for two of the finest. "A cab-driver who has just lost his son, has to go on working just the same. He tries to speak of his grief to his fares, but finds only indifference." Another equally famous story began with three little sentences: "Some officers on manoeuvres are invited to a house where there are several young women. One of them kisses one of the officers, a shy and reserved young man, in the dark. He looks for her, but in vain." These are the plain, experienced reality, but the stories written out of them are the heightened over-reality.

Poor Chekhov, tending the sick with his own fatal illness corrupting his lungs. When he died in Germany, his coffin was taken to Moscow in a baggage car marked "Oysters." Yet he never allowed a scrap of self-pity to interfere with the absolute integrity of his dedication to writing. "My own experience is that once a story has been written, one has to cross out the beginning and the end. It is there that we authors do most of our lying. . . . One must always tear up the first half. I mean that seriously. Young writers begin by, as one says, 'placing the story'—whereas the reader ought, on the contrary, to be able to grasp what it is all about by the way it is told, without any explanations from the author, from the conversation and the actions of the characters. . . . One must ruthlessly suppress everything that is not concerned with the subject. If, in the first chapter, you say there is a gun hanging on the wall, you should make quite sure that it is going to be used further on in the story."

Chekhov felt strongly the distinction between direct reality as it is lived and the imagined reality of art. In 1898 he went to a rehearsal of *The Sea Gull* at the Moscow Art Theatre and was told by an actor that backstage there would be sounds of frogs croaking, grasshoppers scraping, and dogs barking. He asked why, and was told this would be realistic. But the theater is not realism, it is art, he argued. If you put a real nose into a painting of a face, the nose will be realistic but the picture will be ruined. You do not use fiction to resolve the existence of God; you exhibit characters conducting lives, and show the way in which they discuss God.

Similarly Tolstoy remarked that *Anna Karenina,* that massive novel, was just a simple story about a married woman who falls in love with an officer. This sort of reducing of any piece of writing to its essence is a part of that control over material which is indispensable to the practicing writer. Such definition comes out of enormous and confusing reaches of experience. No one has more imaginatively stated the mysterious and at the same time real nature of human existence than Virginia Woolf when she wrote that "Life is a luminous halo, a semi-transparent envelope surrounding us from the beginning."

Virginia Woolf also wrote a paragraph defining the nature of this envelope more precisely. "Examine for a moment an ordinary mind on an ordinary day. The mind receives myriad impressions—trivial, fantastic, evanescent, or engraved with the sharpness of steel. From all sides they come, an incessant shower of innumerable atoms; and as they fall, as they shape themselves into the life of Monday or Tuesday, the accent falls differently from of old; the moment of importance came not here but there; so that, if the writer were a freeman and not a slave, if he could write what he chose, not what he must, if he could base his work upon his own feeling and not upon convention, there would be no plot, no comedy, no tragedy, no love interest or catastrophe in the accepted style."

The simple, often grunt-like puffs of air which we call words must be used by the writer with such skill that they can bring to a reader, who cannot even hear whatever tone of voice the writer would give them, a form and sense which will move him. This is by no means as easy as lifting bricks all day or breaking stone. Flaubert testifies to that: "My head reels and my throat aches with chasing after, slogging over, delving into, turning round, groping after, and bellowing, in a hundred thousand different ways, a sentence that I've at last finished. It's good. . . ." One sentence!

No one knew the tortures, or the necessity, for this sort of harsh self-discipline better than that most exuberant and debauched poet, Baudelaire. In his *Flowers of Evil*, he wrote, there was a cold and sinister beauty. How did that beauty happen? This first of the Beatniks differed from these later brothers not in his contempt for the vulgarity of middle-class life, nor in his concern for the flaunting immorality which repudiated that life, but in his attitude toward his art. Yearning to have his book appear so that it could prove to his mother, his formidable stepfather General Aupick, and his friends, that he was an authentic poet, he nevertheless kept the printer waiting several months while he revised a few lines into perfection. It may actually be that much writing is created into excellence, and then revised into greatness. This is true of the play, the story, the novel, the poem, the article, of whatever form men choose to make words move other men.

Form and Expression
in the Short Story

R. V. CASSILL

The most remarkable thing about the modern short story is its multiplicity of successes. If all the fine stories of the last half century were taken merely to be a reportage of the manners, the speech, the high life and low life, the psychological shallows and depths, the local color, the poverty, violence, frustration, or the unprecedented confrontations of an increasingly mobile population, even then they would amount to a documentation of inestimable value. Let no one underestimate the value of the short story as report.

Yet the miracle beyond this is that so many writers have found so many ways to organize their material into meanings that transcend reportage, so that finite encounters have very often been unfolded into the adventures of infinity. The short story has done the poetic work of journalism and the yeoman work of poetry.

Limited as it is in actual physical dimensions, overworked (or so it would seem) by a horde of practitioners, outclassed (some would say) by the stage or the big and little screens in its variety of technical resources, the short story shows no signs of being exhausted. It comes on like artesian water in a thirsty land and time.

There is hardly a master of modern fiction who has not given us short stories as famous as his novels: Lawrence's "Rocking Horse Winner," Mann's "Disorder and Early Sorrow," Joyce's "The Dead," Hemingway's "The Snows of Kilimanjaro," and Faulkner's "A Rose for Emily."

There are literally hundreds of short stories one ought to read to grasp the full delicacy and strength of the modern literary spirit. Look at the anthologies. Go to the collected stories of Frank O'Connor, Jean Stafford, George P. Elliott, J. D. Salinger, Bernard Malamud, John Updike, Mary McCarthy, Eudora Welty, Katherine Anne Porter, J. F. Powers, Hortense Calisher, Herbert Gold, Flannery O'Connor, Richard Yates, and . . . One stops the list because no listing of authors quite defines the limit of masterly work accomplished by our contemporaries.

Beyond their work there are thousands of other stories in which passion and experience have been crafted into meanings unknown before. It is not only in published stories or in those that make the anthologies that the valuable fusion of material and spirit coincides in short story form. I have read too many fine unpblished things to be tempted to measure the present art of short fiction by its best advertised segment.

Thank God, the popularity of the short story eludes the horrible definitions of popularity that would reduce us all to "a market" or the productive units of a superstate. Probably the most important thing is that stories continue to be written by amateurs and professionals in all those bright-dark, secret-public, somber-happy redoubts where the real literary life of the republic bides its time.

The avenues for publishing short fiction are far from satisfactory. A dwindling handful of big circulation commercial magazines publishes first-rate stuff. *The New Yorker* and *Esquire,* among these, deserve special citation for effort and excellence, though *The New Yorker*'s formula has aged to a cliché and *Esquire* means to *look* serious even at the cost of paying more attention to literary fashions than to merit or meaning. A perennial platoon of little magazines and literary quarterlies publishes new fiction in every issue. Without such publications, the serious story might disappear completely underground. If it did, it might not die, but something would.

The best one can say of the publishing situation is that it might change. Somehow and sometime it could become responsive to the actual capacities of American writers and readers. They might reclaim their birthright of communicating freely with each other, limited only by their talents and the brevity of their lives. In the meantime, writing and reading short stories can still be the pleasure of those who seek it hard enough. As long as the libraries are fat, as long as there are pencil, paper, and heart, we can go on learning the major and minor premises of short fiction.

Like us, Tolstoy went on learning how to write by reading. And he, who should have known if anyone ever did, thought that the Biblical story of Joseph was the finest model of storytelling in the world's literature. This is not the same as saying that the contemporary writer might learn all, or even a formidable fraction, of his art by studying the Book of Genesis. Perhaps if each of us were Tolstoy we could. But each of us has his own name, and where we learn what we need to know when we need to know it is not easily prescribed. Yet some things which may be said of the Joseph story ought to guide any writer from the time of his apprenticeship until he buries the staff of his art.

Read the Joseph story. Note this above all—that the end of the story is in the beginning. Everything that will count, that will be developed as the narrative moves on, is planted in the account of Joseph's boyhood. His authority, the "gift" that enables him to reconcile Egypt and Israel, and the homage of his brothers are all prefigured in the dreams that begin the narrative as well as in his situation as his father's favorite.

At the same time, though the end is in the beginning, it is embryonic there, hidden, enfolded, so that only the progress of time (and the parallel progress of the tale, where the time of the story re-creates in miniature the passage of years) can fully disclose it.

In the beginning Joseph's authority is mere presumption. His brothers show their good sense in resenting it. His gift is merely a difference, an eccentricity, not to be distinguished by practical minds from pretense or what they must have called in all ages *phoniness*. The homage from his common brothers occurs only in his dream, as a wish fulfillment, suggesting not so much an actually recognizable superiority to them as the younger brother's need to catch up and excel them, the immoderate goad of the late starter, which might as easily produce a criminal as a creative man.

So, because all that which will become great is, in the dawning of Joseph's story, no more than egotism and pretense, his brothers do a very natural thing when they sell him into slavery in Egypt. It serves him right. (How right, how marvelously, miraculously right this mischance serves him will be revealed only in the full development of his future. If good luck appeared instantly, or without disguise, there would be no story.)

In the second phase of the narrative we read how that which was *given* in the beginning has been altered and developed in consequence of the brothers' understandable but shortsighted revenge. Back home they could say of Joseph, with unrebuked derision, "Behold, this dreamer cometh." Of course dreams and dreamers are more trouble than they're worth for honest shepherds going about their routine lives. But in urban Egypt, where Joseph's fortunes alter precisely because he remains himself, dreams are a more viable commodity. What has been the pure offense of his difference becomes the means of his success.

Then, as the story approaches its term, as the shortsightedness of the brothers brings them first into Egypt to seek Joseph's bounty and then to his feet to ask forgiveness, the climactic moment of revelation comes. Joseph makes himself known to his brothers—but he does not exactly forgive them. To do so would be to deny the emergent meaning of what has befallen him—which, of course, is not entirely consistent with what his brothers intended when they disposed of him.

Instead of forgiving he says, "Now it was not you who sent me hither, but God." He means they were only, after all, instruments of a destiny which he is happy to claim in its entirety.

This is his personal recognition, and not every story will have a central character wise and fortunate enough to articulate the meaning of his own adventure. Further, within the conventions of modern fiction, the entire form of the story is generally shaped to deliver such thematic statements instead of entrusting them to a spokesman character. But however the theme is conveyed, I think that in every fully formed story a moment will come when we hear an echo of Joseph's words. *It was not you who sent me but God.* It was not what this or that character intended which counted, but how their acts combined with their desires and with what Hardy called the "crass casualty" of the universe—the accident of circumstance—to produce an unforeseen result.

A story is never merely an account of what happened first and what happened next. There must be a meaningful connection between events and, as they follow each other, there must be a transformation in what is expected of them. A man sets out with a treasure map, and we expect that he will either find gold or not find it. But when he comes to his treasure island we expect that he will either save his life or lose it. In the event of his saving it our expectations are again transformed. We expect him to save it at a cost he can or cannot afford. In the movement of any real story we can see this spiral of changing expectations.

Ordinarily the movements of a story originate in the human will, as when Joseph's brothers decide to sell him into slavery. The movements terminate when will is transformed into fate— when the brothers' cruelty is transformed into Joseph's good fortune. Nothing in fiction is more fundamental than these transformations. No skill with language and no wisdom in portraying reality will make up for their absence.

Remember, as a general prescription of what a story must tell, Gonzalo's speech in *The Tempest:*

> O rejoice
> Beyond a common joy! and set it down
> With gold on lasting pillars: In one voyage
> Did Claribel her husband find at Tunis
> And Ferdinand, her brother, found a wife
> Where he himself was lost, Prospero his dukedom
> In a poor isle, and all of us ourselves
> When no man was his own.

Stories tell how things are found. In one fashion or another they always tell how men find themselves, to their consternation or their satisfaction, in pursuing something else.

But when we realize that fundamentally a story depicts the transformation of a quest, still we know that some stories are better than others, quite apart from the inherent interest of this transformation. They are better in respect to the richness and depth and concreteness of their picture of life. The better stories are not necessarily produced by "born storytellers."

Some people who have a gift for storytelling turn out to be poorer writers than those whose very honesty and responsibility to their experience make it hard for them to fashion stories. Experience almost never offers itself in story form—at least not unless one has the gift for discerning the story pattern in it; and even then the people who find stories in the actual routine of life are more apt to turn into gossips than good writers. The person who finds stories ready-made generally trims away so much human complexity to find them that their remaining resemblance to life is trivial.

The good writer makes a story by adding one part of his experience to another, fitting, adjusting, tinkering, building up, until a form emerges in which both the complexity of life and the transformation of the story are equally evident. He is willing to wait until, as in Joseph's case, his handicap becomes his opportunity, to substitute for his lack of glibness in storytelling the prolonged devotion of an experimenter. He looks for the story that can emerge from the recombinations of experience that he constructs with words on paper.

Drawing a meaningful composite from the scattered corners of one's experience is not, of course, entirely a process of trial and error. It is a series of imaginative acts pyramiding into the imaginative conception of a story as a unity quite distinct from the experiences with which he started.

Such unity is something we expect of a finished story, but long before the writer himself has perceived it clearly, the initial imaginative steps of the creative act have begun in his observations of life. These observations are already in the nature of choices, discriminations that single out some facts as being richer in potential for development than others. The writer's eye skims past all the brothers and comes to rest on Joseph's many-colored coat. It doesn't matter that the brothers are as real and as human as Joseph himself. They lack that flash of significant color and they will not be chosen.

The writer may not know in the beginning *why* his eye lights on Joseph and finds him interesting, quite in advance of knowing the story in which he may figure. In the beginning it is enough for the writer to trust his interest, for it is this interest and not the objective fact that will be the real source of his story. The story will come out of him. The objective world only catches a thread in him and begins to unravel it, and what we call the choice of a subject is more apt to be a matter of the subject choosing some potential in the writer and giving it a chance to be born. At any rate the fiction writer never renounces his identity in face of what science or the law would call evidence.

In gathering his material he does not merely open a lens and record the panorama around him. Observation is not a passive occupation. It has to represent a constant synthesis of the observer's interest—all those predispositions that make him a special individual—with the color and shine of a world far too full of details ever to be reproduced in full.

At the very least observation is selection. Nietzsche pointed out that a participant in an event has a far better chance to observe it truly than someone sitting on the sidelines with his notebook in his hand. This is so because the concentration of one's attention on a goal screens the mind against irrelevancies as nothing else can. Men of action have a real advantage as writers, provided they have the wit and opportunity to take the advantage up, for the emotion that rises from engagement is the only real means for following the threads of consequence that link events in a pattern worth reproducing in a story.

To see how very strongly observation partakes of the qualities of creation, look at a few entries from Chekhov's notebook:

"A certain captain taught his daughter the art of fortification."

"He dreamt of winning three hundred thousand in lottery, twice in succession, because three hundred thousand would not be enough for him."

"A clever girl: 'I cannot pretend . . . I never tell a lie . . . I have principles'—and all the time 'I, I, I . . .' "

" 'Oh my dear little pimple!' said the bride tenderly. The bridegroom thought for a while, then felt hurt—they parted."

About each of these entries there is something bewitchingly cryptic. One is tempted to say of them that they tell stories in capsule form. But that is not quite true, though they are story-like. They "do" what passages of fiction always ought to do—set up a lively response of curiosity and interpretation in the mind of the reader who encounters them.

Rather than being stories, these miniatures are like the dreams at the beginning of the Joseph story. They have that in them which might become a story, or a new branch growing from the trunk of a story already begun. Because they represent some initial step of the imagination, they impel a continuation, but there is nothing in them to determine which way and how far the imagination will run. Just as we are apt to feel that a dreamy, favorite younger son like Joseph might turn out well or badly, we can see that the captain's daughter who learned fortifications might, thereafter, have become an adventuress, a spinster, or a nun. Something in the bride's past must have determined her tendency to unfortunate compliments—and the story to be made around Chekhov's glowing fragment would have to tell us what it was. The man who dreamed of winning twice in the lottery is obviously a brother to those of us who dream of winning what we need in a lump sum, but a peculiar sort of desperate modesty distinguishes him and demands further explanation.

A writer's notebook may—and Chekhov's did—contain many

entries simpler and less piquant than those I have quoted. Lists of proper names, fragments of dialogue overheard or invented, newspaper clippings, gleanings from poetry or prose, moral epigrams, individual words—all these are part of the ragbag each writer carries around with him on paper or in his memory. Anything may go in—only provided that it be somehow charged with the emotion of the person who selected it. It is, it has to be, from combinations of the materials in the ragbag that stories are made.

How?

By organizing all that is newest, most personal, and most vital in the writer's observations within the oldest and most venerable conventions of storytelling. There may seem to be a paradox in this. Very well. Art is a paradox—but one we have long accepted as familiar. The art of the short story is one small province within the great art of language, and we are well accustomed to casting our freshest thoughts in words and syntactical patterns older than history. Just as no one in his right mind undertakes to invent all over again the conventions of language, in the same way no one need suppose he has to invent—or can do without—the conventions of storytelling.

The fundamental conventions are those of plot, character, tone, narrative, scene, setting, diction, climax, and theme. No one who has heard or read stories is totally unaware of these conventions. It is our common experience that we absorb them from our reading before we get around to admitting a need for formal definition. The ordinary, responsive reader may be better off if he never bothers with definitions, for—though all fiction is artifice, something put together by human ingenuity—the purpose of the artifice is to give the sense that reality is being witnessed through a sort of peephole. An awareness that language is not a peephole but a complexly engineered structure of meaning may actually inhibit receptivity to that meaning. All honor, long life, and good health to the reader who never riles his appetite by resorting to formal critical examination.

The writer, though, is not in the same case as the ordinary

reader. He is the one who must do the engineering. A formal definition of the conventions is part of his equipment—useless in itself, of course, but useful in so far as he understands how they relate and discipline the material of observation. Such definitions as I have to give here are not intended to be exhaustive, merely basic.

PLOT: A causal sequence of actions. A chain reaction corresponding to our notion that nothing happens without sufficient motive. As a device for conveying meaning it draws on our belief that an event is understood by explaining how it came about.

CHARACTER: The drawing of individual personalities who take part in action. In life character is observed. In fiction it has to be created.

TONE: The author's attitude toward his material. His contempt, pity, awe, love, distrust, amusement, or sympathy will be conveyed, at least partly, by his choice of language, though whether he makes the plot come out happily or unhappily and the way he sets up his cast of characters are also part of his resources in controlling tone.

NARRATIVE: Those passages in a story which telescope extended periods of time or represent complex actions in a kind of general summary.

SCENE: The parts of a story where the pace of presentation is slowed to the point that the reader sees and hears approximately all he would if he were actually witnessing the action of the characters. Often, but not always, consists of dialogue plus detailed description.

SETTING: Usually the physical location or background of a story. The generally prevailing situation to which the chief action is directly related. It shows off the action as a frame shows off a painting or a stage shows off the actors.

DICTION: The particular—and always limited—vocabulary chosen to help reveal the special qualities of the subject.

CLIMAX: That point in a story at which the conflicting forces meet in a decisive encounter. We ought to feel at the end of each story, "Things can never again be as they were." The climax, whether or not it comes as an overt action, shows why they can't.

THEME: The over-all meaning of a story. It is never, properly, a moral tacked onto illustrative actions, but emerges from the unity of the work in somewhat the same way power is created by the harmoniously working parts of a machine.

It should go without saying that these definitions are valuable only when they are supported and amplified by a great number of examples from existing fiction. Perhaps the minimal illustrations I can give here will be somewhat useful in relating my definitions to the short stories you will find in this book and to your other reading in fiction.

Suffice it for the moment to say that the conventions I have defined are well-nigh inescapable in telling a story. No one need worry that his originality will be aborted by observing them. The only real worry one need have is how well he manages them. His management of them will depend on what he learns from reading, but will always be conditioned by the insistent and peculiar qualities of his own observations. Originality—that bright goal of bright young writers, and, indeed, a priceless objective—does not have to be sought in a trackless wilderness. It will be evident in the faithful attempt to marry the conventions of the art with the barely tractable materials the imagination offers. The imagination thrives, and goes on making its contributions to the story, as the writer scouts for ways to fit the formless into a form.

The conventions are not impediments. They are opportunities. To form a plot by bringing one's observations into a causal sequence of action is an obligatory part of bringing them into an expressive unity. I suppose that plot, properly understood, is the very most important component of fictional expression.

It is all the better, of course, when it is so neatly immersed in the fictional medium that the easy reader sees no plot at all—as in Chekhov's story "Typhus," which at first glance may seem merely a sketch.

Actually it is more than a description of how it feels to be very ill. We must not suppose that plot is lacking merely because what happens goes beyond the conscious intention of Klimov or the other characters. In this case plot blends intention, chance, and unconscious determination in such a way as to show us profoundly what we mean when we speak of our *selves*.

It is by chance that Klimov falls ill as the train is carrying him toward home. He *intends* merely to withdraw as well as he can from the uncomfortable and presently agonizing onslaught of his illness. He intends to hold on until he arrives where his orderly and sister can take care of him. And we see how these limited intentions ride like froth on the swollen force of a wave, rolling him toward an eventuality and a cruel responsibility that will reshape his life forever. Of course it is no part of his intent to transmit his disease to his sister, but his intents are responsive to irrational forces that will make him do just that.

Yet the shock of illumination provided by the turn of the plot is not to be found in the irony that he has unintentionally brought about his sister's death. Rather it comes from his shocking—but ah, so natural—response to the news that she is dead. "Animal joy" at his own recovery completely overshadows the significance of this news, though his mind "fully grasped" it. At this point we understand that in his bout with death Klimov has become that natural man idealized by romantic literature. In his victory he has gone beyond the range of human concerns. He is like a god, or like man before the Fall. He is more and less than human. And when the "clang of old iron rails" recalls him to his humanity like an alarm clock waking a dreamer, he realizes—and the reader grasps the theme at the same moment—that the price of being human is boredom verging on despair.

There is not much intricacy or complication in such a plot. It is more like the plot of a poem than that of a drama or novel. It lacks the turns and the involvement of numerous contributing defined phases, each with its definitive realignment of forces in characters characteristic of the novel. It is not divisible into clearly conflict, as the plot of a play usually is. We should not take it as an example that defines the limit of plot in the short story form, but rather as a case where even the simplest of accounts depends for its meaning on the significant shape of plot. Without this much plot the thematic statement could not emerge.

Of course it is never plot alone that delivers a story's meaning. So it is never pertinent to judge the merit of a plot in isolation. The question is: How well is the plot suited to the total purpose in the story?

The plot of Mr. Hall's "A View of the Beach" is hardly more complicated than Chekhov's. A boy rides to Florida in search of an Eldorado whose glamour is defined for him by a rather commercialized image of flamingos and "great hotels anchored by the ocean's shore." Arrived in the actual Florida, he finds that, after all, he was really looking for a girl, and since Ceely is handy, he adorns her with the exotic attributes of the night around her and expects that in possessing her he will possess "it all."

By accident—and it is an accident strongly conditioned by the boy's ineptness—the girl is frightened almost at the moment of yielding. She runs "into the shadow"—that is, back into the realms of inaccessible dream from which his need had so briefly summoned her. He runs, too. That is, he repudiates the dream which alone could justify his pursuit and regresses into a vegetable life. Back in Ohio.

Note that a part of the plot action has been displaced from its normal position. Near the end of Section II when Ceely jumps from the sea wall we are not told that she lands on a drunken cook. That information, which seems at first thought to belong here, is withheld until the following section while we are told cryptically instead that the travelers begin their dreary return to the North.

Why this break in continuity? Probably the episode with the cook—that fabulous serpent rising out of the dark beyond the sea wall like the repugnant physicality of sex soiling the fantasies of a virgin boy—was moved from its normal place in the sequence of action to indicate that it was less important at the time it happened than it became in retrospect. By frustrating our expectations of an explanation in Section II the author makes us all the more eager to fasten the occurrence somewhere in the narrator's life. And we will think that the revulsion which might have been transient if it were attached to that passing moment on the beach is, in being detached, permanent in the narrator's life thereafter.

Devices like this displacement—the sum of them amounting to a variety of techniques that may quite effectively cloak the causal sequence of action—may give the unwary reader the notion that contemporary short fiction depends little on plot. Not so. Writers in our century have merely found new ways to adapt it, either to the illusion of reality they learned from the naturalists or to an expressive commerce with the reader which they learned from poets and symbolists.

In spite of new techniques the fundamentals of the short story remain what they have been for the last century. The major technical achievement for a writer is almost always the marriage of plot with character. Anyone can see that there is no excess space in the short story where character might be created independently in a purely static fashion. If the reader does not come to know the characters by what they do, by their contrast with others in the same story, and by the way their positions change in relation to each other, he has little chance of knowing them at all.

The character lives while the story runs. The chief concern of the writer is to make it run with one hand while he shapes the character into its motion with the other. When he says to himself, "I *know* dozens of things about the people I mean to write about," his story smiles wickedly and says, "I'm not offering you any place to write those 'things' down." An itemized tally of characteristics belongs outside a story, not inside. Inside, the characteristics merely show in passing.

It is terribly important that the author know his characters well before he goes into the story, whether they are wholly imaginary or drawn from life. But until he has structured them into his narrative, adapting them, changing them, making them the creatures of his fiction rather than creatures of his fancy or experience, they can't be fully known to anyone else.

It is a common mistake to try to remain true to a model, real or imaginary, as one builds characters into a story. A character must be born within the environment of the fiction, must grow to fit not only the meaningful action required of him but the rest of the cast. A liar must tell those lies that will succeed with the other characters the author assembles around him. An ungrateful son will take his fictional character from the fictional father assigned to him, whether or not the author begins from real-life observation of such a boy.

Beyond this, in the creation of characters one must give the impression that they are acting of their own volition, for we know people best when we can see them choose among alternatives and guess the dynamism with which they pursue their choice. I suppose that this illusion of a personal will is made when the author merges his identity with that of his characters and, so to speak, *acts* out the role he has commenced by delineating. In "A View of the Beach" the moment when Ceely turns in anger on the narrator for not having worn a tie is, we would say, well chosen. It is time that Ceely voiced exasperation if she is going to be Ceely. And how could the moment have been chosen so surely if the author had not felt the same sort of exasperation, making Ceely real by having her voice his own response?

Particularly in first-person narration the voice of the narrator—the way a story is told, what is emphasized, what is ignored, what is unrecognized by the narrator though understood well enough by the reader— is one of the most flexible means for creating character. Within the tight confines of the short story it is attractive because all the while the narrator is demonstrating his own nature he is telling us about what's going on around him. Degrees of distinction between author and narrator are almost infinitely numerous, and each degree provides a different terrain for the exploitation of language.

The writer may completely suppress his own natural expression and let his narrator speak consistently in characteristic language. More often—and this is true of "A View of the Beach"—the author will suppress his own language in relation to certain parts of the story, all the while reserving some other crucial areas for his own statement, identifying at such moments, though only then, completely with his speaker.

Thus, through most of Mr. Hall's story we are aware of a distinction. The character telling the story is an emasculated, withered bumpkin. A good bit of the humor here is achieved by letting him reveal in his own insufficient terms his justification for biting off his nose to spite his face after the bad luck on the beach with Ceely. But, in respect to his heartbreak and to his beaten vision of oceanic glamour, the author identifies completely with his spokesman. Language of author and language of narrator, the concreteness to which they refer in shaping images equivalent to their emotion, and the implied values of each, are fused, become the same.

In this we may see that the ultimate objective of the modern short story is not to reveal character or to create an action whose meaning is sufficient in itself. These things are only contributory to an expressive unity, the lyric address of author to reader, by which his theme is clarified. The lyric and purely expressive play of language unites the small-scale actions of the story with their mothering myth and affords a visionary penetration through the appearances of every day.

Mr. Hall's story ends with an overwhelmingly petty statement about trivialities. "I cook for just the two of us. Salads mostly." But because of its relation to the rest of the story, this banality means: "Now it is not Ceely who fled me, but God's promise." And if the note here is bleaker than Joseph's, yet the small story has turned out to have a scope of expression almost as broad. Neither the brief length nor the comedy mixed with pathos nor the small consequence of the main character on the world's stage marks the limit of the story's significance.

❆ TYPHUS

Anton Chekhov

A young lieutenant called Klimov was travelling from Petersburg to Moscow in a smoking carriage of the mail train. Opposite him was sitting an elderly man with a shaven face like a sea captain's, by all appearances a well-to-do Finn or Swede. He pulled at his pipe the whole journey and kept talking about the same subject:

"Ha, you are an officer! I have a brother an officer too, only he is a naval officer. . . . He is a naval officer, and he is stationed at Kronstadt. Why are you going to Moscow?"

"I am serving there."

"Ha! And are you a family man?"

"No, I live with my sister and aunt."

"My brother's an officer, only he is a naval officer; he has a wife and three children. Ha!"

The Finn seemed continually surprised at something, and gave a broad idiotic grin when he exclaimed "Ha!" and continually puffed at his stinking pipe. Klimov, who for some reason did not feel well, and found it burdensome to answer questions, hated him with all his heart. He dreamed of how nice it would be to snatch the wheezing pipe out of his hand and fling it under the seat, and drive the Finn himself into another compartment.

"Detestable people these Finns and . . . Greeks," he thought. "Absolutely superfluous, useless, detestable people. They simply fill up space on the earthly globe. What are they for?"

And the thought of Finns and Greeks produced a feeling akin to sickness all over his body. For the sake of comparison he tried to think of the French, of the Italians, but his efforts to think of these people evoked in his mind, for some reason, nothing but images of organ-grinders, naked women, and the foreign oleographs which hung over the chest of drawers at home, at his aunt's.

Altogether the officer felt in an abnormal state. He could not arrange his arms and legs comfortably on the seat, though he had the whole seat to himself. His mouth felt dry and sticky; there was a heavy fog in his brain; his thoughts seemed to be straying, not only within his head, but outside his skull, among the seats and the people that were shrouded in the darkness of night. Through the mist in his brain, as through a dream, he heard the murmur of voices, the rumble of wheels, the slamming of doors. The sounds of the bells, the whistles, the guards, the running to and fro of passengers on the platforms, seemed more frequent than usual. The time flew by rapidly, imperceptibly, and so it seemed as though the train were stopping at stations every minute, and metallic voices crying continually:

"Is the mail ready?"

"Yes!" was repeatedly coming from outside.

It seemed as though the man in charge of the heating came in too often to look at the thermometer, that the noise of trains going in the opposite direction and the rumble of the wheels over the bridges was incessant. The noise, the whistles, the Finn, the tobacco smoke—all this mingling with the menace and flickering of the misty images in his brain, the shape and character of which a man in health can never recall, weighed upon Klimov like an unbearable nightmare. In horrible misery he lifted his heavy head, looked at the lamp in the rays of which shadows and misty blurs seemed to be dancing. He wanted to ask for water, but his parched tongue would hardly move, and he scarcely had strength to answer the Finn's questions. He tried to lie down more comfortably and go to sleep, but he could not succeed. The Finn several times fell asleep, woke up again, lighted his pipe, addressed him with his "Ha!" and went to sleep again; and still the lieutenant's legs could not get into a comfortable position, and still the menacing images stood facing him.

At Spirovo he went out into the station for a drink of water. He saw people sitting at the table and hurriedly eating.

"And how can they eat!" he thought, trying not to sniff the air,

that smelt of roast meat, and not to look at the munching mouths,
—they both seemed to him sickeningly disgusting.

A good-looking lady was conversing loudly with a military man
in a red cap, and showing magnificent white teeth as she smiled;
and the smile, and the teeth, and the lady herself made on Klimov
the same revolting impression as the ham and the risoles. He could
not understand how it was the military man in the red cap was
not ill at ease, sitting beside her and looking at her healthy, smiling
face.

When after drinking some water he went back to his carriage,
the Finn was sitting smoking; his pipe was wheezing and squelch-
ing like a galosh with holes in it in wet weather.

"Ha!" he said, surprised; "what station is this?"

"I don't know," answered Klimov, lying down and shutting his
mouth that he might not breathe the acrid tobacco smoke.

"And when shall we reach Tyver?"

"I don't know. Excuse me, I . . . I can't answer. I am ill. I caught
cold today."

The Finn knocked his pipe against the windowframe and began talking of his brother, the naval officer. Klimov no longer heard
him; he was thinking miserably of his soft, comfortable bed, of a
bottle of cold water, of his sister Katya, who was so good at making
one comfortable, soothing, giving one water. He even smiled when
the vision of his orderly Pavel, taking off his heavy stifling boots
and putting water on the little table, flitted through his imagination. He fancied that if he could only get into his bed, have a drink
of water, his nightmare would give place to sound healthy sleep.

"Is the mail ready?" a hollow voice reached him from the distance.

"Yes," answered a bass voice almost at the window.

It was already the second or third station from Spirovo.

The time was flying rapidly in leaps and bounds, and it seemed
as though the bells, whistles, and stoppings would never end. In
despair Klimov buried his face in the corner of the seat, clutched
his head in his hands, and began again thinking of his sister Katya

and his orderly Pavel, but his sister and his orderly were mixed up with the misty images in his brain, whirled round, and disappeared. His burning breath, reflected from the back of the seat, seemed to scald his face; his legs were uncomfortable; there was a draught from the window on his back; but, however wretched he was, he did not want to change his position. . . . A heavy nightmarish lethargy gradually gained possession of him and fettered his limbs.

When he brought himself to raise his head, it was already light in the carriage. The passengers were putting on their fur coats and moving about. The train was stopping. Porters in white aprons and with discs on their breasts were bustling among the passengers and snatching up their boxes. Klimov put on his great-coat, mechanically followed the other passengers out of the carriage, and it seemed to him that not he, but someone else was moving, and he felt that his fever, his thirst, and the menacing images which had not let him sleep all night, came out of the carriage with him. Mechanically he took his luggage and engaged a sledge-driver. The man asked him for a rouble and a quarter to drive to Povarsky Street, but he did not haggle, and without protest got submissively into the sledge. He still understood the difference of numbers, but money had ceased to have any value to him.

At home Klimov was met by his aunt and his sister Katya, a girl of eighteen. When Katya greeted him she had a pencil and exercise book in her hand, and he remembered that she was preparing for an examination as a teacher. Gasping with fever, he walked aimlessly through all the rooms without answering their questions or greetings, and when he reached his bed he sank down on the pillow. The Finn, the red cap, the lady with the white teeth, the smell of roast meat, the flickering blurs, filled his consciousness, and by now he did not know where he was and did not hear the agitated voices.

When he recovered consciousness he found himself in bed, undressed, saw a bottle of water and Pavel, but it was no cooler, nor softer, nor more comfortable for that. His arms and legs, as before, refused to lie comfortably; his tongue stuck to the roof of his mouth, and he heard the wheezing of the Finn's pipe. . . . A stalwart, black-bearded doctor was busy doing something beside the bed, brushing against Pavel with his broad back.

"It's all right, it's all right, young man," he muttered. "Excellent, excellent . . . goo-od, goo-od. . . !"

The doctor called Klimov "young man," said "goo-od" instead of "good" and "so-oo" instead of "so."

"So-o . . . so-o . . . so-o," he murmured. "Goo-od, goo-od. . . .! Excellent, young man. . . . You mustn't lose heart!"

The doctor's rapid, careless talk, his well-fed countenance, and condescending "young man," irritated Klimov.

"Why do you call me 'young man'?" he moaned. "What familiarity! Damn it all!"

And he was frightened by his own voice. The voice was so dried up, so weak and peevish, that he would not have known it.

"Excellent, excellent!" muttered the doctor, not in the least offended. . . . "You mustn't get angry, so-o, so-o, so-o . . ."

And the time flew by at home with the same startling swiftness as in the railway carriage. . . . The daylight was continually being replaced by the dusk of evening. The doctor seemed never to leave his bedside, and he heard at every moment his "so-o, so-o, so-o." A continual succession of people was incessantly crossing the bedroom. Among them were: Pavel, the Finn, Captain Yaroshevitch, Lance-Corporal Maximenko, the red cap, the lady with the white teeth, the doctor. They were all talking and waving their arms, smoking and eating. Once by daylight Klimov saw the chaplain of the regiment, Father Alexandr, who was standing before the bed, wearing a stole and with a prayer-book in his hand. He was muttering something with a brave face such as Klimov had never seen in him before. The lieutenant remembered that Father Alexandr used in a friendly way to call all the Catholic officers "Poles," and wanting to amuse him, he cried:

"Father, Yaroshevitch the Pole has climbed up a pole!"

But Father Alexandr, a light-hearted man who loved a joke, did not smile, but became graver than ever, and made the sign of the cross over Klimov. At night-time by turn two shadows came noiselessly in and out; they were his aunt and sister. His sister's shadow knelt down and prayed; she bowed down to the ikon, and her grey shadow on the wall bowed down too, so that two shadows were praying. The whole time there was a smell of roast meat and the Finn's pipe, but once Klimov smelt the strong smell of incense. He felt so sick he could not lie still, and began shouting:

"The incense! Take away the incense!"

There was no answer. He could only hear the subdued singing of the priest somewhere and someone running upstairs.

When Klimov came to himself there was not a soul in his bedroom. The morning sun was streaming in at the window through the lower blind, and a quivering sunbeam, bright and keen as the sword's edge, was flashing on the glass bottle. He heard the rattle of wheels—so there was no snow now in the street. The lieutenant looked at the ray, at the familiar furniture, at the door, and the first thing he did was to laugh. His chest and stomach heaved with delicious, happy, tickling laughter. His whole body from head to foot was overcome by a sensation of infinite happiness and joy in life, such as the first man must have felt when he was created and first saw the world. Klimov felt a passionate desire for movement, people, talk. His body lay a motionless block; only his hands stirred, but that he hardly noticed, and his whole attention was concentrated on trifles. He rejoiced in his breathing, in his laughter, rejoiced in the existence of the water-bottle, the ceiling, the sunshine, the tape on the curtains. God's world, even in the narrow space of his bedroom, seemed beautiful, varied, grand. When the doctor made his appearance, the lieutenant was thinking what a delicious thing medicine was, how charming and pleasant the doctor was, and how nice and interesting people were in general.

"So-o, so, so . . . Excellent, excellent! . . . Now we are well again. . . . Goo-od, goo-od!" the doctor pattered.

The lieutenant listened and laughed joyously; he remembered

the Finn, the lady with the white teeth, the train, and he longed to smoke, to eat.

"Doctor," he said, " tell them to give me a crust of rye bread and salt, and . . . and sardines."

The doctor refused; Pavel did not obey the order, and did not go for the bread. The lieutenant could not bear this and began crying like a naughty child.

"Baby!" laughed the doctor. "Mammy, bye-bye!"

Klimov laughed, too, and when the doctor went away he fell into a sound sleep. He woke up with the same joyfulness and sensation of happiness. His aunt was sitting near the bed.

"Well, aunt," he said joyfully. "What has been the matter?"

"Spotted typhus."

"Really. But now I am well, quite well! Where is Katya?"

"She is not at home. I suppose she has gone somewhere for her examination."

The old lady said this and looked at her stocking; her lips began quivering, she turned away, and suddenly broke into sobs. Forgetting the doctor's prohibition in her despair, she said:

"Ah, Katya, Katya! Our angel is gone! Is gone!"

She dropped her stocking and bent down to it, and as she did so her cap fell off her head. Looking at her grey head and understanding nothing, Klimov was frightened for Katya, and asked:

"Where is she, aunt?"

The old woman, who had forgotten Klimov and was thinking only of her sorrow, said:

"She caught typhus from you, and is dead. She was buried the day before yesterday."

This terrible, unexpected news was fully grasped by Klimov's consciousness; but terrible and startling as it was, it could not overcome the animal joy that filled the convalescent. He cried and laughed, and soon began scolding because they would not let him eat.

Only a week later when, leaning on Pavel, he went in his dressing-gown to the window, looked at the overcast spring sky and listened to the unpleasant clang of the old iron rails which were being carted by, his heart ached, he burst into tears, and leaned his forehead against the windowframe.

"How miserable I am!" he muttered. "My God, how miserable!" And joy gave way to the boredom of everyday life and the feeling of his irrevocable loss.

❧ A VIEW OF THE BEACH

James B. Hall

I

Into Kentucky, between burley leaf and the blue grass she steered us, and Kentucky gave us wonders through her lecturing tongue. She was a school teacher on vacation and now the things she always had written on blackboards were just beyond our windshield. She could not bear to drive past any historical marker, or to cross any bridge if her book said once the Sharden Brothers ran a ferry at this spot, well-known to pioneers on the Westward Trek.

In the front seat the three of them. Her husband Ray was no traveler and very early in the morning always suggested a place to stop for supper if we could only get there before dark. That summer Ceely rode between them and began to use much lipstick and each mile she placed her legs carefully on one side or the other of the gearshift lever.

I was their back seat passenger and we were headed South. I was sent because my father telegraphed money from "that Hell hole he preferred to a decent home" and because my mother believed travel was broadening. So I listened to Mrs. Herdston's lecturing tongue, but I thought only of the flamingo's infectious color, and of the great hotels anchored by the ocean's shore, in Florida.

"Jefferson, you can get out and look," Mattie would call while I was still in the back seat shuffling her boxes that fell over me whenever she stopped, "Come look if you want."

After she called I could elect to do the right thing, or I could sleep. Her school-room voice always put it that way and as she often said when I was in her room at school, "That's America for you."

By the time I got out of the car Mrs. Herdston would be standing on the entrance steps to some county museum, her face pressed against the windows. Mattie was shaped like a stump, one that is left in cut-over land, when there has been two years' growth of briar. Yet a white oak stump is solid there among vines, under the crow's far picket call.

A great teacher, my mother always said. That is, Mrs. Herdston told you the Right or Wrong of it. If a boy were running around until all hours of the night she would have a little talk with him, to save him from the Workhouse, or Marriage Too Young. Or she saw to it about the Army or the Navy. A little enlistment, she felt, never hurt anyone. Over the years, though, the school board tried to fire all married teachers, but she had scotched that by petitions. A few laughed because she wore the same velveteen dress the year around, but no one laughed to her face.

So we stopped where a Union spy was taken; the birthplace of an Opera singer; where a regiment of Illinois Volunteers was "cut a-sunder by Jensen's intrepid cavalry"; and we saw the farthest reach of a cave where hollowed-out logs were used for pipes when soldiers labored in the foul air to mine saltpetre, so that other soldiers could unloose a fusillade at Indians concealed among trees.

Towards midnight they would argue and would finally decide on a motel. Then Ceely and her mother disappeared through a door into their room, and I heard two suitcases snap open. Usually Ray and I also shared the same bed, to save money. Ray would stretch his arms towards the ceiling and would say, "Day's work, wahn't it?"

If I got to sleep, the great black square trucks passed again and again inside my head, or black seals like black projectiles broke upward from the beach and the sand of my dreams.

II

The first morning I awoke at Miami Beach, they had already gone out. Mrs. Herdston was up at daylight, and saw the ocean off Collins avenue before anyone else. Together Mattie and Ray strolled past all of the un-opened shops, and saw a candy store lined entirely with red satin. By noon she was back again at our hotel. I was almost awake. She poked me in the ribs and tried to be forgiving. More than half our time in the Playland of the South was already gone, she said, and outside were new frontiers.

Above my bed the black fan blades chopped at the hot ceiling; outside a palm frond rowed in the breeze. The sun washed each stucco wall, and through the window I could see farther up the beach where the really big hotels reared into the sky, monuments erected by lovers of the sun.

So I dressed and walked outside to see the beach. The children ran crying to their mothers when the sea sucked lettuce crates and the floating husks of coconuts through the iron groins. When the children cried the women got up from the sand, the sun guards of white celluloid taped firmly like beaks across the nose. The women turned their backs to the sun and the ocean and stood there: waves bent above their coiled shell-children on the sand.

No one swam far from shore so the life guard dozed in his high white chair under a canvas. His hands remained crossed upon his belly of golden flesh. The dark glasses which were his eyes were sightless from his profession of watching an empty sea. And this was the beach in the afternoon.

But when the sun was down the spot lights on the walls and in the palm trees turned everything which was not dark to silver. The upper stories of the hotels were a floating terrace of lights overhead. The cars that had been roosting under the palm fronds came out into the streets and drilled past. Inside these cars the quick puff of light from a match showed the driver's face and perhaps, also, the bare shoulders of the woman beside him.

That night after dark I really did meet someone I knew. That's the way they say it happens. I saw her walking along the other side of the street, her head erect. I ran across the street, through traffic, and from behind, I called her name.

Ceely turned around and waited. When she noticed I was panting she laughed and said she thought I fell in the ocean, and I said Fancy meeting you here, and she said Dr. Jefferson I presume, and I said The condemned man ate a hearty meal.

Ceely's blue organdy sash blew very slightly ahead of us in the breeze, so we walked off together in that direction. She wore the white opened-toed sandals. Her hair was nearly blonde from our travel. She was not really as tall as I was, though at first you might think so. As we walked she put her arm through mine. Ahead, on each side of the street, were neon lights. Inside the heavy slab-glass doors the men in burnt umber, or mauve, or turquoise dinner jackets waited near the bars, or they sat at tables farther back where the music was.

The Maritime. It's the one with nets and sponges outside, and porthole windows. The night club was like some illuminated crustacean rolled from the ocean floor, come to rest and finally secured on this street beside the ocean after a hurricane.

Inside the Club Maritime we waited in line. Through the low sea-fog smoke inside the yellow candles burned like buoy lights along some easy summer coast; beyond the ledge of tables the dance floor was small and polished and almost concealed by the high gold satin panels above the dance band. The musicians were from the Barbados—all black, except for their girl singer.

The head waiter leaned towards me and said softly, "Oh, you two have been waiting. That's too bad. And you two are out for a date?"

I said we thought we would dance some.

The music began when someone from the Barbados pounded on the smallest drum. We did not hear the whole piece. We were out on the street again very quickly, walking away very fast. I could not tell Ceely that the head waiter whispered into my ear, "No tie. Gotta have a tie."

We ended up on a bench, in a small park which faced the ocean. Ahead the breakers tripped and fell, one after the other, upon the shore. Behind us the door of some hotel kitchen opened. The spear of light from the opened door came across the darkness and ticked for a moment across her face. For one frozen, light-flicked moment, I saw her face, immobile in the spear of light, staring out across the ocean.

"Not a nice walk," Ceely said, without taking her face from the ocean. I was trying to see the brighter side of things, since both of our mothers advised this.

"Dammit," she said and spat once into the sand, "I have put up with that mother of mine all through Tennessee and Georgia. And we finally get where we are going. And you (Ceely turned on me) *you* don't have sense enough to wear a tie!"

I did not say anything. I knew that I had not wanted to dance, really, because I could dance only a little, and not at all to the small drums from the Barbados.

Not a nice walk for me either, but I could not say that. The car sickness came on me all over again and I thought of the automobile we had passed in Georgia, its wheels in the air, aimed at a ditch. Near the roadside there was something under a bed quilt, but we did not stop. It was not a point of interest.

As I sat on the bench in the cooling salt tide of air, I seemed to see us from a distance, as though I were standing nearby, staring ahead at the two figures and the organdy sash trembling in the breeze. The voice in my ear was my father's voice, and I remembered him standing on our porch, on Fancy Street, a billed cap of white duck slanted across his face. That last time I saw him he was standing beside me at the porch rail, looking out as though our dun-colored street were the wake of a ship somewhere off Penang. "How about you, Johnny-boy?" he said. "You getting any? Are you?" He was a merchant sailor. The next day he was gone.

My arm, as I watched it, went out and around Ceely's small shoulders. I was surprised at how easy it was. She seemed to lie athwart my arms, as though I had suddenly, by my touch, turned her straight small back into a length of some easy, clinging thing. In that moment when all the moonlight was cut off by the clouds, I quickly kissed her.

Ceely did not stiffen in my arms and it was curious how I could tell this although I seemed, still, to be divorced from those two people on the bench in the darkness. She really was yielding, as all the stories said. Then she put her head even closer to my shirt, and I could feel her small breath very close to my skin. Because I did not know what to do, or because I was afraid, we sat there for a very long time.

After she put my hand down there she said, Oh, now we are in Florida and are on the beach . . . now. And it was Ceely, herself, who got up and took me by the hand.

Ahead was the retaining wall. The darkness on the other side would conceal us. She knew this, also, and she led me to the wall. Ahead the wall curved away under the palm trees in the darkness, and beyond was the sand, and beyond the sand the breakers which tripped over themselves in the moonlight, and broke into foam.

For a moment Ceely stood on the retaining wall, facing the beach and the sea. She raised herself on tip toe. She released my hand. I understood I was to follow. But instead I pushed her. Forward. With a little cry, Ceely leaped down. And into the shadow.

. . . towards the everglades, and the sky beyond the Tamiami Trail: Ray was expecting a hurricane, so we got out of the State. We saw the old fortifications at Vicksburg, and paused at Muscle Shoals where generators are buried in the deepest foundations of those dams, to fire great surges of current along the cables, to make lights burn somewhere on a farm so that a man does not have to milk in the early morning darkness in winter. It was dark and raining when we crossed the river back into Ohio and it was midnight when we drove along under the trees of the little town we had started from. At our house there was a light on the porch and my mother was up because Mrs. Herdston's cards had come through all right. . . .

III

Ray married again. His next wife owned the eight-room hotel and some other property in Blanton. At three p.m. Ray becomes her night clerk. His health is better because of his year-around regular hours.

Ceely married. She ran off to Kentucky with a man who sold

aluminum ware, house-to-house. One morning he knocked and Ceely answered the door. When the man is not on the road they live in a trailer park in El Dorado, Arkansas. Ceely, they say, did not inherit her mother's brains.

As they had planned in the beginning, the School Board waited until Mrs. Herdston took off on our vacation and then they fired all married teachers. They say it killed her. They found her in bed, wearing the velveteen dress that clung to her big hips like bark around a tree stump. Perhaps all the swelling was from the years of standing on her feet, marking the Right and the Wrong of it on a hundred black boards. Except for my mother no one ever mentions Mrs. Herdston, but as yet they have not found anyone quite like her for the job.

Just before graduation I left High School and my mother's complaints about being on her feet all day in the local bank. I made a break, I went all the way back down to Miami Beach. For almost a year I worked in a hotel. I worked in the kitchen. Salads, mostly.

But going and coming from work I often stopped to look at the exact place where Ceely jumped from the retaining wall, where I pushed her down and away from me that night she took my hand and led me from the bench. The wall seemed lower now, but that night I pushed her, Ceely's face looked up once at me from the shadows and she cried out.

Like a serpent groping in that shadow a man's pale arm encircled her knees. Her lips shaped. She screamed my name. Like some white climbing animal she tried to scramble back up the wall. I did not move. Ceely fell back again upon him. She kicked furiously at the groping arms. Before I could move or could call out or could follow, Ceely ran down the ocean side of the wall, and out of sight under the palm trees.

The man was some great crustacean, abandoned there by the tides; the waves kept us from hearing his snores. After she was gone the man sat slowly upright. He was huge in the darkness, in a muddy cook's apron, wearing his cook's white, muddy, hat.

His bulged face, glazed as a bun, floated upward to my feet. His face was directly in the cleaver edge of light above the top of the wall. I thought it was whiskey in his hand, but it was a square sullen bottle of lemon extract. His mouth opened. A gold cap on a tooth in the back of his throat caught the light.

"Ev-ry-body," he said hoarsely, "Every-body . . . gets a dance with me. . . ."

Then the cook that was muddy turned towards the ocean. He walked with his feet wide apart, the square bottle in one hand, towards the lines of foam along the water's edge.

But the reason I came home was this: somewhere in the North Japan Sea, at the edge of a typhoon, my father washed overboard from a tanker. Mother said I should come home and live with her on the insurance. And that is how it all came out.

Now I sit on the porch and look at the ocean-colored street and sometimes I think back on the big trip to Florida, when Mrs. Herdston's lecturing voice explained all the points of interest.

Although I remember everything very clearly that happened, it is nothing. Nothing at all for there is no one else around now who also remembers. Except perhaps mother. She still stands on her feet all day in the bank, and she still complains at night. She works at the bank so that we can both have a decent home, she says. And I cook for just the two of us. Salads, mostly.

Writing the
Commercial Short Story
JEAN TODD FREEMAN

Two myths about the commercial short story are firmly entrenched in the minds of many writers. The first myth concerns the blindness of magazine editors: "They won't publish anything but slick formula fiction, or Big Names." The second myth proclaims the decline of the story form: "Writers are turning in desperation to non-fiction, novels, television, because there is no longer a market for short fiction."

Most myths contain a kernel of truth; so do these. But to accept either statement as strict fact is to oversimplify the position of the commercial story, and story writer, in today's world.

It is true that some editors like to publish Names-for-Namesake, but the policy of printing inferior or bottom-desk-drawer stories by writers with big reputations does not pay off in the end, since magazines are edited for *readers* and not for autograph hounds, and no intelligent editor forgets that fact. It is also true that magazines publish some stories which may correctly be described as "slick" or "formula"—but the formulas are often highly complex and the slickness is really deftness, having little to do with patness, predictability, or triviality. What's more, editors have become surprisingly experimental in recent years. In the pages of mass-audience magazines for women may be found heroines who drink martinis, have extramarital love affairs, and sometimes dislike their mothers. Magazines once devoted largely to western serials have turned literary, and literary magazines are printing stories about a side of life once explored (though in less eloquent prose) by the pulps.

The fact is that American readers are growing more sophisticated, demanding more than conventional light romances or situation adventure stories. They want to read about human conflict, to meet characters who are not just stereotypes, to enter into fictional situations that are more persuasive and meaningful than those found in conventional escape fiction. When they want stories about "happy people with happy problems" they turn, not to magazines, but to television. And magazine editors, aware that it makes no sense to compete with television by publishing exclusively TV fiction, are only too glad to buy stories that are original and offbeat —when they can find them.

This brings us to the second myth: that story writing is declining because of declining markets. Certainly the demise of several major magazines in recent years has cut down, physically, the *number* of markets. But the surprising fact is that magazines still publishing short fiction are having more and more difficulty finding enough good stories to fill their pages.

Why? I think part of the blame must fall on the writers.

Some of them, becoming discouraged, have indeed turned to non-fiction, television, and novels. But far more serious is the failure of many writers to recognize just those changes I have mentioned —the increasing sophistication and intellectual range of their potential audience. Often it is the writer, not the editor, who is blind. He continues to produce precisely, and monotonously, the same glib, superficial boy-meets-girl story he has been writing for twenty years; or, especially if he is a new writer, he dismisses commercial magazine fiction as "phony," and indulges in formless, self-absorbed, precious reminiscences aimed at literary quarterlies.

I refuse to believe that a writer must choose between these extremes. During my years as a magazine editor I occasionally found, with delight and thanks to God, a story that fell somewhere in the happy middle: a story which, while exhibiting the positive qualities so often associated with the slicks (strong plot, professional skill, a recognizable ending), revealed additional qualities of originality, emotional depth, serious purpose. Few stories of this caliber were turned down.

Such a story was "Sorrow Rides a Fast Horse," by Dorothy Gilman Butters, published in the September, 1962, issue of the *Ladies' Home Journal*.[1] Here is a story with all the ingredients necessary for a successful magazine story: quality writing, unusual plot, appealing and convincing characters, suspense, drama, and an ending which, though far from pat or happy in a conventional sense, still leaves the reader with a feeling of inevitability and satisfaction.

The story begins quietly.

> When my mother died everyone in Green Valley said what a selfless and patient woman she had been, and how wonderfully she had managed to raise two sons alone. "A modest, uncomplaining woman," the minister said at her funeral. "A woman who was born in this town and who died in this town and never went beyond it, but cultivated wisdom in her own small garden."

Quiet, yes; but the alert reader senses a note of irony in the description, and the next sentence confirms it:

> When he said this my brother Rufus nudged me and smiled.

Obviously the brothers know more about their mother than the minister knows. As readers, our interest is instantly aroused. We read on, and through a series of skillful flashbacks begin to get hints about "That Year," which the boys have never discussed with each other, nor even with their mother. The first clue comes when we learn that one of the sons, in the ninth grade, is able to describe to his teacher the interior of the Taj Mahal. Astonished, she asks how he knows what it looks like.

> "I've been there. I've seen the Taj Mahal."

The teacher is skeptical, for in those days no one in Green Valley traveled abroad. But the reader is willing to suspend disbelief.

[1] For complete text, see p. 67.

Another flashback, to an earlier scene. The sons are seven and nine; their father has died unexpectedly, leaving $15,000 in insurance. We see the mother holding the check.

> . . . so meaningless to her that she only wanted to destroy it, and if not to destroy it, at least to abuse it . . . her eyes glittered strangely . . . it seemed to us that we had lost mother, too; when we spoke to her she looked at us blankly, as though she had forgotten who we were.

Now we begin to see what the author is doing. She has presented us first with the ironic ending of a story, and now she is leading us back to its beginning. And finally, if the story is to be successful, she must lead us again to the ending—an ending which inevitably will seem different, because of all we have learned in the course of the story.

"Sorrow Rides a Fast Horse" is an ambitious story, and in less skillful hands might have turned out to be only an interesting failure. That it succeeded is due to several important factors. The author has a story to tell. She presents it in an original way. Her characters, although experiencing unusual adventures in exotic settings, at all times behave like real people, react with recognizable emotions. There are surprises along the way, but the ending, when we reach it, seems logical.

How would one classify this story? It is not a run-of-the-mill formula story, although it employs several familiar devices (story within story, flashbacks, "I" narrator). Neither is it a literary story, although it is a work of genuine imagination. Deceptively simple, it holds appeal both for the serious student of writing and the casual reader.

It is an example of what I believe to be the commercial short story of the future, the happy-medium story I believe writers should be aiming for today. It could even qualify as a touchstone for ambitious writers.

TOUCHSTONE: 1. A smooth, fine-grained, black or dark-colored variety of quartz or jasper, used for testing the

quality of gold and silver alloys by the color of
the streak produced by rubbing them upon it.
2. (*fig.*) That which serves to test or try the genu-
ineness or value of anything; a test, criterion.
Oxford Universal Dictionary

The idea of judging an untried work of art by comparing it with
a work of art *known* to be great is not a new one. One of my favorite literary critics is Longinus, who lived in the third century
A.D. and even then was complaining about "the world-wide bar-
renness of literature that now pervades our life." In a charming
little essay casually called *Concerning Sublimity*, he advised his
students that the way to the sublime was through "imitation and
emulation of great writers and poets who have been before us"; and
he was quite idealistic about the mass appeal of excellence: "That
which is really great . . . is hard, nay impossible to resist . . . those
are beautiful and genuine effects of sublimity which please always,
and please all."

We know, of course, that Shakespeare enjoyed a popular, as
well as a critical success. But if he had limited himself to outwrit-
ing his contemporaries and pleasing his audiences, instead of
matching his talent against the great dramatists of the past, would
he ever have achieved a *King Lear?*

In the nineteenth century, Matthew Arnold urged critics to
judge contemporary works not against each other, but against
proven classics. Although he is speaking here of poetry, his touchstone theory can be applied to all arts.

We must accustom ourselves to a high standard and to a strict
judgement . . . there can be no more useful help for discovering
what poetry belongs to the class of the truly excellent, and can
therefore do us most good, than to have always in one's mind
lines and expressions of the great masters, and to apply them as
a touchstone to other poetry. . . .If we have any tact, we shall find
them, when we have lodged them well in our minds, an infallible
touchstone for detecting the presence or absence of high poetic
quality in all other poetry which we may place beside them. (from
A Study of Poetry)

Arnold's touchstone method of criticism, adapted to modern needs, works very well indeed in keeping standards high. In a world in which we are constantly exposed to mediocrity, it is easy to let our senses get dulled, to think, "This is magnificent!" when in fact the story or song or painting is only a little superior to most of what we read, hear, see. But this is relative judgment, based on easy comparisons of near-averages. What we need is a firmer standard by which to judge. As an editor concerned with reading thousands of stories, many of them inferior, I found myself losing sight of what actually constituted a good short story, and turned for help to the touchstone stories of Hemingway, Fitzgerald, Katherine Anne Porter, Faulkner, Katherine Mansfield, Isak Dinesen. By comparing the manuscripts I was reading with these, I managed to retain my sanity and a certain critical objectivity.

But isn't this all a bit esoteric? After all, we're discussing the *commercial* story, not great art. And isn't this advice more meaningful, really, to editors than to writers?

No. Writing a good commercial story *is* art; and art often has high commercial value—all the abovementioned writers have been published in popular magazines. Moreover, a writer is editor as well, and maintaining objectivity in judging his own work and that of others is no less important to a writer than to an editor or critic. Just as an ambitious tennis player tries to find a partner better than he, a writer should keep in touch with the work of his superiors. One-level reading leads to superficial thinking and, inevitably, to shallow writing. Even though the best examples of commercial writing are far from shallow, the writer who reads only contemporary magazine fiction will suffer from overexposure to the genre; he will find his imagination failing, his work becoming sterile. Too much concentration upon the stories of direct competitors can also lead to a dangerous practice and a dangerous state of mind.

The dangerous practice is *slanting*—studying one magazine assiduously with the object of writing a story precisely suited to that magazine. The trouble with slanting is that it doesn't work. If the editor himself does not have a precise idea of what he wants— and most editors prefer to keep an open, rather than a closed and prejudiced mind—how can a writer expect to know? And beware: the deliberately slanted story has a faint but detectable odor of unhealth, for by its very nature it is dishonest.

A writer who has slanted stories to a particular market for some time without capturing that market often falls into the dangerous attitude of *bitterness*. It seems obvious to him that his story is as good or better than the ones he has seen published in that magazine; therefore the editor is a poor judge, or unfair.

If slanting has a use at all, it is in placing the story after it is written. Certainly it is sensible to exercise some judgment here; to send *Playboy* a delicate study of a young girl's gradual awakening to life in Hastings, Nebraska, is probably a waste of postage. Still, editors are full of surprises. If a magazine publishes predominently domestic drama, chances are that 80 per cent of the stories that magazine receives are domestic dramas— and the editor's taste may be revived by something quite offbeat and unexpected.

Freshness, in fact, has high market value. While it is true that the oldest plot in the world can occasionally be handled with such originality that it seems new, there *are* certain stories that are written over and over and over. An editor soon learns to recognize such category stories as the Scurryback, the CTR, the Sensitive Adolescent Taking a First Step into Maturity, the Boss to Dinner, the Whamsical story, the Trick story, and the Cinderella story.

Here is a typical Scurryback plot: Jane Jones is a thirty-five-year-old housewife who wakes up one morning to discover she has a gray hair. She begins to worry about her vanishing youth. That same day she has a telephone call from the man she almost married. He is in town and wants to see her. Heart aflutter, she pulls out the gray hair and hastens to the assignation.

At this point, the story can take either of two directions. In Version 1, Jane Jones is disillusioned by her old love's balding head and thickening waistline. In Version 2, she finds him madly attractive and is on the point of running away with him when she learns that her child is (a) sick, or (b) lost. In both versions she scurries back home to (if Version 1) cook her husband's favorite meal, or (if Version 2) save the child.

CTR stands for "comes-to-realize." In this story, the protagonist, after nineteen pages of conflict over some agonizing problem, comes to realize on page twenty what the reader has known since page two. Usually the great insight turns out to be a cliché: that a husband may love his wife although he doesn't tell her so, that children must learn to stand on their own feet, that a happy marriage is more important than money, etc.

There is no reason to object to the CTR story if the protagonist has a real problem to begin with, a genuine change of attitude or insight, and if that change is justified by what happens during the course of the story. But nine times out of ten, the solution to the dilemma is facile and improbable: i.e., the wife who feels unloved is reassured when her husband brings her flowers. The reader is more skeptical than the wife. If her doubts have enough validity to occupy her thoughts (and the reader's time) for nineteen pages, are they really going to be dispelled by a dozen roses? And what, other than the writer's need to end the story, prompted the husband to buy the flowers on this particular evening?

The Sensitive Adolescent Taking a First Step into Maturity explains itself. There's nothing wrong with this story except that it exists in epidemic proportions. Every writer was once a sensitive adolescent. Every writer has total recall about that First Step. Every writer has written about it, at least once.

The Boss to Dinner story depends for its humor on the reversal of a fictional convention. The convention (which no magazine reader should believe by now anyway) is that men are promoted according to their wives' ability to cook. Linda Lou Landry, a newlywed, is panic-stricken because her husband's boss is coming to dinner. She spends the entire day making elaborate preparations, for she knows that unless the evening is a success, her husband will not get the raise. The dinner starts off smoothly; then Something Terrible happens. What that something is provides the only opportunity for variation on the theme: the soufflé may not rise; the wife may make a gaffe, revealing her lack of stability, culture, or tact; the dinner may be high in cholesterol and the boss on a diet. But (surprise!) the boss likes the wife better *because* of the disaster, and of course her husband gets the raise.

To the best of my knowledge, it was Hugh McNair Kahler, senior editor at the *Ladies' Home Journal* for many years and contributor of some 150 stories to *The Saturday Evening Post,* who invented the word "whamsy." A story qualifies as whamsy if it sets out to be whimsy, and fails. Stories about fairies, talking dogs, and the imaginary companions of children may be diverting to write, but it is rare indeed that such a story appears in the pages of a national magazine.

The Trick story more often tricks the writer than the reader. In a short-short, an unexpected twist is desirable; and in any story, a surprising ending which seems believable in retrospect may be refreshing. But surprise is quite different from deceit. A reader justifiably feels cheated when, at the end of what he was led to believe was the account of a star-crossed love affair, he is told that the lovers have actually been married for twenty years. Nor is he mollified by the coy revelation that the couple, to enliven their marriage, celebrate their anniversary every year by pretending they are having an illicit assignation.

Surprisingly enough, the Cinderella story has great vitality still. Perhaps it is a collective human dream to become suddenly beautiful, rich, desired, or famous. For of all the hackneyed plots, this one seems most likely to succeed.

Even though a writer may successfully avoid falling into the trap of tired plots, he still must circumvent the snares of poor characterization, overdependence on the-way-it-happened, unconvincing dialogue, bad pacing, and wrong point of view.

Why so many neophytes choose to write in the first person is a mystery. Perhaps telling a story as seen through one's own eyes, or the eyes of an objective observer removed from the action, may seem easier; in fact it is often extremely difficult. An "I" narrator must be on hand to witness every scene and overhear every word of dialogue; frequently this proves inconvenient, and the writer is reduced to hiding him, like Polonius, behind an arras. Also, to be justified, the narrator should be an interesting character in his own right, with an individual voice, and must be dramatically involved in the story as well. When employed by a writer of great skill,[2] first-person narration can be highly effective and lend the story a sense of immediacy; when abused, the technique is tiring and tends to keep the reader at arm's length—the narrator blocking his view of the story.

Oddly, it is the story without a narrator which usually earns the criticism of being "too told." As children, we were bored with stories that seemed to be all description; as adults, we become impatient with stories that are too expository, stories unrelieved by dialogue, which *tell* us what is happening rather than letting the story happen to us. One way to avoid such monotony is to think of the story as a play. Set the stage, produce the characters, let them talk to each other and act and react against each other, and then, when the scene is finished, lower the curtain—and begin with another scene.

Dialogue is almost as important in a short story as in a play. If it sounds false, it can alienate the reader; if it is overly realistic, it can bore him. Unfortunately, the conversation of real people in real life is seldom interesting enough for fiction, as anyone can prove to himself by recording, word for word, the dialogue he overhears in a restaurant or at a party:

"Well, Henry! How *are* you?"

"Oh, fine, fine. How are you? Haven't seen you in a long time."

"Oh, we're all fine, too. How are Mary and the children?"

"They're just fine, too. What about old John? Still working hard?"

Obviously, in a short story there isn't *time* for this sort of thing.

[2] For an example of skillful first-person narration, see p. 78.

Every word of dialogue must count, must further the action or deepen the characterization. Short cuts must be taken, allowing the speakers to reach in a few sentences a point it might have taken half an hour to reach in real life.

Since time is so important in a story (I immediately suspect a story that is longer than twenty manuscript pages) the writer must be careful about pacing. Ordinarily, a light story moves along swiftly; a serious one goes more slowly. Important scenes are given more space, inconsequential moments dealt with quickly or skipped altogether. There is nothing more pathetic than watching an amateur trying to get a character offstage: "Joe put down his coffeecup, rose from the chair, and stood up. He walked across the room, went into the hall, and down the hall to the front door. He opened it, went out, and closed the door behind him." Now, unless the story demands that Joe's exit be made to seem important, there is no excuse for this sort of blow-by-blow description—we all know how to walk out of a house. Extraordinary attention to detail slows the pace of the story and cuts down on the time that should be allotted to more important matters.

Bad pacing, however, is a correctable fault, and will hardly ruin a story all by itself. A more common editorial reason for turning down a manuscript is: "I don't believe it." And the most frequent defense of the injured writer is: "But that's the way it really happened!"

The fact that it happened that way in reality is no excuse for an implausible story. A serious writer soon discovers that part of his job is to impose order on life, which is so often full of coincidence, chance, and irrelevance. He must make coincidence seem foreordained, turn chance into cause-and-effect, and rule out irrelevancies altogether.

Here is an example of irrelevance: a married couple are taking an automobile trip. They are quarreling because the wife wants to make a side trip to a small town which is off their route but is reported to be charming. The husband flatly refuses, but gives no logical reason for his refusal. They pick up a hitchhiker, drive him a few miles, and let him out. Then the quarrel resumes, and we eventually learn that the husband was once in love with a girl who lived in the charming town, and is reluctant to revive old memories by revisiting it.

A neat enough plot—but what purpose does the hitchhiker serve? The reader expects him to figure in the plot; in fact, he does not affect the action at all. Then why was he in the story in the first place?

The answer is that he was there in real life, and the writer could not bear to leave him out of the story, even though he had no place there and was, in fact, misleading.

Irrelevance can be damaging to characterization as well as to plot. The writer who takes his characters straight from life runs the risk not only of offending Uncle Willie or Cousin Charlotte, but also of failing to convince the reader. Most real people are full of contradictions and inconsistencies; they do not remain "in character" as fictional people must. A simple test is to write down every characteristic of a person you know well, then ask if the resulting image is clear. Probably it will be out of focus. In creating a truly believable character, even when drawing from life, the wirter must select those aspects of personality and behavior which contribute to a clear image, and reject those that detract or mislead.

But not many writers attempt to lift an Uncle Willie straight from the backyard hammock and plunk him, unchanged, into a story. The more common error is in the opposite direction, toward stereotype. The slender blonde heroine, the craggy, handsome hero (whose name is Rick or Jon or Craig), the awkward adolescent, the repressed spinster aunt, the sage grandfather, the trusting child—these paper-thin people have walked across the pages of magazine fiction so often that they can be recognized at a glance. The lazy writer capitalizes on just this familiarity. Why should he trouble himself with creating complex, three-dimensional characters when with a few easy phrases he can evoke from the well-trained reader an instant response? The confirmed formula writer has the trust of a mathematician:

Dark, sardonic face+charm+mysterious behavior=hero of Gothic romance
Thirty-five-year-old woman+children+1 gray hair=frustrated housewife

Sometimes, as in the case of a story with a highly complicated plot (a mystery story, for example), the judicial use of stereotypes may be justified, since elaborate characterization may slow down the pace. But a writer who depends upon stock characters is not facing up to his responsibility to originate. Instead of creating characters, he is using characters that have already been created.

A writer who has mastered the arts of characterization, plotting, dialogue, pacing, and point of view may still be bothered by *balance*—that fine art of walking the tightrope between the obvious and the understated. An obvious, or sledge-hammer-approach writer underestimates his audience. Not content to make his point once, he hammers it home until the intelligent reader feels insulted and irritated. It is usually the obvious writer who is addicted to stories with a message—and the message is not conveyed dramatically, through the actions of characters in a given situation, but is tacked on to the ending, as prominently as a billboard sign or the commercial on a television program.

On the contrary, the subtle writer is probably not thinking of his audience at all. It is *his* story, and *he* knows what it means. Of course he knows what it means, because he is unconsciously supplying to the story the between-the-lines information he has in his own head, but has not put down on paper. The reader, without access to the writer's unconscious mind, is baffled. This sort of elliptical writing is common, and forgivable, among the very young. It can even be rather attractive, since a gifted writer can convey the impression that he is saying something important, almost but not quite within the grasp of less perceptive readers. But it is not, in the end, fair to reader or to writer, since the reader eventually feels cheated; and the writer forms the bad habit of promising what he cannot deliver.

Most writers quail at the prospect of revision, especially revision suggested by an editor. This is understandable. By the time a story is submitted for publication the writer, presumably, has revised it several times already, and considers it perfect—or at least as good as he can make it.

But it is hard to be objective about one's own work. For years I maintained a kind of double-standard attitude toward revision: as an editor, I was quite willing to recommend changes in the work of other writers, but as a writer, I bristled at the thought of revising my own stories. My capitulation was tardy, but total. The change came about when a story of mine was returned by an editor for revision. Being "objective," I was willing to concede that the story was slight, and probably would have been less resentful if it had been turned down outright. But at that time I still subscribed to the rather mystical belief that stories existed Somewhere Out There in Space, waiting to be discovered by clever writers, and that to change a word would amount to sacrilege.

That this was a ridiculous attitude goes without saying; I had to learn from experience. Feeling extremely self-righteous, convinced that revision would utterly ruin the story, and eager to prove the editor wrong, I sat down to rewrite it precisely to his specifications. And something surprising happened. I found myself getting interested; I saw depths in the characters that I had not seen before, new ways to strengthen the rather tenuous plot, a more plausible ending. As revised, the story was not quite as the editor had envisioned it, not at all as I had first conceived it, yet satisfactory to us both.

Now, I still believe a writer should regard suggestions for revision with a certain amount of caution. After all, no one understands what he is trying to say as well as he does, and if he is too passive and eager to please everyone, he will end with pleasing no one. But fresh minds can often provide fresh insights. A story worth telling can be told in several different ways, and a simple change in point of view, a scene added or deleted, an ending clarified, may prove the difference between success and failure. A writer should never agree to make changes if he sincerely believes them to be detrimental to the story, but he should not let artistic temperament blind him to suggestions that are genuinely helpful.

Artistic temperament is valuable, and so is sensitivity. But the artistic impulse should be channeled directly into the writing of the story, and used up in the creative process. Once the story is finished, supersensitivity ceases to be an asset. It does nothing but harm to brood over rejected stories, quiver at criticism, fall into moods of self-doubt. If a story is returned with suggestions for revision, then by all means revise it. If it is returned with a few kind words or none at all, weep no sad tears, but send it out to another market and begin another story as quickly as possible. Above all, beware of those fascinating and fruitless discussions and comparisons with other writers, which serve no purpose but that of keeping you away from your typewriter.

I once shared an office with a writer-editor whose work I very much admired. She happened to write slowly, whereas I normally write fast. After a few weeks I discovered that I was beginning to feel peculiarly guilty—and so, to my surprise, was she. My clattering typewriter keys said to her, "What you're writing can't be good, since you're taking so much time and having so much difficulty eking it out." Her thoughtful, deliberate tap-tap-tapping warned me, "Slow down, slow down; what you're writing can't be anything but glib and superficial, or you couldn't do it so quickly."

In fact, I think speed and slowness have no direct relationship to excellence. Some writers are speedy, others more deliberate, just as some people work better facing a blank wall while others prefer a view, and some require absolute silence and solitude while others can work in the midst of chaos. I know a writer who prefers to write on trains, with clipboard and pencil, and another who professes to be unable to write on any kind of paper but heavy white bond—even the *first* draft. But do these minor eccentricities have anything to do with the success or failure of a story? I doubt it.

When my own writing is not going well, and I find myself

blaming a worn typewriter ribbon, the shouting of children out-side my window, the telephone, or the heat, I recall that the first story I ever sold was written in the midst of preparations for a wedding—*literally* in the midst, for my typewriter was set up at one end of the dining room table, and at the other end my sister and her bridesmaids were opening wedding presents with loud and distracting exclamations. I can even remember my sister's quite justified accusation: "*Must* you sit there writing, now of all times, when we have so much to do?"

If a writer has a story to tell, he will not be stopped by the necessity of picking up a wedding cake from the bakery, or chang-ing a typewriter ribbon. It is only when he has nothing to say that minor frustrations defeat him.

The art of writing a story is mysterious, and textbook analysis is often inadequate to explain that mystery. Some stories follow the rules, and fail. Others depart from all known paths, and succeed. As an editor, I decided that judging stories is like testing Christ-mas tree lights: some light up and others don't. If a story doesn't light up, then no matter what it says or how carefully it was de-vised, it isn't right. If it *does* have that undefinable but unmistak-able spark, it is on its way to success. An editor may quibble over details, suggest cuts or changes, and may even turn the story down. But a story with a spark will never be dismissed lightly.

What usually provides the spark is the writer's commitment to his story. If the writer does not care about his people, his places, his plots, it is highly unlikely that his readers will care about them. Belief, or even the more demanding suspension of disbelief, is contagious. And if the writer himself is convinced by what he is writing, he will probably convince his readers as well.

To quote Curtiss Anderson, former editor of the *Ladies' Home Journal,* "A good writer cannot avoid publication, even if he tries."

SORROW RIDES A FAST HORSE

Dorothy Gilman Butters

(*Ladies Home Journal*, September, 1962)

When my mother died everyone in Green Valley said what a selfless and patient woman she had been, and how wonderfully she had managed to raise two sons alone. "A modest, uncomplaining woman," the minister said at her funeral. "A woman who was born in this town and who died in this town and never went beyond it, but cultivated wisdom in her own small garden."

When he said this my brother Rufus nudged me and smiled. People forget, of course—and anyway, the minister had lived in Green Valley for only twelve years, so he couldn't have known. Certainly mother would never have told him about what Rufus and I tacitly referred to as That Year; when it was over, mother never talked of it with us or anyone. I don't think she was ashamed or sorry so much as embarrassed about it because she could not explain her actions even to herself. Only once did she even admit that it had taken place, and I can imagine the effort this cost her. It happened when I was in the ninth grade at Green Valley School and Miss Larkin showed us a film slide of the Taj Mahal. She made a few remarks about it, saying she was sorry she could not show us a picture of the interior, but that no photographs of it had as yet been allowed.

I raised my hand and told her that inside it was glittering and white, with words from the Koran carved on the walls, and flower designs, and colored stones set into the marble.

"And from what book did you get that, John?"

"I didn't get it from a book," I told her. "I've been there. I've seen the Taj Mahal."

After school Miss Larkin took me aside and told me sternly that I must not tell lies like that; I had done it only to gain attention, but people would like me much better if I told the truth. "Now

I want you to admit that you've never visited the Taj Mahal."

"But I have," I protested.

She rapped my knuckles and said I would have to stay after school every day until I confessed to the class that I had never seen the Taj Mahal and had not been telling the truth. I almost lost my paper route from being punished and that was how mother learned about it. The next day she walked into Miss Larkin's room looking pale and nervous. Standing just inside the door she said stiffly, "Miss Larkin, John was not lying; he has seen the Taj Mahal," and without another word she walked out of the room.

Since that day two wars ago the boys and men of Green Valley have seen quite a few exotic corners of the earth, but when I was a child no one in Green Valley traveled abroad. There was neither the time nor the money for such frivolity. The town was—and still is—farmland with only a few stores, two churches and one school. My father taught in that school until one day he was reading lines from Kubla Khan to his class and reached the words "Down to a sunless sea" and crumpled suddenly to the floor. Three hours later he died of a cerebral hemorrhage.

My brother Rufus was seven and I was nine. It's difficult to realize that my mother was only thirty-one. She didn't cry when they told her; she stiffened as if she had been hit, her chin went up and her eyes glittered strangely. The first thing she did when everyone had gone was to go into the kitchen and begin scrubbing the floor. Even after the relatives arrived nobody could make her stop working; our Aunt Agatha said she was like a woman possessed.

After the funeral we were glad to go back to school because it seemed to us we had lost a mother, too; when we spoke to her she looked at us blankly, as if she'd forgotten who we were. She was still that way when the insurance man arrived. He spent an hour in the study with mother and when he left she looked chilled.

"What's that pink paper you've got?" Rufus asked.

"It's a check," mother said, staring down at it contemptuously. "A check for fifteen thousand dollars. When I think of what it

could have bought us—the things we could have done together—"
For one moment I thought she was going to cry and then her face
froze and she walked back into the kitchen. But the check must
have put the idea into her mind; here was all this money, so
utterly meaningless to her now that she wanted only to destroy it,
and if not to destroy at least abuse it. And besides, she had cleaned
the house from attic to cellar and there was nothing left to clean.

Two weeks later Rufus and I came home from school to find
mother standing in the hall with three suitcases on the floor. She
was dressed in her good black coat and the plain blue dress that
she wore to Sunday school. In those days her brown hair was
parted in the center and pulled into a tight bun at her neck, but
little tendrils always succeeded in escaping to soften her small,
delicate-boned face. "You won't be going to school tomorrow,"
she told us. "We're going away."

"When will we be back?" I asked.

She gave me that impatient blind glance that I was growing
accustomed to now. "I don't know when we'll be back," she said
in a voice that meant she didn't care when we came back. "We're
going around the world."

"I can't go around the world tomorrow," I told her. "I've got an
arithmetic exam."

"I'm sorry," she said politely. "But we are leaving in one hour
and we are going around the world."

It was late October when we landed in England, and in London
we settled into a hotel room and mother made arrangements for
two weeks of sight-seeing. After we'd watched the changing of
the guard at the palace Rufus and I decide England might be fun,
but after four days of London mother decided we must go to
Wales. A week later we were in Holland and soon after that we
left for Austria. I remember that we spent Christmas in Paris, but
we had no sooner visited the Eiffel Tower and the Bastille than
mother announced that we must pack our bags again. That was
the way it was all through the winter and spring—we packed and
unpacked our bags through Spain, Portugal and Morocco. We

were like bees flitting nervously from flower to flower: one week
riding a camel in Morocco, the next week a rented bicycle in Italy.
Rome held us briefly, but mother found Naples too beautiful and
so we did not even unpack our bags there but left immediately
for Florence. Then we moved to Greece, Rufus and I picking up
foreign words like crumbs begged from shopkeepers, concierges,
sailors and chambermaids. We behaved very badly as well, I remember, and despaired when mother did not notice. We were
alone, really alone, for the first time in our young and sheltered
lives and we resented being shut out of mother's life. But in the
manner of children everywhere, I suppose some kind of adjustment took place in us. It was to me that Rufus looked for comfort,
and I to him; and if we hated mother's indifference we also took
advantage of it, eating sweets when we chose and going to bed
when we pleased and saying "No" to her in half a dozen languages.

   In July we came to Baghdad, a city of houses the color of yellow
sand, and of blazing sun and minarets puncturing the sky with
their polished gold domes. The streets were narrow and dim,
overflowing with dust, sheep and people, the men with tender
dark eyes, the women soft and mysterious behind veils. In the
sugs Rufus and I ate yogurt with our fingers from earthenware
pots, we drank bitterly strong coffee and sat cross-legged for hours
watching men work gold or silver into filigree or hammer out
huge jugs of copper. We did not go back to our hotel except at
night. There were other Americans in that hotel because the first
oil well had been brought in only a few years earlier, but we
scorned these men; they talked only of geological surveys and
gushers and pipelines.

   No one had questioned mother until we reached Baghdad, when
an English colonel stopped one night beside our table in the dining room. It was Rufus's eighth birthday and we were attempting
some kind of celebration. The colonel told mother that Rufus
reminded him of his grandson, and after a few minutes he sat
down and asked us where we were going. Mother explained that
we were on our way to India to see the Taj Mahal and to spend a

week in Kashmir. But first, she added, we were going across the mountains to Tehran and then to Meshed to see the place where Harun al-Rashid, the caliph of the *Arabian Nights,* was buried.

The colonel's jaw dropped. "Across the mountains! What on earth can you be thinking of? This isn't England, you know."

"I didn't think it was," mother told him with asperity.

"You're in Asia now. Those mountains are full of smugglers and thieves—not safe at all. Unthinkable. I can't imagine who planned your itinerary."

"My husband did," said mother in an even voice. "Some years ago."

The colonel snorted. "Well, you can't just look at a map and go the shortest way in these countries. If you won't listen to me I'll go to your consul first thing in the morning and tell him what you're up to. He'll stop you."

But of course by the next day we were gone. Mother had already visited the consulates and she had had the foresight to acquire a visa for Persia and a man to drive us across the border and over the mountains. In those days the idea of a woman traveling alone in Asia with two children was so unthinkable that it must never have occurred to anyone—except the colonel—to ask her questions. I think the authorities, most of whom spoke little or no English, assumed mother was traveling with one child and a husband, and mother did not discourage them. Certainly she did not look like an adventuress and she met no one wise enough to see her ruthlessness. They did not know that mother was courting self-destruction. As for endangering the lives of two children, no appeal in that direction could have touched her because she was, as Aunt Agatha said, a woman possessed. We scarcely existed for her then.

Our driver was an Afghan named Mohammed Aslam and there was so much affection in his first glance at us that we stopped acting like spoiled and precocious children. As mother handed him our three suitcases, she inquired—dutifully and with not much interest —if there really were thieves in the mountains ahead.

Aslam gave her a gay smile accompanied by a shrug. "A few,

perhaps. The people are poor, poorer than anybody else in that country. But in my car, we go fast."

We looked at his car, a patched and ancient Ford truck. "She goes," he told us proudly, patting its fender. And indeed she did go; and did not break down until we needed her most.

A child does not remember the same things an adult remembers. You may take a child to the Louvre, and he will remember the guard who picked his nose, or the organ grinder on the street outside, or the chocolate treat on the way home. Only the adults remember the *Mona Lisa*. For us this journey into Persia was Aslam, dust and heat and picnics eaten beside the truck. In this queer, convulsed corner of the world even mother seemed more cheerful, as if its bleakness matched hers. We slept for two nights on rugs beside the car with a canvas stretched from the truck to a pole. No one passed us along the way; we might have been the only four people in the world. At dawn we would eat *mast*, a kind of curds dried into a hard white ball, and mother and Aslam would drink *chai* while we had milk from a goatskin kept cool in a bucket of water. Then we would be off, climbing slowly toward the mountain range before us. It was barren, desolate country covered not with scrub but with thistles, as tall as a man and bearing blossoms the size of an apple. The truck gave out when we had reached what seemed like the top of the world. It simply stopped. We piled out, trying not to look into the canyon below, and waited while Aslam cheerfully peered under and into the engine. At last he shook his head. "*No benzine.*"

"You're out of gas?"

"*Bali.*" He led us to the rear and showed us the gas tank, which had a hole in it the size of a twenty-five-cent piece.

Mother appeared unconcerned; she asked Aslam what he proposed to do next. He replied—still very cheerfully—that we must not worry, he would get us to Hamadan, *inshallah*. I did not remind mother that *inshallah* meant if God wills it. He asked for money, which mother trustingly gave him, and said he would be back in a few hours with donkeys. Five hours later, when we were nearly prostrate from the heat, he did indeed return, from heaven knows where, leading four emaciated donkeys. He had bought them in a Lur village some miles away and he said he would return them when he came back for his truck. The donkeys, Aslam told me, were for my *mader,* my *barader* and me; upon the fourth he would pile our baggage and food and water while he himself would walk. Although we protested at this he was very insistent, saying that he could walk faster than any of us. I did not realize until later that he was afraid. It did not occur to us that in these mountains a man with enough money to buy donkeys draws attention to himself.

We made poor time, but we traveled until long past sunset. The border was far behind us now. Another day's traveling, Aslam said, and we would reach Kermanshah, where he could purchase *benzine* and—he hoped—the means to repair his tank. In the meantime we would stop here—we had reached a plateau rimmed with jagged rocks—and cook a little rice and spread our rugs. He began to make a small fire, leaning over it, blowing on it and crooning to it. Mother sat slumped on her donkey, too tired to dismount, while Rufus and I stood beside ours wondering how to tether them.

It was several moments before we realized we were not alone.

There were six of them, and they had stepped out of the darkness like wraiths. The poverty of them, and the desolateness of our surroundings, made my heart jump in a sickening fashion. They were bearded, fierce and ragged. They wore loose, pantaloonlike black trousers, but neither sashes nor shirts. Only three of them owned turbans. They looked so terribly poor—and so fierce—that I suddenly realized how wealthy we must look to them with our rugs and our donkeys.

"Who are they?" asked mother with a faint look of surprise.

Aslam stood up cautiously and spoke to them. The tallest of the six men—heavily bearded and wearing a turban so that only his eyes and the sharpness of his cheekbones showed—replied at some length. When he had finished speaking he laughed and showed Aslam the heavy stick he carried in one hand.

"Who are they?" repeated mother, still not afraid.

Aslam looked a little sick. "Bandits."

"Then give them food," mother said impatiently.

Aslam said uneasily, "They do not want food."

"Then give them what money we have."

Still Aslam hesitated.

"Well?" asked mother curtly. "What is it they want?"

Keeping his eyes on the ground, Aslam said, "They want you and the children as well as the food and money. I have told them you are American, but they do not know what American is."

Mother frowned. "They intend to *capture* us?"

Aslam gave her a fleeting look of surprise. "They have already captured us."

"But what on earth do they want us for?"

Aslam's eyes returned to the ground. He said nothing, which was thoughtful of him, for none of the possibilities would have pleased us. The leader of the bandits stepped forward and made a gesture to mother to get down from her donkey. She stared at him unbelievingly and then she turned to look at the five other men and at Rufus and me. Her gaze moved from us to the deep night sky and then to the jagged black rocks and I saw a shudder run through her as if she were shaking herself out of a deep trance. The blind look had gone from her eyes. I realized that at last she was clearly seeing us and her surroundings. Such a look of horror crossed her face that I thought she was going to scream.

"Please," Aslam begged in a low voice. "There is no hope just now. Wait. Do nothing to resist. These men are dangerous."

Mother seemed dazed. "Not resist? Aslam, they must not capture us!"

Aslam said sadly, "It must be your *qismat*—your fate—to stop here."

Mother gave a bitter, half-strangled laugh. Her cheeks were flushed and her hair undone; she looked wild and strange. "My *qismat*?" she said harshly. "Tell this man I must travel like the wind—that is my *qismat*. Tell him," she went on fiercely, "that

Sorrow rides behind me on a fast horse—if he listens closely he may hear the hoofbeats. Tell him that if he captures me he will capture Sorrow as well—because where I go Sorrow follows and where I stop Sorrow will stop."

Where did she find these words? I don't know. My mother had never spoken in that manner before and I never heard her speak that way again. Aslam obediently translated her words for the bandit chief and I saw him narrow his eyes. I wondered if instead of capturing us they might kill us then and there. The bandits began to speak among themselves and to gesticulate, one of them pointing in the direction from which we had come, and another giving us an angry, accusing glance. After interminable moments the bandit chief turned to mother and spoke.

Aslam said breathlessly, "He says it has been a hard year, with many people dead in their village. Sheep have sickened and died. He says they do not wish for more Sorrow. If Sorrow follows behind you then you must leave these mountains at once. You must not stop even to sleep."

Mother closed her eyes. She looked suddenly drained.

"He and his men will guide us out of the mountains to speed us on our way."

Mother opened her eyes and said with dignity, "Tell him that we are ready to go."

The bandits were as good as their word. All night we rode behind them and when dawn came we were only an hour from Kermanshah. We dismounted and the bandits took the donkeys from us, as well as our food and money, but left us our baggage. As they turned to go the bandit chief walked up to mother and gave her a hard, searching glance. Aslam, translating his words, said, "He wants you to know that his wife died last month and a son last year. He is well acquainted with Sorrow. He has taken your food and money, but he gives you the gift of a copper water jug. Which he probably captured from somebody else," Aslam added dryly. "He says to you '*Istali mashi*,' which means 'May you never be tired.' In return you must say to him '*Kwar mashi*,' which means 'May you never be poor.' "

There were tears in mother's eyes. "*Kwar mashi*," she replied to the bandit chief.

We stood and watched them ride away on our donkeys and then mother said quietly, "I think it is time we began making arrangements to go home now."

We had left Green Valley in October and we returned in October and when we entered our front yard mother looked at the sagging front steps and said in a matter-of-fact voice, "You and I will have to mend those tomorrow, John." She took off her black coat and hung it in the hall closet and said to Rufus, "You're beginning to look like your father, Rufus." Then she went upstairs to unpack our suitcases, still only three in number because mother had not brought home any Persian rugs or Haviland china or any of the souvenirs that tourists collect; there was only the copper jug which she wrapped and put away in a chest. To the neighbors she said, "We did a little traveling, here and there." And in the spring she went to work in the public library and never, never did she talk to us of That Year so that after a while it seemed to Rufus and me like a dream that we happened to dream at the same time.

After the funeral Rufus and I came back to the empty house and rebuilt the fire on the kitchen hearth and made coffee. When it had been poured we sat quietly for a few minutes, neither of us speaking, and then Rufus got up and went to the chest in the living room and brought back a bulky package of flannel and newspaper. He unwrapped the copper jug.

" 'A quiet, uneventful life,' " I quoted dryly.

Rufus nodded. "She would have agreed with the minister, you know."

"It was insane, every moment of it," I said. "We were fortunate to escape with our lives."

Rufus smiled. "There is a proverb that says to nearly lose your life is to find it. Of course it was madness, all of it. And yet—"

"Yes?" I said curiously, for it had been a long time since we had talked of this.

He said softly, "We learned from her how perverse, how unpredictable, how astonishing and how courageous a human being can be."

I lifted my cup. "To our legacy, then," I said, smiling at him. *"Istali mashi."*

"Kwar mashi," he replied, and we drank to That Year.

ꕔ ALL THE TEA IN CHINA

Katharine Topkins

(ALL THE TEA IN CHINA, by Katharine Topkins, is the story of an
American marriage, as seen through the eyes of a teen-age girl,
Emily Showcrafter. In this excerpt, she describes the first meeting
of her sister, Eleanor, and El's future husband Mike.)

The way Mike and El met in the first place was complicated, like
the rest of their life together. El was home from U.C.L.A. for
Christmas vacation—it was her freshman year—and it was Christmas Eve and she was going over to Warren Titus's. They were
engaged. The Tituses lived in Denny Blaine, which is one of
Seattle's older but better districts and about ten miles from us, the
way the crow flies. Our house is on a hillside up on a bluff in
Carleton Park, which is also considered a first-rate residential
section.

Well, there was a big family conference about whether or not
El should be allowed to take the Olds herself or daddy should
drive her. In the end they decided to let her go. (Warren had
broken his ankle skiing, so he couldn't pick her up.) She started
out the door in this gray gabardine coat that she had this real
thing about, even though it was a million years old and mother said
goodness she couldn't go like that, with a spot down the front of
her coat, what would Mrs. Titus think? on Christmas Eve? So in
the end she wore mother's beaver coat and mother wet her fore-
finger and smoothed down El's eyebrows which had a tendency
to go every which way, and we all sat tensely waiting for the
sound of the motor. After we heard the car bump over the curb
(we have a narrow driveway) I went back to the tree, which was
trimmed on only the street side. They keep this weird-looking
unhinged angel that I made in kindergarten for the top of the
tree and a Santa Claus with a cotton beard and brass paper tacks
for buttons and fitful coloring that El did. I was looking for the

Santa Claus when the phone rang and mother just kept saying who? who? my daughter? and she shouted that El had been in an accident five blocks away. It wasn't serious, this woman who called kept saying. El had smashed into a parked car in front of their house and jarred her teeth a little, nothing to worry about.

We all flew over there in the Chrysler. El said she was just leaning down to adjust the heater and she didn't notice this parked car.

The Olds was still drivable and daddy took it, with us following. Mother kept on about thank God it wasn't serious, just enough to teach her a lesson, and El, who was shivering, kept trying to explain how it happened. The main damage was the windshield, which was cracked.

When we got home mother got El the heating pad to break her chill and daddy called our insurance agent who was either crocked or unreceptive to being called on Christmas Eve. He did cough up the name of this place, Tri-State Auto Glass Craft, which as it turned out happened to belong to Mike, and Mike said yes, he would come out with the mobile unit to install the windshield. (We found out later that Mike didn't have any family himself and so he really didn't have anything special to do on Christmas Eve, he having just broken up with his fiancée, Aime—pronounced m-a—and I think he welcomed the call.)

Even by porch light Mike was really breathtaking. That was six years ago and he must have been twenty-six then and really in his prime. Mike had a terrific sense of timing. I mean he just stood there with his fists on his hips shaking his head and looking from the windshield back to El until finally she started to giggle out of nervousness.

Daddy and El stayed out there with him for a while, but eventually the three of them came in and mother said they must be simply frozen. Daddy introduced her—"This is Edward Michaels; my wife, Mrs. Showcrafter"—and Mike said, "Just call me Mike," and reached out to shake hands with mother, looking around at things. "You have quite a layout here, Mrs. Showcrafter," and mother said something about how he was seeing us in a rather confused state, she was afraid. But Mike just stood there looking up at the spiral stairway. It really is kind of impressive. I mean we have this round Chinese Oriental rug in the hall and then this open stairway with a wrought-iron banister and everything like that.

Well, Mike kept standing there even after daddy had signed the receipt Mike gave him for the insurance company and so finally daddy, who had a Christmas Eve habit of reading us Dickens aloud by the fire, invited Mike to join us if he cared to. "A Christmas Carol," daddy began. "Stave One—Marley's Ghost." Mike and El sat on the quilted sofa, facing the fire, with Nicki, our Persian, on the cushion between them, like a breathing pillow, and daddy sat in his leather chair and mother sat on the needlepoint desk chair and I kept on tinseling because I could observe better from there. Nicki kept standing up on El's lap and stretching. Just as Mike said something to El, there went the plume of Nicki's tail into his face, and I think it made Mike feel cut off. He and Nicki never did see eye to eye on things.

Around about where Mr. Fezziwig's fiddler plunges his hot face into a pot of porter, Mrs. Evans, who lives kitty-corner to us, came over for a minute with *pfeffernüss* cookies on a paper plate with a napkin over them and some English holly. Daddy introduced Mike, who told Mrs. Evans that he was imposing on our hospitality, joining in a family celebration, but it really meant a lot to him. Then later on one of the strings of lights on the tree went out and Mike got it going again. About eleven-thirty Mike left, thanking the folks for letting him share Christmas Eve with them, and mother put an arm around Mike's shoulder and said it was all their pleasure, and she hoped they would have occasion to see him again without the necessity of a broken windshield.

Once we heard the truck backing out of the driveway, mother said what a fine boy that was and daddy said yes, that he seemed to be one of the few younger men who understood the necessity for hard work and he would certainly be a catch for some girl, and then mother told El for heaven's sake not to slouch down that way, it was bad for her lungs.

Well, the day after Christmas, Mike called and asked El to go to the ice show with him and she was really flustered, explaining that she was engaged and she couldn't, she really couldn't. Then she just sat there with her hand on the receiver after she had hung up, and her toes hooked around the rung of the phone stool, and mother said wasn't it sweet of that boy to want to return the hospitality, which he certainly didn't need to, that way.

"What makes you think he's just returning the hospitality?" said El.

That was the last we saw of Mike until he and El arrived home from their honeymoon.

The Article

BROCK BROWER

Of all extant literary forms, I'm afraid the general article asks the greatest general sufferance of us right at the moment, because it is concurrently in its dotage as journalism and in its nonage as literature. It is, in too many cases, simply senile—a reiterated banality wheezed to formulae for the engineered readerships of certain unreconstructed mass magazines ("What is a good article made of?" singsongs a wordsmith at her forge in *The Writer's Digest*. "STATISTICS, QUOTES, AND ANECDOTES!"). Yet it has proved itself, in some recent instances, to be a precocious instrument—a remarkably free engine for prose that such editors as Norman Podhoretz of *Commentary* and John Fischer of *Harper's* see as the most pertinent and immediate means of expression our culture can offer a writer. As a result, those of us who write it— and try to write it better than the newspapers are written—live in a din of huzzahs and alarums, and none of us knows exactly whether the article is ignominiously sinking, like the old *Collier's*, or emerging triumphant over itself, like a change in the language. The only thing that *is* certain is that it will not "survive"—in the sense that other troubled literary forms, such as the short story and the novel, are predicted to "survive" any current abatement of interest or debility of art—because there are enough of us around who won't *let* it "survive." The article must now either go under along with all magazines that persist in believing some millions of readers can still be united by a single endocrinal response to "a sparkling lead," "a clear, lucid style," "universal reader appeal," et cetera, or become an entirely new and disturbing and quite different thing, put to broad general use much as Norman Mailer and James Baldwin have put it to more intensive personal use in their efforts to sear public awareness with their own convictions.

In other words, the impact of an article is coming to depend more and more upon the writer's individual intelligence and resolve, and less and less upon the corporate noodling of the journal in which it appears; and this shift proves out an interesting juggle that has occurred lately in the handling of our sense of reality. At about the same time that magazines began, I fear, to let reality slip, a number of fine writers—novelists, short story writers, some of the young and uncommitted—began desperately trying to close with reality. "Making a living is nothing; the great difficulty is making a point, making a difference—with words," Elizabeth Hardwick has summed up this impulsive search. These writers found that the point, the difference had to be made with more than fictions— that the "lies like truth" would no longer do for the Truth—and so they turned precipitously to the concreteness of fact. Or perhaps, in the end, Fact actually turned on them, like a cornered assassin, and almost defensively they reached for the first weapon at hand. The article, whatever else it may be, has always been bluntly at hand, if only because it has never been put by any definition out of reach.

It's important to understand how open and available a form it really is—much more so than the short story or novel—despite the false restrictions that popular journalism has imposed upon it. Of course, as long as only journalists wrote the article, it was bound to follow the journalistic crotchets—a "news peg to hang it on," "lots of quotes, high up in the story," "color," "the flavor of the man," and so on *ad nauseam*—but it was never bonded to journalism. In fact, by definition, the article is bonded to no one. The word itself (if a brief look into the N.E.D. can be excused here) comes from the Latin *articulus,* the diminutive of *artus,* or "joint." "*Articulus* in L. was extended from the joint, to the parts jointed on, limbs, members, 'joints' of the finger, etc; whence *transf.* to the component parts of discourses, writings, actions." An article then is "A literary composition forming materially part of a journal, magazine, encyclopaedia, or other collection, *but treating a specific topic distinctly and independently.*" (Italics added.) It serves no genre, no subject matter, no periodical; it should never be written *for*—in that slavish sense—*The Saturday Evening Post, The New Yorker,* or any other master. It should simply be "jointed on" its literary surroundings, as indeed the best articles always are, outlandish among the Contents.

Actually, there is only one specific obligation that touches the form of the article, and it derives from another branch of the above etymology. (Which is my only reason for quoting such wondrous and cumbersome stuff. Usually this is the kind of research a writer of an article does "to have the facts behind him"—and *leave* behind him.) From the same word *articulus* also comes the idea of breaking down a whole into its jointed parts, and treating each part carefully in sequence. For instance, in speaking—as so many of us were painfully taught to do—we *articulate.* "To express distinctly; to give utterance to. . . . To form or fit into a systematically interrelated whole." That is really all an article is obliged to do. It articulates any subject, person, or idea, and it may do so in any style that pleases the writer, so long as he does not fail to exercise at least two of his faculties: his own voice, so that his article will be distinct, and his own reason, so that his article will be independent.

Patently, neither of these faculties has ever been included in the basic equipage of a journalist, which may explain the vapidity of so much that has been published in magazines. Journalism is routinely voiceless, or whenever it gains a voice, it is a street voice, caterwauling for attention, not understanding. But far worse, journalism is routinely mindless. Its vaunted objectivity—its habit of piling the greater fact on top of the lesser fact, like Pelion on top of Ossa on top of a pebble—this is only an escape from the need to reason. When finally faced with a controversial point which demands some interpretation, the journalist is famous for the "Lib-

Lab," i.e., "on the one hand, *this,* and on the other hand, *that,*" but neither hand is his. The easy generalization ("the greatest living . . . single most . . . best known . . . fastest rising . . . nonesuch on the immediate horizon") and the endless qualifier ("perhaps") are the two stylistic counterweights with which the journalist maintains his own commitment, and hence his own existence, at constant zero. The total impression is at last one of immobility, as if words indeed made no point, no difference, and the writing strikes us as literally inarticulate—that is, random, disconnected, *disjointed.*

The obvious effect of this practice on our sense of reality is to sap it, and for some time this seemed to be the deliberate case with many magazines. However, nothing can remain unreal for very long and still circulate, so that something of a panic has finally overtaken these magazines, and happily just at the moment when some of the better writers have independently hit upon their own means of articulating reality. In several cases—still far too few—there have been some most fortunate meetings of minds, and the article has begun to appear with both a voice and an independence within it. Put another way, the facts, which would have only been gathered and sieved by a journalist, have been enclosed within a single intelligence, and a mind has set to work, making independent observations that are far more capacitous than those of the tape recorder or the TV camera.

Actually, this is not a new thing, but only a resurrected approach; in fact, one of the best examples of this kind of writing in American letters is an article from *The Southern Literary Messenger,* April, 1836. It appeals to me especially because it shows, long before twentieth-century journalism elaborated itself into a huge staff operation with its own infernal technology, how far superior the work of a single good mind really is.

The subject of this article is what must have been one of the first computers. Or rather, it purported to be such. The machine was an Automaton Chess-Player, displayed by a German named Johann Nepomuk Maelzel, and it played chess against the local human competition (just as IBM7090 has been partially programmed to do) through a dummy seated at a chest, on which were a chessboard and six differently tapered candles. The chest was full of machinery—supposedly—and the dummy, called the Turk, was run by the machinery—supposedly. People had their doubts, of course, though they were allowed in a limited way to examine the mechanism before the Turk started his chess game. But the man who settled those doubts—and proved that a human being *had* to be inside the machine, even if he were a midget—was a writer of occasional articles named Edgar Allan Poe.

Now the remarkable thing about Poe's article, entitled "Maelzel's Chess-Player," is that he disproved the reality of the mechanism—dismantled it and looked inward at its chicane vitals—by simply reasoning it onto the logical scrap heap. He never had to go near the Chess-Player to demolish it. He never got "behind the scenes," or talked intimately with members of the Maelzel household, or met the midget in a bar and got him drunk. He merely observed, reasoned, and concluded. "Ratiocination," Poe was later to call this exercise of intelligence. He even managed by ratiocination to show that the man inside the Chess-Player had to be righthanded—a conclusion that follows irrefutably from the fact that the Turk plays a left-handed game. Poe adduced sixteen other refutations altogether (some of them are given in the selection from "Maelzel's Chess-Player" at the end of this chapter), but two should suffice here to show the style of mind that he brought to bear upon just such a critical question of reality.

3. The Automaton does not invariably win the game. Were the machine a pure machine this would not be the case—it would always win. The *principle* being discovered by which a machine can be made to *play* a game of chess, an extension of the same principle would enable it to *win* a game—a farther extension would enable it to *win all* games—that is, to beat any possible game of an antagonist. A little consideration will convince anyone that the difficulty of making a machine beat all games, is not in the least degree greater, as regards the principle of the operations necessary, than that of making it beat a single game. If then we regard the Chess-Player as a machine, we must suppose, (what is highly improbable,) that its inventor preferred leaving it incomplete to

perfecting it—a supposition rendered still more absurd, when we reflect that the leaving it incomplete would afford an argument against the possibility of its being a pure machine—the very argument we now adduce.

4. When the situation of the game is difficult or complex, we never perceive the Turk either shake his head or roll his eyes. It is only when his next move is obvious, or when the game is so circumstanced that to a man in the Automaton's place there would be no necessity for reflection. Now these peculiar movements of the head and eyes are movements customary with persons engaged in meditations, and the ingenious Baron Kempelen would have adapted these movements (were the machine a pure machine) to occasions proper to their display—that is, to occasions of complexity. But the reverse is seen to be the case, and this reverse applies precisely to our supposition of a man in the interior. When engaged in meditation about the game, he has no time to think of setting in motion the mechanism of the Automaton by which are moved the head and the eyes. When the game, however, is obvious, he has time to look about him, and accordingly, we see the head shake and the eyes roll.

In these passages, the *style* of the intelligence is inimitable, but the *role* of the intelligence emphatically is not. In fact, it is precisely the role that every writer engaging reality must set for his own reason to play—first confrontory, then encompassing, and finally critical. Yet, under the circumstances that usually attend the writing of an article, it is the hardest role to assign independent reason. It is so easily usurped by the "actual assignment—what we want you to do with this one," the pressure of time, the ephemera around the subject, et cetera. The great usurper once was the magazine itself with its Draconic point of view, but this is not now so important as the bad habits this usurpation bred. It is so easy to quote, generalize, qualify, extrapolate *neutrally* around a subject—*Let the reader draw his own conclusions*—instead of facing it directly as something that must be plumbed by a dropline of pure thought.

In writing articles, I've always tried in some way to drop such a line—except when I've been dragooned into assignments that have turned out hopeless and ashen—and I find I'm most comfortable making the effort when I can draw as near as possible to

Poe's exercise of pure mind. That is, I prefer to try to imbue an entire matter with an impersonal intelligence which infuses everything like a sudden freshness in the whole air than to set upon a subject with a rush of personality which bestirs everything like too sharp an individual breeze. I suspect this approach (that is, Poe's) is probably best for anybody initially attempting an article—unless he has a Nobel Prize, or expects one soon—but it certainly isn't, by any means, the only style the mind can assume. Much that has been achieved recently with expository prose has been exactly opposite in nature: highly personal, and as far removed from Poe's ratiocination as his terrors are from our own. But this still doesn't change the essential role that reason plays, for there must inevitably be the same force of intelligence in, say, one of James Baldwin's refutations as there is in one of Poe's.

The American Negro has the great advantage of having never believed the collection of myths to which white Americans cling: that their ancestors were all freedom-loving heroes, that they were born in the greatest country the world has ever seen, or that Americans are invincible in battle and wise in peace, that Americans have always dealt honorably with Mexicans and Indians and all other neighbors or inferiors, that American men are the world's most direct and virile, that American women are pure. Negroes know far more about white Americans that that; it can almost be said, in fact, that they know about white Americans what parents— or, anyway, mothers—know about their children, and that they very often regard white Americans that way. And perhaps this attitude, held in spite of what they know and have endured, helps to explain why Negroes, on the whole, and until lately, have allowed themselves to feel so little hatred. The tendency has really been, insofar as this was possible, to dismiss white people as the slightly mad victims of their own brainwashing. One watched the lives they led. One could not be fooled about that; one watched the things they did and the excuses that they gave themselves, and if a white man was really in trouble, deep trouble, it was to the Negro's door that he came. And one felt that if one had had that white man's worldly advantages, one would never have become as bewildered and as joyless and as thoughtlessly cruel as he. The Negro came to the white man for a roof or for five dollars or for a letter to the judge; the white man came to the Negro for love. But he was not often able to give what he came seeking. The price was too high; he had too much to lose. And the Negro knew this, too. When one knows this about a man, it is impossible for one to hate him, but unless he becomes a man—becomes equal—it is also impossible for one to love him. Ultimately, one tends to avoid him, for the universal characteristic of children is to assume that they have a monopoly on trouble, and therefore a monopoly on *you*. (Ask any Negro what he knows about the white people with whom he works. And then ask the white people with whom he works what they know about *him*.)

Nothing could conflict more with the immaculately analytic tone of Poe than this homiletic style of Baldwin's, but despite the difference of a century in moral feeling, there is still the same basic probity in both men. Like Poe, Baldwin is also looking closely to see why "the head shakes and the eyes roll." It is the same intrusive act of mind, a stealing inside all reality's dumb shows to find out how false or true the machinery within actually is, whether it is "operating" an automaton or a white man or a Negro or a President or a revolution.

On a practical working level, there are numerous thoughts about writing an article that follow from this insistence upon independent probity, but basically they all come down to the hard fact that if a writer expects to maintain this independence, he must do everything for himself. If a single good mind is to encompass a matter, then other minds become superfluous. The writer himself, for instance, is always his own best researcher, despite what other adjunctive intelligences may contribute, and the rule is that the research is only done when the writer "meets himself coming back the other way," i.e., when among all possible informants, the writer becomes, at least for the moment, the best informed.

Similarly, all the interviewing must be done by the writer himself, *live*—that is, without the excuse of a tape recorder to let him off listening and responding—and all his efforts should be bent upon staging in his own head a kind of symposium attended by his various interviewees. Through him, without ever meeting, they "discuss" the subject. He does not run around collecting opinions, like a pollster. He actively seeks to create a dialogue among people who really only converse through him, and his advantage is that to him each can speak freely, where they might argue with, or shy from, or disdain one another face to face.

And finally, only the writer himself can assume the full burden of knowledge. Behind even the most personal prose, there is always some privacy, or privacies, kept inviolate; there is always information "on the record" and information "off the record." In fact, it is positively the sign of mindless journalistic technology at work when the written instrument exhausts the "available facts." Any writer who is no such technocrat inevitably begins with a much deeper knowledge of his subject than he can possibly put on paper, and the rule is that no writer should set down a word on paper until he knows what he must also leave unsaid.

These are some few of the demands made upon the writer when reason is given its proper role, but they are all made, of course, prior to the actual writing of the article. This is only preparation, and there is still the need to find a voice. That challenge—to discover a voice that will summon reality like a flourish from the horn of Roland—is the hardest to meet in any prose, and it is remarkable how large a success the article has had recently in discovering a variety of such voices. The explanation, of course, is that there has been a heavy borrowing from the house of fiction.

Actually, this is exactly as it should be, though this transposition seems often strangely inhibited. In the past, there existed a much closer tie between expository prose and narrative prose. To return to Poe for a moment, the prose that appears in "Maelzel's Chess-Player" is precisely the prose that he puts in the mouth of his great detective, M. Dupin. "But Truth is often, and in very great degree, the aim of the tale," he wrote in a famous review of Hawthorne's short stories. "Some of the finest tales are tales of ratiocination." As his own indeed proved to be. Even his literary criticism has this same ratiocinative tone as if he only required the one voice to swiftly subsume all forms. The same is true of Melville, whose reportage and fiction (and often their mixture) are given utterance in a single voice that stands reality on its ear.

Such descriptions as he offers in *The Encantadas, or Enchanted Isles*, where "No voice, no low, no howl is heard; the chief sound of life here is a hiss," are enough to buckle our senses.

> . . . behold these really wondrous tortoises—none of your schoolboy mud-turtles—but black as widow's weeds, heavy as chests of plate, with vast shells medallioned and orbed like shields, and dented and blistered like shields that have breasted a battle, shaggy, too, here and there, with dark green moss, and slimy with the spray of the sea. These mystic creatures, suddenly translated by night from unutterable solitudes to our peopled deck, affected me in a manner not easy to unfold. They seemed newly crawled forth from beneath the foundations of the world. Yea, they seemed the identical tortoises whereon the Hindoo plants this total sphere. With a lantern I inspected them more closely. Such worshipful venerableness of aspect! Such furry greenness mantling the rude peelings and healing the fissures of their shattered shells. I no more saw three tortoises. They expanded—became transfigured. I seemed to see three Roman Coliseums in magnificent decay.

Yet these tortoises are not what he "imagined" in fiction, but actual beings he "saw" on board ship, and indeed "next evening, strange to say, I sat down with my shipmates, and made a merry repast from the tortoise steaks and tortoise stews." There is no real discrepancy, for Melville's voice is a master instrument, tuned to mundanity as well as dream, and not a vulnerable lute that must be held safely aloof from the vibrations of reality.

Since the nineteenth century, this magisterial range of voice through any number of forms, particularly the article, has been sorely missed, but suddenly—out of a hunger for impressions that only an extreme sense of isolation could have bred—writers have begun again to attempt it. Nelson Algren writes a travel book that carries him out of his destitute fantasy of Chicago into the real world where he must bring whole nationalities, the Spanish, the French, the English, the Irish, the Turks, around the corner of South Street into his own blind pig. Truman Capote turns profilist, then chronicler of the Moscow *Porgy and Bess* tour, and finally detective, as he offers the police an important clue in a Kansas murder case, the latest grotesque he has chosen from the things of reality to transform directly into an exquisite bibelot of prose. Norman Mailer unleashes a diurnal attack against the culture that has pruned him of his goodly limbs and left him a stark and leafless trunk—a "success"—and out of this shock tactic, out of even the magazine deadline itself, he begins to find his way back from "prophecy" to the novel once more. "The drama of real life will not let down the prose writer," Miss Hardwick comments. "Life inspires. The confession, the revelation, are not reporting, not even journalism. Real life is treated *as if it* were fiction. The concreteness of fact is made suggestive, shadowy, symbolical. The vividly experiencing 'I' begins his search for his art in the newspapers."

And ends by publishing it in the magazines.

So the voice carries over from its beginnings in fiction, and sustains itself at the pitch of real life, perhaps even gains strength, as has certainly been the case with James Baldwin. More than any other writer, Baldwin has achieved his individual voice through the article form. He has even made the article assignment—that purchase order from a magazine for prose on an out-of-stock topic—into an iron link between event and personal vision. In his fiction, this voice has often seemed constricted, even *falsetto,* but set free to find its own natural limits—a liberty which the article form could indulge—it reached a lambency in prose that threw the black sufferings of his people into terrible relief against the white world. At the same time, no writer has set "the vividly experiencing 'I' " to face greater intrinsic peril, simply because every real event for Baldwin seems to catch at some thread in the worn, tacky, durable fabric of his being. He pulls at the thread himself, just a loose end, and then suddenly there is no knowing where the ravel will end or lead us. "On the 19th of December, in 1949, when I had been living in Paris for a little over a year, I was arrested as a receiver of stolen goods and spent eight days in prison," he begins an article for *Commentary,* "Equal in Paris," which I have included in its entirety at the end of this chapter. The stolen goods were only a *drap de lit,* the "theft" only a misunderstanding; the event at bottom was insignificant. But it pulls from Baldwin a thread of existence that supports an awful burden of culture and race and alienation. Yet it never breaks, only delicately shines.

> One had, in short, to come into contact with an alien culture in order to understand that a culture was not a community basket-weaving project, nor yet an act of God; was something neither desirable nor undesirable in itself, being inevitable, being nothing more or less than the recorded and visible effects on a body of people of the vicissitudes with which they had been forced to deal. And their great men are revealed as simply another of these vicissitudes, even if, quite against their will, the brief battle of their great men with them has left them richer.

Am I saying then that only the displaced voice from fiction has sufficient resolve to force a personal articulation of reality upon the article form? Not at all. It is simply that of late the best voices have come over, impassioned or hortatory or simply bully, from fiction, and the writer of an article might better listen to them first if he wishes to find his own voice at all. Obviously no writer need master the short story before trying his hand at an article, but at the same time no writer should ignore the fictional techniques that have so strengthened the embodiment of fact in prose and made it "suggestive, shadowy, symbolical." What the novelists know naturally, the rest of us must learn at our pain.

In my own case, since I invariably keep at an impersonal distance from my subject, my strongest efforts in this area have been bent upon turning fact into imagery in an article. Faced with the usual Augean stable of data, I do not try to sweep it clean—as a journalist would in his Herculean labors—but rather to pick out the most redolent facts and deliberately hoard them for the aura of the stable. That is, I select facts not only as a rationalist, trying to bring an abstract line of reasoning to a conclusion, but also as an imagist, seeking to broach reality for a pattern. It is hard to pick much of an example from what has been a very broadly scattered exercise, but in an article on psychoanalysis, I tried to sum up its early history, while bodying forth the aura of the actual practice, in the following manner:

> That first couch was of horsehair. Pyramided high with pillows. *Berggasse 19, Wien IX.* ("After the—well, later when the Professor

is no longer with us," the porter said one day to the poet H.D. on her way to her fifty-five-minute "hour," "they will call it Freudgasse." They never did.) For some of his taller patients, it was almost too short, and their feet under the couch rug nearly touched the glowing porcelain stove set narrowly in the corner. From the other corner, behind the couch's hard, slightly elevated headpiece, came the cigar smoke and the fatherly voice. "Today we have tunneled very deep. You have discovered for yourself what I discovered for the race." Around him, the sublimations of a frustrated archaeologist: Greek amphorae, Assyrian and Egyptian statuettes, and other tiny, ancient totems, set all in a row. And over the couch—on the wall usually reserved nowadays for the stark probe of a favored pair of analytical eyes—a large steel engraving of the Temple of Arnak, for this was the only consulting room in the history of psychoanalysis where it was not possible to hang on that wall an honorific portrait of an analyst's chosen St. Analyst.

I wanted to begin with the facts at a particular point in time, but I also wanted these same facts to form an image of reality that would give back a semblance of life, of moment to the prose. My own voice, I'm afraid, is factual, not personal, and I depend much more upon a kind of factual density than upon any vision to help me articulate reality. But this is only one other writer's way of struggling for voice, not the lone arduous path to the one true expository style, and the eventual point is that many voices have lifted themselves above the jibber of mere fact to confound directly the reality behind it.

In fact, one of the best is also one of the most prosaic, that of George Orwell. In a way, Orwell preceded all of us into reality. His prose—which is as spare as experience itself really is—seems to have an absolute correspondence with his moment, his existence; his voice is so quietly suasive that reading him is like joining him. His articles don't end; rather, *he* departs, and leaves behind him both a sense of truth and a sense of embarrassment. In his famous article on "Shooting an Elephant," he ends by telling us:

> Afterwards, of course, there were endless discussions about the shooting of the elephant. The owner was furious, but he was only an Indian and could do nothing. Besides, legally I had done the right thing, for a mad elephant has to be killed, like a mad dog,

if its owner fails to control it. Among the Europeans opinion was divided. The older men said I was right, the younger men said it was a damn shame to shoot an elephant for killing a coolie, because an elephant was worth more than any damn Coringhee coolie. And afterwards I was very glad that the coolie had been killed; it put me legally in the right and gave me a sufficient pretext for shooting the elephant. I often wondered whether any of the others grasped that I had done it solely to avoid looking a fool.

Orwell has already told us his pathetic reasons for having to shoot the elephant, even as he lies down in the road to do it, but this last is still a shock, the kind of humbling shock that a work of fiction can never bring home. It is, finally, too real.

Orwell, of course, wrote fiction, but in the end he is the strongest argument for the future of the article, for it was in this form that he expressed his best thinking in his most characteristic voice. He could not have told of "A Hanging" or "How the Poor Die" or "'Such, Such Were the Joys . . .'" without the excuse that journalism offered him (though it was not journalism that he wrote). Fiction helped him find a voice, but it was a voice unnatural to fiction. It had to be heeded elsewhere.

It is quite possible that things have now gone even farther, and fiction itself has become unnatural to the voices *we* heed. In that sense, Baldwin has, much like Orwell, found a more proper form, and it could happen that the next generation of writers in America will not need to "come over" from fiction, but will only look back on it nostalgically as a point of departure. If this is anything like the case, the article obviously will flourish, and might attain the kind of excellence that existed in English prose during the eighteenth century.

But if anything like this *is* to happen, the reasons for writing about reality will have to attain to something like Orwell's humility in truth, for there is no gainsaying the disappointment and denial that will be let loose. "Go, go, go, said the bird:" in T. S. Eliot's poem, "human kind/Cannot bear very much reality." Few, including most magazine publishers, have any real desire to test the machinery inside, or to discover whether these be automata or men that play the great chess game in the world. Few even wish to be articulate. It is over this guise of indifference—which is really the universal wish to "avoid looking the fool"—that voice and reason will have to triumph. The dead language of journalism has kept the article a corporate instrument in America far too long, but if it can finally achieve the sanctions which so naturally attend fiction, it will emerge as the one form with enough space to contain the risks of actual existence—the only form in which a man has enough room to shoot an elephant and admit his shame and folly.

✕ MAELZEL'S CHESS-PLAYER

Edgar Allan Poe

(*Excerpted from* THE SOUTHERN LITERARY MESSENGER, April, 1836)

In this analysis of the operations of the Automaton, we have purposely avoided any allusion to the manner in which the partitions are shifted, and it will now be readily comprehended that this point is a matter of no importance, since, by mechanism within the ability of any common carpenter, it might be effected in an infinity of different ways, and since we have shown that, however performed, it is performed out of the view of the spectators. Our result is founded upon the following *observations* taken during frequent visits to the exhibition of Maelzel.[1]

1. The moves of the Turk are not made at regular intervals of time, but accommodate themselves to the moves of the antagonist —although this point (of regularity) so important in all kinds of mechanical contrivance, might have been readily brought about by limiting the time allowed for the moves of the antagonist. For example, if this limit were three minutes, the moves of the Automaton might be made at any given intervals longer than three minutes. The fact then of irregularity, when regularity might have been so easily attained, goes to prove that regularity is unimportant to the action of the Automaton—in other words, that the Automaton is not a *pure machine.*

2. When the Automaton is about to move a piece, a distinct motion is observable just beneath the left shoulder, and which motion agitates in a slight degree, the drapery covering the front of the left shoulder. This motion invariably precedes, by about

---

[1] Some of these observations are intended merely to prove that the machine must be regulated by mind, and it may be thought a work of supererogation to advance farther arguments in support of what has been already fully decided. But our object is to convince, in especial, certain of our friends upon whom a train of suggestive reasoning will have more influence than the most positive a priori demonstration.

two seconds, the movement of the arm itself—and the arm never, in any instance, moves without this preparatory motion in the shoulder. Now let the antagonist move a piece, and let the corresponding move be made by Maelzel, as usual, upon the board of the Automaton. Then let the antagonist narrowly watch the Automaton, until he detect the preparatory motion in the shoulder. Immediately upon detecting this motion, and before the arm itself begins to move, let him withdraw his piece, as if perceiving an error in his manoeuvre. It will then be seen that the movement of the arm, which, in all other cases, immediately succeeds the motion in the shoulder, is withheld—is not made—although Maelzel has not yet performed, on the board of the Automaton, any move corresponding to the withdrawal of the antagonist. In this case, that the Automaton was about to move is evident—and that he did not move, was an effect plainly produced by the withdrawal of the antagonist, and without any intervention of Maelzel.

This fact fully proves, 1—that the intervention of Maelzel, in performing the moves of the antagonist on the board of the Automaton, is not essential to the movements of the Automaton, 2—that its movements are regulated by *mind*—by some person who sees the board of the antagonist, 3—that its movements are not regulated by the mind of Maelzel, whose back was turned toward the antagonist at the withdrawal of his move.

3. The Automaton does not invariably win the game. Were the machine a pure machine this would not be the case—it would always win. The *principle* being discovered by which a machine can be made to *play* a game of chess, an extension of the same principle would enable it to *win* a game—a farther extension would enable it to *win all* games—that is, to beat any possible game of an antagonist. A little consideration will convince anyone that the difficulty of making a machine beat all games, is not in the least degree greater, as regards the principle of the operations necessary, than that of making it beat a single game. If then we regard the Chess-Player as a machine, we must suppose, (what is highly improbable,) that its inventor preferred leaving it incomplete to perfect-

ing it—a supposition rendered still more absurd, when we reflect that the leaving it incomplete would afford an argument against the possibility of its being a pure machine—the very argument we now adduce.

4. When the situation of the game is difficult or complex, we never perceive the Turk either shake his head or roll his eyes. It is only when his next move is obvious, or when the game is so circumstanced that to a man in the Automaton's place there would be no necessity for reflection. Now these peculiar movements of the head and eyes are movements customary with persons engaged in meditation, and the ingenious Baron Kempelen would have adapted these movements (were the machine a pure machine) to occasions proper for their display—that is, to occasions of complexity. But the reverse is seen to be the case, and this reverse applies precisely to our supposition of a man in the interior. When engaged in meditation about the game, he has no time to think of setting in motion the mechanism of the Automaton by which are moved the head and the eyes. When the game, however, is obvious, he has time to look about him, and accordingly, we see the head shake and the eyes roll.

5. When the machine is rolled round to allow the spectators an examination of the back of the Turk, and when his drapery is lifted up and the doors in the trunk and thigh thrown open, the interior of the trunk is seen to be crowded with machinery. In scrutinizing this machinery while the Automaton was in motion, that is to say while the whole machine was moving on the castors, it appeared to us that certain portions of the mechanism changed their shape and position in a degree too great to be accounted for by the simple laws of perspective; and subsequent examinations convince us that these undue alterations were attributable to mirrors in the interior of the trunk. The introduction of mirrors among the machinery could not have been intended to influence, in any degree, the machinery itself. Their operation, whatever that operation should prove to be, must necessarily have reference to the eye of the spectator. We at once concluded that these mirrors

were so placed to multiply to the vision some few pieces of machinery within the trunk so as to give it the appearance of being crowded with mechanism. Now the direct inference from this is that the machine is not a pure machine. For if it were, the inventor, so far from wishing its mechanism to appear complex, and using deception for the purpose of giving it this appearance, would have been especially desirous of convincing those who witnessed his exhibition, of the *simplicity* of the means by which results so wonderful were brought about.

6. The external appearance, and especially, the deportment of the Turk, are, when we consider them as imitations of *life*, but very indifferent imitations. The countenance evinces no ingenuity, and is surpassed, in its resemblance to the human face, by the very commonest of wax-works. The eyes roll unnaturally in the head, without any corresponding motions of the lids or brows. The arm, particularly, performs its operations in an exceedingly stiff, awkward, jerking, and rectangular manner. Now, all this is the result either of inability in Maelzel to do better, or of intentional neglect—accidental neglect being out of the question, when we consider that the whole time of the ingenious proprietor is occupied in the improvement of his machines. Most assuredly we must not refer the unlifelike appearances to inability—for all the rest of Maelzel's automata are evidence of his full ability to copy the motions and peculiarities of life with the most wonderful exactitude. The rope-dancers, for example, are inimitable. When the clown laughs, his lips, his eyes, his eye-brows, and eye-lids,—indeed, all the features of his countenance—are imbued with their appropriate expressions. In both him and his companion, every gesture is so entirely easy, and free from the semblance of artificiality, that, were it not for the diminutiveness of their size, and the fact of their being passed from one spectator to another previous to their exhibition on the rope, it would be difficult to convince any assemblage of persons that these wooden automata were not living creatures. We cannot, therefore, doubt Mr. Maelzel's ability, and we must necessarily suppose that he intentionally

suffered his Chess-Player to remain the same artificial and un-natural figure which Baron Kempelen (no doubt also through design) originally made it. What this design was it is not difficult to conceive. Were the Automaton lifelike in its motions, the spectator would be more apt to attribute its operations to their true cause (that is, to human agency within) than he is now, when the awkward and rectangular manoeuvres convey the idea of pure and unaided mechanism.

7. When, a short time previous to the commencement of the game, the Automaton is wound up by the exhibiter as usual, an ear in any degree accustomed to the sounds produced in winding up a system of machinery, will not fail to discover, instantaneously, that the axis turned by the key in the box of the Chess-Player, cannot possibly be connected with either a weight, a spring, or any system of machinery whatever. The inference here is the same as in our last observation. The winding up is inessential to the operations of the Automaton, and is performed with the design of exciting in the spectators the false idea of mechanism.

8. When the question is demanded explicitly of Maelzel—"Is the Automaton a pure machine or not?" his reply is invariably the same—"I will say nothing about it." Now the notoriety of the Automaton, and the great curiosity it has everywhere excited, are owing more especially to the prevalent opinion that it *is* a pure machine, than to any other circumstance. Of course, then, it is the interest of the proprietor to represent it as a pure machine. And what more obvious, and more effectual method could there be of impressing the spectators with this desired idea, than a positive and explicit declaration to that effect? On the other hand, what more obvious and effectual method could there be of exciting a disbelief in the Automaton's being a pure machine, than by withholding such explicit declaration? For, people will naturally reason thus—It is Maelzel's interest to represent this thing a pure machine—he refuses to do so, directly, in words, although he does not scruple, and is evidently anxious to do so, indirectly by actions —were it actually what he wishes to represent it by actions, he

would gladly avail himself of the more direct testimony of words —the inference is, that a consciousness of its *not* being a pure machine, is the reason of his silence—his actions cannot implicate him in a falsehood—his words may.

9. When, in exhibiting the interior of the box, Maelzel has thrown open the door No. 1, and also the door immediately behind it, he holds a lighted candle at the back door (as mentioned above) and moves the entire machine to and fro with a view of convincing the company that the cupboard No. 1 is entirely filled with machinery. When the machine is thus moved about, it will be apparent to any careful observer that, whereas that portion of the machinery near the front door No. 1 is perfectly steady and unwavering, the portion farther within fluctuates, in a very slight degree, with the movements of the machine. This circumstance first aroused in us the suspicion that the more remote portion of the machinery was so arranged as to be easily slipped, *en masse*, from its position when occasion should require it. This occasion we have already stated to occur when the man concealed within brings his body into an erect position upon the closing of the back door.

10. Sir David Brewster states the figure of the Turk to be of the size of life—but in fact it is far above the ordinary size. Nothing is more easy than to err in our notions of magnitude. The body of the Automaton is generally insulated, and having no means of immediately comparing it with any human form, we suffer ourselves to consider it as of ordinary dimensions. This mistake may, however, be corrected by observing the Chess-Player when, as is sometimes the case, the exhibitor approaches it. M. Maelzel, to be sure, is not very tall, but upon drawing near the machine, his head will be found at least eighteen inches below the head of the Turk, although the latter, it will be remembered, is in a sitting position.

11. The box behind which the Automaton is placed is precisely three feet six inches long, two feet four inches deep, and two feet six inches high. These dimensions are fully sufficient for the accommodation of a man very much above the common size—and

the main compartment alone is capable of holding any ordinary man in the position we have mentioned as assumed by the person concealed. As these are facts, which anyone who doubts them may prove by actual calculation, we deem it unnecessary to dwell upon them. We will only suggest that, although the top of the box is apparently a board of about three inches in thickness, the spectator may satisfy himself by stooping and looking up at it when the main compartment is open, that it is in reality very thin. The height of the drawer also will be misconceived by those who examine it in a cursory manner. There is a space of about three inches between the top of the drawer as seen from the exterior, and the bottom of the cupboard,—a space which must be included in the height of the drawer. These contrivances to make the room within the box appear less than it actually is, are referrible to a design on the part of the inventor, to impress the company again with a false idea, viz., that no human being can be accommodated within the box.

12. The interior of the main compartment is lined throughout with *cloth*. This cloth we suppose to have a twofold object. A portion of it may form, when tightly stretched, the only partitions which there is any necessity for removing during the changes of the man's position, viz: the partition between the rear of the main compartment and the rear of cupboard No. 1, and the partition between the main compartment, and the space behind the drawer when open. If we imagine this to be the case, the difficulty of shifting the partitions vanishes at once, if indeed any such difficulty could be supposed under any circumstances to exist. The second object of the cloth is to deaden and render indistinct all sounds occasioned by the movements of the person within.

13. The antagonist (as we have before observed) is not suffered to play at the board of the Automaton, but is seated at some distance from the machine. The reason which, most probably, would be assigned for this circumstance, if the question were demanded, is, that were the antagonist otherwise situated, his person would intervene between the machine and the spectators, and preclude

the latter from a distinct view. But this difficulty might be easily obviated, either by elevating the seats of the company, or by turning the end of the box toward them during the game. The true cause of the restriction is, perhaps, very different. Were the antagonist seated in contact with the box, the secret would be liable to discovery, by his detecting, with the aid of a quick ear, the breathings of the man concealed.

14. Although M. Maelzel, in disclosing the interior of the machine, sometimes slightly deviates from the *routine* which we have pointed out, yet *never* in any instance does he *so* deviate from it as to interfere with our solution. For example, he has been known to open, first of all, the drawer—but he never opens the main compartment without first closing the back door of cupboard No. 1—he never opens the main compartment without first pulling out the drawer—he never shuts the drawer without first shutting the main compartment—he never opens the back door of cupboard No. 1 while the main compartment is open—and the game of chess is never commenced until the whole machine is closed. Now, if it were observed that *never, in any single instance,* did M. Maelzel differ from the routine we have pointed out as necessary to our solution, it would be one of the strongest possible arguments in corroboration of it—but the argument becomes infinitely strengthened if we duly consider the circumstance that he *does occasionally* deviate from the routine, but never does *so* deviate as to falsify the solution.

15. There are six candles on the board of the Automaton during exhibition. The question naturally arises—"Why are so many employed, when a single candle, or, at farthest, two, would have been amply sufficient to afford the spectators a clear view of the board, in a room otherwise so well lit up as the exhibition room always is —when, moreover, if we suppose the machine a *pure machine,* there can be no necessity for so much light, or indeed any light at all, to enable *it* to perform its operations—and when, especially, only a single candle is placed upon the table of the antagonist?" The first and most obvious inference is, that so strong a light is re-

quisite to enable the man within to see through the transparent material (probably fine gauze) of which the breast of the Turk is composed. But when we consider the *arrangement* of the candles, another reason immediately presents itself. There are six lights (as we have said before) in all. Three of these are on each side of the figure. Those most remote from the spectators are the longest— those in the middle are about two inches shorter—and those nearest the company about two inches shorter still—and the candles on one side differ in height from the candles respectively opposite on the other, by a ratio different from two inches—that is to say, the longest candle on one side is about three inches shorter than the longest candle on the other, and so on. Thus it will be seen that no two of the candles are of the same height, and thus also the difficulty of ascertaining the *material* of the breast of the figure (against which the light is especially directed) is greatly augmented by the dazzling effect of the complicated crossings of the rays—crossings which are brought about by placing the centres of radiation all upon different levels.

16. While the Chess-Player was in possession of Baron Kempelen, it was more than once observed, first, that an Italian in the suite of the Baron was never visible during the playing of a game at chess by the Turk, and secondly, that the Italian being taken seriously ill, the exhibition was suspended until his recovery. This Italian professed a *total* ignorance of the game of chess, although all others of the suite played well. Similar observations have been made since the Automaton has been purchased by Maelzel. There is a man, *Schlumberger,* who attends him wherever he goes, but who has no ostensible occupation other than that of assisting in the packing and unpacking of the Automaton. This man is about the medium size, and has a remarkable stoop in the shoulders. Whether he professes to play chess or not, we are not informed. It is quite certain, however, that he is never to be seen during the exhibition of the Chess-Player, although frequently visible just before and just after the exhibition. Moreover, some years ago Maelzel visited Richmond with his automata, and exhibited them, we

believe, in the house now occupied by M. Bossieux as a Dancing Academy. *Shlumberger* was suddenly taken ill, and during his illness there was no exhibition of the Chess-Player. These facts are well known to many of our citizens. The reason assigned for the suspension of the Chess-Player's performances, was *not* the illness of *Schlumberger*. The inferences from all this we leave, without farther comment, to the reader.

17. The Turk plays with his *left* arm. A circumstance so remarkable cannot be accidental. Brewster takes no notice of it whatever, beyond a mere statement, we believe, that such is the fact. The early writers of treatises on the Automaton, seem not to have observed the matter at all, and have no reference to it. The author of the pamphlet alluded to by Brewster mentions it, but acknowledges his inability to account for it. Yet it is obviously from such prominent discrepancies or incongruities as this that deductions are to be made (if made at all) which shall lead us to the truth.

The circumstance of the Automaton's playing with his left hand cannot have connexion with the operations of the machine considered merely such. Any mechanical arrangement which would cause the figure to move, in any given manner, the left arm—could, if reversed, cause it to move, in the same manner, the right. But these principles cannot be extended to the human organization, wherein there is a marked and radical difference in the construction, and at all events, in the powers, of the right and left arms. Reflecting upon this latter fact, we naturally refer the incongruity noticeable in the Chess-Player to this peculiarity in the human organization. If so, we must imagine some *reversion*—for the Chess-Player plays precisely as a man *would not*. These ideas, once entertained, are sufficient of themselves to suggest the notion of a man in the interior. A few more imperceptible steps lead us, finally, to the result. The Automaton plays with his left arm, because under no other circumstances could the man within play with his right—a *desideratum*, of course. Let us, for example, imagine the Automaton to play with his right arm. To reach the machinery which moves the arm, and which we have before explained to lie just beneath the shoulder, it would be necessary for the man within either to use his right arm in an exceedingly painful and awkward position (viz., brought up close to his body and tightly compressed between his body and the side of the Automaton), or else to use his left arm brought across his breast. In neither case could he act with the requisite ease or precision. On the contrary, the Automaton playing, as it actually does, with the left arm, all difficulties vanish. The right arm of the man within is brought across his breast, and his right fingers act, without any constraint, upon the machinery in the shoulder of the figure.

We do not believe that any reasonable objections can be urged against this solution of the Automaton Chess-Player.

✕ EQUAL IN PARIS
James Baldwin

(COMMENTARY, March, 1955)

On the 19th of December, in 1949, when I had been living in Paris for a little over a year, I was arrested as a receiver of stolen goods and spent eight days in prison. My arrest came about through an American tourist whom I had met twice in New York, who had been given my name and address and told to look me up. I was then living on the top floor of a ludicrously grim hotel on the rue du Bac, one of those enormous dark, cold, and hideous establishments in which Paris abounds that seem to breathe forth, in their airless, humid, stone-cold halls, the weak light, scurrying chambermaids, and creaking stairs, an odor of gentility long long dead. The place was run by an ancient Frenchman dressed in an elegant black suit which was green with age, who cannot properly be described as bewildered or even as being in a state of shock, since he had really stopped breathing around 1910. There he sat at his desk in the weirdly lit, fantastically furnished lobby, day in and day out, greeting each one of his extremely impoverished and *louche* lodgers with a stately inclination of the head that he had no doubt been taught in some impossibly remote time was the proper way for a *propriétaire* to greet his guests. If it had not been for his daughter, an extremely hardheaded *tricoteuse*—the inclination of *her* head was chilling and abrupt, like the downbeat of an ax—the hotel would certainly have gone bankrupt long before. It was said that this old man had not gone farther than the door of his hotel for thirty years, which was not at all difficult to believe. He looked as though the daylight would have killed him.

I did not, of course, spend much of my time in this palace. The moment I began living in French hotels I understood the necessity of French cafés. This made it rather difficult to look me up, for as soon as I was out of bed I hopefully took notebook and fountain pen off to the upstairs room of the Flore, where I consumed rather a lot of coffee and, as evening approached, rather a lot of alcohol, but did not get much writing done. But one night, in one of the cafés of St. Germain des Près, I was discovered by this New Yorker and only because we found ourselves in Paris we immediately established the illusion that we had been fast friends back in the good old U.S.A. This illusion proved itself too thin to support an evening's drinking, but by that time it was too late. I had committed myself to getting him a room in my hotel the next day, for he was living in one of the nest of hotels near the Gare St. Lazare, where, he said, the *propriétaire* was a thief, his wife a repressed nymphomaniac, the chambermaids "pigs," and the rent a crime. Americans are always talking this way about the French and so it did not occur to me that he meant what he said or that he would take into his own hands the means of avenging himself on the French Republic. It did not occur to me, either, that the means which he *did* take could possibly have brought about such dire results, results which were not less dire for being also comic-opera.

It came as the last of a series of disasters which had perhaps been made inevitable by the fact that I had come to Paris originally with a little over forty dollars in my pockets, nothing in the bank, and no grasp whatever of the French language. It developed, shortly, that I had no grasp of the French character either. I considered the French an ancient, intelligent, and cultured race, which indeed they are. I did not know, however, that ancient glories imply, at least in the middle of the present century, present fatigue and, quite probably, paranoia; that there is a limit to the role of the intelligence in human affairs; and that no people come into possession of a culture without having paid a heavy price for it. This price they cannot, of course, assess, but it is revealed in their personalities and in their institutions. The very word "institutions," from my side of the ocean, where, it seemed to me, we suffered so cruelly from the lack of them, had a pleasant ring, as of safety and order and common sense; one had to come into contact with these institutions in order to understand that they were also outmoded, exasperating, completely impersonal, and very often cruel. Similarly, the personality which had seemed from a distance to be so large and free had to be dealt with before one could see that, if it was large, it was also inflexible and, for the foreigner, full of strange, high, dusty rooms which could not be inhabited. One had, in short, to come into contact with an alien culture in order to understand that a culture was not a community basket-weaving project, nor yet an act of God; was something neither desirable nor undesirable in itself, being inevitable, being nothing more or less than the recorded and visible effects on a body of people of the vicissitudes with which they had been forced to deal. And their great men are revealed as simply another of these vicissitudes, even if, quite against their will, the brief battle of their great men with them has left them richer.

When my American friend left his hotel to move to mine, he took with him, out of pique, a bedsheet belonging to the hotel and put it in his suitcase. When he arrived at my hotel I borrowed the sheet, since my own were filthy and the chambermaid showed no sign of bringing me any clean ones, and put it on my bed. The sheets belonging to *my* hotel I put out in the hall, congratulating myself on having thus forced on the attention of the Grand Hôtel du Bac the unpleasant state of its linen. Thereafter, since, as it turned out, we kept very different hours—I got up at noon, when, as I gathered by meeting him on the stairs one day, he was only just getting in—my new-found friend and I saw very little of each other.

On the evening of the 19th I was sitting thinking melancholy thoughts about Christmas and staring at the walls of my room. I imagine that I had sold something or that someone had sent me a Christmas present, for I remember that I had a little money. In those days in Paris, though I floated, so to speak, on a sea of acquaintances, I knew almost no one. Many people were eliminated from my orbit by virtue of the fact that they had more money than I did, which placed me, in my own eyes, in the humiliating role of a free-loader; and other people were eliminated by virtue of the fact that they enjoyed their poverty, shrilly insisting that this wretched round of hotel rooms, bad food, humiliating concierges, and unpaid bills, was the Great Adventure. It couldn't, however, for me, end soon enough, this Great Adventure; there was a real question in my mind as to which would end soonest, the Great Adventure or me. This meant, however, that there were many evenings when I sat in my room, knowing that I couldn't work there, and not knowing what to do, or whom to see. On this particular evening I went down and knocked on the American's door.

There were two Frenchmen standing in the room, who immediately introduced themselves to me as policemen; which did not worry me. I had got used to policemen in Paris bobbing up at the most improbable times and places, asking to see one's *carte d'identité*. These policemen, however, showed very little interest in my papers. They were looking for something else. I could not imagine what this would be and, since I knew I certainly didn't have it, I scarcely followed the conversation they were having with my friend. I gathered that they were looking for some kind of gangster and since I wasn't a gangster and knew that gangsterism was not, insofar as he had one, my friend's style I was sure that the two policemen would presently bow and say *Merci, messieurs,* and leave. For by this time, I remember very clearly, I was dying to have a drink and go to dinner.

I did not have a drink or go to dinner for many days after this, and when I did my outraged stomach promptly heaved everything up again. For now one of the policemen began to exhibit the most vivid interest in me and asked, very politely, if he might see my room. To which we mounted, making, I remember, the most civilized small talk on the way and even continuing it for some moments after we were in the room in which there was certainly nothing to be seen but the familiar poverty and disorder of that precarious group of people of whatever age, race, country, calling, or intention which Paris recognizes as *les étudiants* and sometimes, more ironically and precisely, as *les nonconformistes*. Then he moved to my bed, and in a terrible flash, not quite an instant before he lifted the bedspread, I understood what he was looking for. We looked at the sheet, on which I read, for the first time, lettered in the most brilliant scarlet I have ever seen, the name of the hotel from which it had been stolen. It was the first time the word *stolen* entered my mind. I had certainly seen the hotel monogram the day I put the sheet on the bed. It had simply meant nothing to me. In New York I had seen hotel monograms on everything from silver to soap and towels. Taking things from New York hotels was practically a custom, though, I suddenly realized, I had never known anyone to take a *sheet*. Sadly, and without a word to me, the inspector took the sheet from the bed, folded it under his arm, and we started back downstairs. I understood that I was under arrest.

And so we passed through the lobby, four of us, two of us very clearly criminal, under the eyes of the old man and his daughter, neither of whom said a word, into the streets where a light rain was falling. And I asked, in French, "But is this very serious?"

For I was thinking, it is, after all, only a sheet, not even new.

"No," said one of them. "It's not serious."

"It's nothing at all," said the other.

I took this to mean that we would receive a reprimand at the police station and be allowed to go to dinner. Later on I concluded that they were not being hypocritical or even trying to comfort us. They meant exactly what they said. It was only that they spoke another language.

In Paris everything is very slow. Also, when dealing with the bureaucracy, the man you are talking to is never the man you have to see. The man you have to see has just gone off to Belgium, or is busy with his family, or has just discovered that he is a cuckold; he will be in next Tuesday at three o'clock, or sometime in the course of the afternoon, or possibly tomorrow, or, possibly, in the next five minutes. But if he is coming in the next five minutes he will be far too busy to be able to see you today.

So that I suppose I was not really astonished to learn at the commissariat that nothing could possibly be done about us before The Man arrived in the morning. But no, we could not go off and have dinner and come back in the morning. Of course he knew that we *would* come back—that was not the question. Indeed, there was no question: we would simply have to stay there for the night. We were placed in a cell which rather resembled a chicken coop. It was now about seven in the evening and I relinquished the thought of dinner and began to think of lunch.

I discouraged the chatter of my New York friend and this left me alone with my thoughts. I was beginning to be frightened and I bent all my energies, therefore, to keeping my panic under control. I began to realize that I was in a country I knew nothing about, in the hands of a people I did not understand at all. In a similar situation in New York I would have had some idea of what to do because I would have had some idea of what to expect. I am not speaking now of legality which, like most of the poor, I had never for an instant trusted, but of the temperament of the people with whom I had to deal. I had become very accomplished in New York at guessing and, therefore, to a limited extent manipulating to my advantage the reactions of the white world. But this was not New York. None of my old weapons could serve me here. I did not know what they saw when they looked at me. I knew very well what Americans saw when they looked at me and this allowed me to play endless and sinister variations on the role which they had assigned me; since I knew that it was, for them, of the utmost importance that they never be confronted with what, in their own personalities, made this role so necessary and gratifying to them, I knew that they could never call my hand or, indeed, afford to know what I was doing; so that I moved into every crucial situation with the deadly and rather desperate advantages of bitterly accumulated perception, of pride and contempt. This is an awful sword and shield to carry through the world, and the discovery that, in the game I was playing, I did myself a violence of which the world, at its most ferocious, would scarcely have been capable, was what had driven me out of New York. It was a strange feeling, in this situation, after a year in Paris, to discover that my weapons would never again serve me as they had.

It was quite clear to me that the Frenchmen in whose hands I found myself were no better or worse than their American counterparts. Certainly their uniforms frightened me quite as much, and their impersonality, and the threat, always very keenly felt by the poor, of violence, was as present in that commissariat as it had ever been for me in any police station. And I had seen, for example, what Paris policemen could do to Arab peanut vendors. The only difference here was that I did not understand these people, did not know what techniques their cruelty took, did not know enough about their personalities to see danger coming, to ward it off, did not know on what ground to meet it. That evening in the commissariat I was not a despised black man. They would simply have laughed at me if I had behaved like one. For them, I was an American. And here it was they who had the advantage, for that word, *Américain,* gave them some idea, far from inaccurate, of what to expect from me. In order to corroborate none of their ironical expectations I said nothing and did nothing—which was not the way any Frenchman, white or black, would have reacted. The question thrusting up from the bottom of my mind was not *what* I was, but *who.* And this question, since a *what* can get by with skill but a *who* demands resources, was my first real intimation of what humility must mean.

In the morning it was still raining. Between nine and ten o'clock a black Citroën took us off to the Ile de la Cité, to the great, gray Préfecture. I realize now that the questions I put to the various policemen who escorted us were always answered in such a way as to corroborate what I wished to hear. This was not out of politeness, but simply out of indifference—or, possibly, an ironical pity—since each of the policemen knew very well that nothing would speed or halt the machine in which I had become entangled. They knew I did not know this and there was certainly no point in their telling me. In one way or another I would certainly come out at the other side—for they also knew that being found with a stolen bedsheet in one's possession was not a crime punishable by the guillotine. (They had the advantage over me there, too, for there were certainly moments later on when I was not so sure.) If I did *not* come out at the other side—well, that was just too bad. So, to my question, put while we were in the Citroën —"Will it be over today?"—I received a *"Oui, bien sûr."* He was not lying. As it turned out, the *procès-verbal* was over that day. Trying to be realistic, I dismissed, in the Citroën, all thoughts of lunch and pushed my mind ahead to dinner.

At the Préfecture we were first placed in a tiny cell, in which it was almost impossible either to sit or to lie down. After a couple of hours of this we were taken down to an office, where, for the first time, I encountered the owner of the bedsheet and where the *procès-verbal* took place. This was simply an interrogation, quite chillingly clipped and efficient (so that there was, shortly, no doubt in one's own mind that one *should* be treated as a criminal), which was recorded by a secretary. When it was over, this report was given to us to sign. One had, of course, no choice but to sign it, even though my mastery of written French was very far from certain. We were being held, according to the law in France, incommunicado, and all my angry demands to be allowed to speak to my embassy or to see a lawyer met with a stony *"Oui, oui. Plus tard."* The *procès-verbal* over, we were taken back to the cell, before which, shortly, passed the owner of the bedsheet. He said he hoped we had slept well, gave a vindictive wink, and disappeared.

By this time there was only one thing clear: that we had no way of controlling the sequence of events and could not possibly guess what this sequence would be. It seeemed to me, since what I regarded as the high point—the *procès-verbal*—had been passed and since the hotel-keeper was once again in possession of his sheet, that we might reasonably expect to be released from police custody in a matter of hours. We had been detained now for what would soon be twenty-four hours, during which time I had learned only that the official charge against me was *receleur*. My mental shifting, between lunch and dinner, to say nothing of the physical lack of either of these delights, was beginning to make me dizzy. The steady chatter of my friend from New York, who was determined to keep my spirits up, made me feel murderous; I was praying that some power would release us from this freezing pile of stone before the impulse became the act. And I was beginning to wonder what was happening in that beautiful city, Paris, which lived outside these walls. I wondered how long it would take before anyone casually asked, "But where's Jimmy? He hasn't been around"—and realized, knowing the people I knew, that it would take several days.

Quite late in the afternoon we were taken from our cells; handcuffed, each to a separate officer; led through a maze of steps and corridors to the top of the building; finger-printed; photographed. As in movies I had seen, I was placed against a wall, facing an old-fashioned camera, behind which stood one of the most completely cruel and indifferent faces I had ever seen, while someone next to me and, therefore, just outside of my line of vision, read off in a voice from which all human feeling, even feeling of the most base description, had long since fled, what must be called my public characteristics—which, at that time and in that place, seemed anything but that. He might have been roaring to the hostile world secrets which I could barely, in the privacy of midnight, utter to myself. But he was only reading off my height, my features, my approximate weight, my color—that color which, in the United States, had often, odd as it may sound, been my salvation—the color of my hair, my age, my nationality. A light then flashed, the photographer and I staring at each other as though there was murder in our hearts, and then it was over. Handcuffed again, I was led downstairs to the bottom of the building, into a great enclosed shed in which had been gathered the very scrapings off the Paris streets. Old, old men, so ruined and old that life in them seemed really to prove the miracle of the quickening power of the Holy Ghost—for clearly their life was no longer their affair, it was no longer even their burden, they were simply the clay which had once been touched. And men not so old, with faces the color of lead and the consistency of oatmeal, eyes that made me think of stale *café-au-lait* spiked with arsenic, bodies which could take in food and water—any food and water—and pass it out, but which could not do anything more, except possibly, at midnight, along the riverbank where rats scurried, rape. And young men, harder and crueler than the Paris stones, older by far than I, their chronological senior by some five to seven years. And North Africans, old and young, who seemed the only living people in this place because they yet retained the grace to be bewildered. But they were not bewildered by being in this shed: they were simply bewildered because they were no longer in North Africa. There was a great hole in the center of this shed, which was the common toilet. Near it, though it was impossible to get very far from it, stood an old man with white hair, eating a piece of Camembert. It was at this point, probably, that thought, for me, stopped, that physiology, if one may say so, took over. I found myself incapable of saying a word, not because I was afraid I would cry but because I was afraid I would vomit. And I did not think any longer of the city of Paris but my mind flew back to that home from which I had fled. I was sure that I would never see it any more. And it must have seemed to me that my flight from home was the cruelest trick I had ever played on myself, since it had led me here, down to a lower point than any I could ever in my life have imagined—lower, far, than anything I had seen in that Harlem which I had so hated and so loved, the escape from which had soon become the greatest direction of my life. After we had been here an hour or so a functionary came and opened the door and called out our names. And I was sure that *this* was my release. But I was handcuffed again and led out of the Préfecture into the streets—it was dark now, it was still raining—and before the steps of the Préfecture stood the great police wagon, doors facing me, wide open. The handcuffs were taken off, I entered the wagon, which was peculiarly constructed. It was divided by a narrow aisle, and on each side of the aisle was a series of narrow doors. These doors opened on a narrow cubicle, beyond which was a door which opened onto another narrow cubicle: three or four cubicles, each private, with a locking door. I was placed in one of them; I remember there was a small vent just above my head which let in a little light. The door of my cubicle was locked from the outside. I had no idea where this wagon was taking me and, as it began to move, I began to cry. I suppose I cried all the way to prison, the prison called Fresnes, which is twelve kilometers outside of Paris.

For reasons I have no way at all of understanding, prisoners whose last initial is A, B, or C are always sent to Fresnes; everybody else is sent to a prison called, rather cynically it seems to me, La Santé. I will, obviously, never be allowed to enter La Santé, but I was told by people who certainly seemed to know that it was infinitely more unbearable than Fresnes. This arouses in me, until today, a positive storm of curiosity concerning what I promptly began to think of as The Other Prison. My colleague in crime, occurring lower in the alphabet, had been sent there and I confess that the minute he was gone I missed him. I missed him because he was not French and because he was the only person in the world who knew that the story I told was true.

For, once locked in, divested of shoelaces, belt, watch, money, papers, nailfile, in a freezing cell in which both the window and the toilet were broken, with six other adventurers, the story I told of *l'affaire du drap de lit* elicited only the wildest amusement or the most suspicious disbelief. Among the people who shared my cell the first three days no one, it is true, had been arrested for anything much more serious—or, at least, not serious in my eyes. I remember that there was a boy who had stolen a knitted sweater from a *monoprix*, who would probably, it was agreed, receive a six-month sentence. There was an older man there who had been arrested for some kind of petty larceny. There were two North Africans, vivid, brutish, and beautiful, who alternated between gaiety and fury, not at the fact of their arrest but at the state of the cell. None poured as much emotional energy into the fact of their arrest as I did; they took it, as I would have liked to take it, as simply another unlucky happening in a very dirty world. For, though I had grown accustomed to thinking of myself as looking upon the world with a hard, penetrating eye, the truth was that they were far more realistic about the world than I, and more nearly right about it. The gap between us, which only a gesture I made could have bridged, grew steadily, during thirty-six hours, wider. I could not make any gesture simply because they frightened me. I was unable to accept my imprisonment as a fact, even as a temporary fact. I could not, even for a moment, accept my present companions as *my* companions. And they, of course, felt this and put it down, with perfect justice, to the fact that I was an American.

There was nothing to do all day long. It appeared that we would one day come to trial but no one knew when. We were awakened at seven-thirty by a rapping on what I believe is called the Judas, that small opening in the door of the cell which allows the guards to survey the prisoners. At this rapping we rose from the floor—we slept on straw pallets and each of us was covered with one thin blanket—and moved to the door of the cell. We peered through the opening into the center of the prison, which was, as I remember, three tiers high, all gray stone and gunmetal steel, precisely that prison I had seen in movies, except that, in the movies, I had not known that it was cold in prison. I had not known that when one's shoelaces and belt have been removed one is, in the strangest way, demoralized. The necessity of shuffling and the necessity of holding up one's trousers with one hand turn one into a rag doll. And the movies fail, of course, to give one any idea of what prison food is like. Along the corridor, at seven-thirty, came three men, each pushing before him a great garbage can, mounted on wheels. In the garbage can of the first was the bread—this was passed to one through the small opening in the door. In the can of the second was the coffee. In the can of the third was what was always called *la soupe*, a pallid paste of potatoes which had certainly been bubbling on the back of the prison stove long before that first, so momentous revolution. Naturally, it was cold by this time and, starving as I was, I could not eat it. I drank the coffee—which was not coffee —because it was hot, and spent the rest of the day, huddled in my blanket, munching on the bread. It was not the French bread one bought in bakeries. In the evening the same procession returned. At ten-thirty the lights went out. I had a recurring dream, each night, a nightmare which always involved my mother's fried chicken. At the moment I was about to eat it came the rapping at the door. Silence is really all I remember of those first three days, silence and the color gray.

I am not sure now whether it was on the third or the fourth day that I was taken to trial for the first time. The days had nothing, obviously, to distinguish them from one another. I remember that I was very much aware that Christmas Day was approaching and I wondered if I was really going to spend Christmas Day in prison. And I remember that the first trial came the day before Christmas Eve.

On the morning of the first trial I was awakened by hearing my name called. I was told, hanging in a kind of void between my mother's fried chicken and the cold prison floor, "*Vous préparez. Vous êtes extrait*"—which simply terrified me, since I did not know what interpretation to put on the word "*extrait*," and since my cell-mates had been amusing themselves with me by telling terrible stories about the inefficiency of French prisons, an inefficiency so extreme that it had often happened that someone who was supposed to be taken out and tried found himself on the wrong line and was guillotined instead. The best way of putting my reaction to this is to say that, though I knew they were teasing me, it was simply not possible for me to totally *dis*believe them. As far as I was concerned, once in the hands of the law in France, anything could happen. I shuffled along with the others who were *extrait* to the center of the prison, trying, rather, to linger in the office, which seemed the only warm spot in the whole world, and found myself again in that dreadful wagon, and was carried again to the Ile de la Cité, this time to the Palais de Justice. The entire day, except for ten minutes, was spent in one of the cells, first waiting to be tried, then waiting to be taken back to prison.

For I was *not* tried that day. By and by I was handcuffed and led through the halls, upstairs to the courtroom where I found my New York friend. We were placed together, both stage-whisperingly certain that this was the end of our ordeal. Nevertheless, while I waited for our case to be called, my eyes searched the courtroom, looking for a face I knew, hoping, anyway, that there was some-one there who knew *me*, who would carry to someone outside the news that I was in trouble. But there was no one I knew there and I had had time to realize that there was probably only one man in Paris who could help me, an American patent attorney for whom I had worked as an office boy. He could have helped me because he had a quite solid position and some prestige and would have testified that, while working for him, I had handled large sums of money regularly, which made it rather unlikely that I would stoop to trafficking in bedsheets. However, he was somewhere in Paris, probably at this very moment enjoying a snack and a glass of wine and as far as the possibility of reaching him was concerned, he might as well have been on Mars. I tried to watch the proceedings and to make my mind a blank. But the proceedings were not reassuring. The boy, for example, who had stolen the sweater *did* receive a six-month sentence. It seemed to me that all the sentences meted out that day were excessive; though, again, it seemed that all the people who were sentenced that day had made, or clearly were going to make, crime their career. This seemed to be the opinion of the judge, who scarcely looked at the prisoners or listened to them; it seemed to be the opinion of the prisoners, who scarcely bothered to speak in their own behalf; it seemed to be the opinion of the lawyers, state lawyers for the most part, who were defending them. The great impulse of the courtroom seemed to be to put these people where they could not be seen—and not because they were offended at the crimes, unless, indeed, they were offended that the crimes were so petty, but because they did not wish to know that their society could be counted on to produce, probably in greater and greater numbers, a whole body of people for whom crime was the only possible career. Any society inevitably produces its criminals, but a society at once rigid and unstable can do nothing whatever to alleviate the poverty of its lowest members, cannot present to the hypothetical young man at the crucial moment that so-well-advertised right path. And the fact, perhaps, that the French are the earth's least sentimental people and must also be numbered among the most proud aggravates the plight of their lowest, youngest, and unluckiest members, for it means that the idea of rehabilitation is scarcely real to them. I confess that this attitude on their part raises in me sentiments of exasperation, admiration, and despair, revealing as it does, in both the best and the worst sense, their renowned and spectacular hard-headedness.

Finally our case was called and we rose. We gave our names. At the point that it developed that we were American the proceedings ceased, a hurried consultation took place between the judge and what I took to be several lawyers. Someone called out for an interpreter. The arresting officer had forgotten to mention our nationalities and there was, therefore, no interpreter in the court. Even if our French had been better than it was we would not have been allowed to stand trial without an interpreter. Before I clearly understood what was happening, I was handcuffed again and led out of the courtroom. The trial had been set back for the 27th of December.

I have sometimes wondered if I would *ever* have got out of prison if it had not been for the older man who had been arrested for the mysterious petty larceny. He was acquitted that day and when he returned to the cell—for he could not be released until morning—he found me sitting numbly on the floor, having just been prevented, by the sight of a man, all blood, being carried back to *his* cell on a stretcher, from seizing the bars and screaming until they let me out. The sight of the man on the stretcher proved, however, that screaming would not do much for me. The petty-larceny man went around asking if he could do anything in the world outside for those he was leaving behind. When he came to me I, at first, responded, "No, nothing"—for I suppose I had by now retreated into the attitude, the earliest I remember, that of my father, which was simply (since I had lost his God) that nothing could help me. And I suppose I will remember with gratitude until I die the fact that the man now insisted: *"Mais, êtes-vous sûr?"* Then it swept over me that he was going *outside* and he instantly became my first contact since the Lord alone knew how long with the outside world. At the same time, I remember, I did not really believe that he would help me. There was no reason why he should. But I gave him the phone number of my attorney friend and my own name.

So, in the middle of the next day, Christmas Eve, I shuffled downstairs again, to meet my visitor. He looked extremely well fed and sane and clean. He told me I had nothing to worry about any more. Only not even he could do anything to make the mill of justice grind any faster. He would, however, send me a lawyer of his acquaintance who would defend me on the 27th, and he would himself, along with several other people, appear as a character witness. He gave me a package of Lucky Strikes (which the turn-key took from me on the way upstairs) and said that, though it was doubtful that there would be any celebration in the prison, he would see to it that I got a fine Christmas dinner when I got out. And this, somehow, seemed very funny. I remember being aston-ished at the discovery that I was actually laughing. I was, too, I imagine, also rather disappointed that my hair had not turned white, that my face was clearly not going to bear any marks of tragedy, disappointed at bottom, no doubt, to realize, facing him in that room, that far worse things had happened to most people and that, indeed, to paraphrase my mother, if this was the worst thing that ever happened to me I could consider myself among the luckiest people ever to be born. He injected—my visitor—into my solitary nightmare common sense, the world, and the hint of blacker things to come.

The next day, Christmas, unable to endure my cell, and feeling that, after all, the day demanded a gesture, I asked to be allowed to go to Mass, hoping to hear some music. But I found myself, for a freezing hour and a half, locked in exactly the same kind of cubicle as in the wagon which had first brought me to prison, peering through a slot placed at the level of the eye at an old Frenchman, hatted, overcoated, muffled, and gloved, preaching in this language which I did not understand, to this row of wooden boxes, the story of Jesus Christ's love for men.

The next day, the 26th, I spent learning a peculiar kind of game, played with match-sticks, with my cellmates. For, since I no longer felt that I would stay in this cell forever, I was beginning to be able to make peace with it for a time. On the 27th I went again to trial and, as had been predicted, the case against us was dismissed. The story of the *drap de lit*, finally told, caused great merriment in the courtroom, whereupon my friend decided that the French were "great." I was chilled by their merriment, even though it was meant to warm me. It could only remind me of the laughter I had often heard at home, laughter which I had sometimes deliberately elicited. This laughter is the laughter of those who consider themselves to be at a safe remove from all the wretched, for whom the pain of the living is not real. I had heard it so often in my native land that I had resolved to find a place where I would never hear it any more. In some deep, black, stony, and liberating way, my life, in my own eyes, began during that first year in Paris, when it was borne in on me that this laughter is universal and never can be stilled.

On the Writing of Poetry

DONALD JUSTICE

Let us begin with three propositions that have to do with the special character of poetry. For the good writer is aware, whether consciously or not, of the special character of his art; and it is this awareness, as much perhaps as the experience out of which he is writing, that will lead the poet, as if by instinct, to scratch out one word in favor of another, and so on through the long series of practical choices which go into the composition of any poem.

The first proposition is this: that the form of a poem is more directly apprehensible than the ordinarily larger and looser forms of the novel or the play.

The second: that the words of a poem are different from the words of a novel in that they demand a more interested attention in their own right.

The third: that the rhythm of a poem, as it binds and sustains the other elements, becomes in itself an object of interest.

The Form

Whatever form the poem may take—from the most rigid and systematic to the most unlicensed and inventive—this form is, in some degree, directly apprehensible. Currently the most flourishing of the poetic kinds, and also, according to the critic and poet Yvor Winters, the greatest, is the lyric or short poem, which as a form seems to demand none of the impurities, the *longueurs* and distractions, built into the other literary types. In a good short poem a fine sense of relations among its parts is felt, word connecting with word, line with line: as with a spider web, touch it at any part and the whole structure responds. And because this whole of interconnected parts may be balanced in the mind at once, the relations of a great many of the parts to one another and to the whole become more readily perceptible. Of course, in the reading of even a very long and complex novel this perception of the whole, or at least of some connection between some of the parts, is given us occasionally, as when the wards of a key fit into the lock and the door swings open; it is this which enables us to say that we have sensed the form of the work. The short poem necessarily lacks the sweep, the accumulative grandeur of some novels, but it compensates in part for this and other lacks by engaging the senses more directly, that is, by keeping the form always before the ear (through rhythm) and, incidentally, in printed verse, the eye (through typographical arrangements). Since this appears to be a special and definitive characteristic of the poem, the poet who, in addition to all the other things he may be, is a conscious rhetorician is not likely to trust the simple power of his feelings or the obvious truth of his assertions to carry his poem (though one of the rhetorical strategies is to pretend to). He does not say merely, I love you; he says, I love you in such and such an order of detail as sustained by such and such a rhythm. This constant sense in poetry that an arrangement of materials has been effected, that an order has been imposed or revealed, that, in short, a form of one sort or another is importantly present and that it is there to be perceived in its minute particulars—this helps to make the poetic experience seem from moment to moment more intense.

Using *form* in its simplest sense, as a predetermined pattern of recurrences (of rhymes, meters, refrains, etc.), we can say that the forms most easily apprehensible, if not necessarily the most attractive, seem to be the most artificial and mechanical, most of which have been adapted to English from Continental sources, and with which most amateurs of poetry are, if anything, too familiar: the triolet, the rondeau, the villanelle, the sestina, the sonnet. Of these, the only ones used seriously in modern verse are the last three, although in the body of work of a poet like Thomas Hardy, whose native roughness and eccentricities of style counteract the tendency of these Continental forms to fall out with an excessive smoothness or lightness, an occasional success with one of the others, such as his triolet "Winter in Durnover Field," can be found. The sonnet, of course, despite William Carlos Williams' claim that it is now dead, has flourished since the Renaissance (with a gap of about eighty years in the neo-classical period), but the villanelle and sestina have been more or less revived for our use in this century—and already used up again, some would say. Kees' sestina "After the Trial" is a deliberately rather prosy example of a once purely lyrical form, and Empson's "Missing Dates" has proved to be an influential villanelle, showing the possibilities of that form for serious wit. The point of their recovery as usable forms would seem to be a new infusion of harshness, wit, or prosiness that sets up a friction against the implicit musicalness of the forms themselves: this tension is felt as a part of the sense of form communicated. It is as if the form, the fairly simple pattern of recurrences, had been redefined, or a new potential discovered in the abstract pattern. Some such sense of redefinition is probably necessary to the success of a poem in so contrived a form, at least for contemporary taste.

Form need not, of course, be understood as relating only, or even very importantly, to such predetermined patterns, though it is convenient to speak of it in this way. As Coleridge wrote:

> The form is mechanic, when on any given material we impress a pre-determined form, not necessarily arising out of the properties of the material;—as when to a mass of wet clay we give whatever shape we wish it to retain when hardened. The organic form, on the other hand, is innate; it shapes, as it develops, itself from within, and the fullness of its development is one and the same with the perfections of its outward form. Nature . . . inexhaustible in diverse powers, is equally inexhaustible in forms;—each exterior is the physiognomy of the being within. . . .

Much nonsense has undoubtedly been perpetrated in the name of "organic form"—from the fashions of Art Nouveau, with Tiffany "creating" a vase shaped like a tulip, to the appendix of the recent anthology of Beat poets, *The New American Poetry*, in which the contributors set forth their latter-day versions of this notion of the Romantic age. Yet it is clearly insufficient to consider what Coleridge calls the "outward form" as the whole form of a poem, as is sometimes a temptation with the artificial forms, the outward form being so manifest. Outwardly the poem may look formally correct; but if this outward form remains inexpressive of something more inward, something which involves more than the mere propriety of rhyme, meter, and the like, the "form" of the poem will seem defective. What this something is is harder to say than what it is not, but the idea of organic form supplies an illuminating figure of speech for it: when form is there, it will seem as if a shape as natural as one of the forms of nature had been found for the complex of perceptions which make up the poem. It is useful to remember, amid some of the controversies which repeatedly crop up in American poetry between the "traditionalists" and the "experimentalists," that this sense of form may be given by a sestina *or* by free verse: the details of the particular form are, before the fact of the poem itself, irrelevant.

THE WORD

The words of a poem, even if by coincidence they should be the same words as those encountered in a passage of prose, call for a different sort of attention on the part of both reader and writer. Without becoming mystical, it is possible to say, with Sir Herbert Read, that "in poetic experience the words are not merely drawn from the store of memory, as from a dictionary: they are born or re-born at the moment of expression." If in a novel the great event is likely to be a death or a wedding, in a poem it may well be a sentence, a line, a phrase, or just possibly a single word. Auden, who calls the poem a "verbal contraption," observes that one sign of poetic talent in the beginner is that he seems "more interested in playing with words than in saying something original." This interest in the word is probably an inheritance from childhood; at any rate, it seems childlike in its nature, for in a poem the sound, weight, and color of words, over and above their denotative or referential character, count in a half-magical way they do not often do for us after the years when we are first learning our native language. Such an interest, being non-practical, is easily enough associated with the games of children, as in poetry with the word-play, the puns, the near pointless ingenuities in which it abounds. All this is the playful overflow of the energy poets discover in or recharge words and dead phrases with, but it can also be, of course, a serious occupation. For words are rarely used outside of poetry—consider any page of any newspaper—with the precision the poem by its very nature requires. Ezra Pound, echoing the Chinese, remarks that sloppy language corrupts government. The care the poet lavishes on his words is a part of the discipline that may keep his own self-government at least secure, and no doubt it does contribute as a by-product to the preservation of a live culture in general. In a poem the word can be used, as R. P. Blackmur argues, with "the sum of all its appropriate history made concrete and particular in the individual context; and in poetry all words act *as if* they were so used, because the only kind of meaning poetry can have requires that all its words resume their full life: the full life being modified and made unique by the *qualifications* the words perform one upon the other in the poem." Thus in Hart Crane's "The Wine Menagerie" the words *thresholds* and *anatomies,* never before linked, so far as I know, combine together in a way which liberates meanings dormant in each apart.[1] The life and activity of the words, then, like the sense of form, also help to keep the poetic experience intense at every point.

Some sense of this value which individual words may have in poetry leads popular critics like J. Donald Adams to compile from

[1] Blackmur describes the process thoroughly in his essay on Crane, to be found in *Form and Value in Modern Poetry,* an Anchor paperback.

time to time lists of the most "poetical" words in the language, but, unfortunately, these lists are generally made up of words that seem beautiful only, which suggests that their compilers subscribe to an incomplete notion of poetry. Even the word *incarnadine*, which often figures on such lists, though it may indeed be beautiful in itself, is probably remembered for its context more than for itself: "The multitudinous seas incarnadine,/Making the green one red." For it is the context—"the *qualifications* the words perform one upon the other"—which adds to the beauty perhaps inherent in the word itself its specifically poetical character. In Shakespeare's pair of lines the words in each line have different etymologies, exist on different levels of usage; *incarnadine*, as the most surprising of the lot, is seen to be so partly because it is fixed so securely by, first, a word having a similar background, *multitudinous*, and then by the so much humbler *green* and *red*, the second of which, being a kind of meaning-rhyme for *incarnadine*, echoes it in sense and qualifies its grandeur and suggestiveness in a matter-of-fact way, defining rather than diminishing its splendor. Somewhat similar effects of balance and contrast in placing words, thus to call forth their maximum life, are a mark of style in the poems of William Carlos Williams. The passage in "To Elsie" beginning "and young slatterns bathed/ in filth" is a fine extended example, but the last three lines of the poem will serve as a brief illustration: "No one/ to witness/ and adjust, no one to drive the car." If *incarnadine* is a poetical word, so, in this context, is the word *car*.

Just as Henry James entered from the London *Times* odd and suggestive character names in his notebooks, some poets store up for future use interesting rhymes and off-rhymes, alliterative sets, etc. (One poet I know has been planning off and on for six months a poem to use the rhymes *jazzes* and *Jesus*.) Du Bellay advised his fellow poets to learn the techncial terms of the various trades so as to have a ready supply of words and images; so some poets look through flower and seed catalogues, others through atlases for the special richness place-names on occasion supply. All such acts are a practical, if in some cases a trivial, testimony to the poet's dependence on his vocabulary, which is his starting ground, and beyond that to the importance and power of the words themselves when put into the context awaiting them.

THE RHYTHM

But it is probably the rhythm of poetry which is its most definitive characteristic. We may leave aside the usual natural analogies, although for some these provide a warrant for the use of rhythm in poetry—the cycles of the seasons, the tides, even the blood-pulse and the process of breathing, all of which are rhythmical; however suggestive, they are, except perhaps for the analogy to breathing, very distant. All successions of spoken words necessarily have a rhythm of sorts, and the rhythm of poetry has a natural enough warrant in this alone, for its rhythm is only the rhythm of speech (or prose) more highly organized and therefore more notable. Its rhythm is not only a significant aspect of the poem's formal character, continually insisting as it does on the fact that the materials of the poem are not haphazardly there but are the result of an at least partially willed arrangement; rhythm is not only one of the significant means by which special attention is called to the words, insinuating as it does their sound-values into our consciousness (beyond whatever aptness the words bear to the plain sense or argument of the poem) and moreover placing and binding them together in a context that is not merely syntactical: the rhythm exists for these purposes, certainly, but for its own sake as well. And all this is true, more or less, whether the poem is written in the traditional meters or in free verse, whether the "music" of the poem approaches the one extreme of song (see the Renaissance songs by Dowland and Peele, and the modern example by Auden, "Lauds") or the other extreme of speech (see Williams' "To Elsie"). It has been suggested that one of the functions the meters serve is to reinforce by their appropriateness the subject of the poem, that is, to imitate: so in Browning's "How

They Brought the Good News from Ghent to Aix" the trisyllabic meters gallop as the horses do, with a desperate kuh-kloppety-klop; and there is a famous passage in Pope's "An Essay on Criticism" which means to illustrate this way of thinking:

> Soft is the strain when Zephyr gently blows,
> And the smooth stream in smoother numbers flows:
> But when loud surges lash the sounding shore,
> The hoarse, rough verse should like the torrent roar:
> When Ajax strives some rock's vast weight to throw,
> The line too labors, and the words move slow;
> Not so, when swift Camilla scours the plain,
> Flies o'er th'unbending corn, and skims along the main.

On the other hand, any imitation so direct is likely to seem primitive or naïve, and John Crowe Ransom has suggested that what the meters imitate is nothing less than an abstraction, a sort of Platonic universal—which is perhaps to say only that the meters operate with less realism than does the argument or "plot" of the poem; in other words, the meters exist as an object of interest apart from the paraphrasable meaning and are therefore capable of their own perfections without respect to their possible function in following the sense.

The traditional meters, being so distinctly audible and so well established by a consistent practice since the early Renaissance, would appear ready to yield at once to a descriptive analysis. This is, however, an illusion. Prosodists such as Sidney Lanier understand the meters as measures of time; the majority, like George Saintsbury, take them to be measures of stress. The nature of the language is so various, so many factors which go into its total sound are analyzable—stress, duration, pitch, pause or juncture, and all these in varying degrees—that a system of measure taking every one of them into account, though perhaps practicable for the linguist, is unnecessarily complicated for the poet himself, even if in his own less scientific way he is obliged to consider them.

The poet is naturally under no obligation to become learned in prosody or to memorize the standard classical names for metrical feet. Among some poets, indeed—Eliot, for example—it is an affectation to pretend innocence in such matters. In any event, the molossus and certain other classical feet have in English verse approximately the mythical status of the griffin and the roc. For the poet who would write in the traditional meters a good training of the ear on the practice of the masters (and his contemporaries) should be sufficient, no matter what set of terms he may choose to account for their practice and his own. It is enough to be aware of what is possible so as to attempt that or something just beyond.

However, we may try for the sake of clarification to describe current practice with as simple and consistent a set of terms as is available. Although other prosodic bases have been tried in English, poets today write in meters that, for our purposes, we may call (1) Accentual, (2) Syllabic, (3) Accentual-Syllabic, or (4) Free.

In Accentuals the norm of the line depends solely on a counting of the stresses. The number of syllables is not a determinate factor; their number will vary, and it will ordinarily be to the advantage of the meters for the syllable-count to vary. Examples: Old English verse, some of the ballads and nursery rhymes, some of Hopkins, some of Ransom, etc. "To Ishtar," by Richard Wilbur, is a good recent example: in each stanza the stress-count by line is 3-4-4-3, but the number of syllables is constantly varying along with the placement of the stresses.

In Syllabics the norm of the line depends solely on a counting of the number of syllables. The number of stresses, not being a determinate factor, will vary, and it is ordinarily to the advantage of Syllabics for the stress-count to vary. Examples: traditional French verse,[2] Marianne Moore, some of Auden, some of Dylan Thomas, some of Robert Bridges. "The Goddess," by Thom Gunn, is a good recent example. (Note that one of Gunn's lines, an effective one, departs from the 7-syllable norm.)

Accentual-Syllabic verse is one term for describing traditional meters, for in such meters (Shakespeare, Pope, Keats, Tennyson,

[2] It is sometimes argued that syllabics are less well adapted to the nature of English than to French, since stress in English speech is more decisive. Baudelaire's "Je n'ai pas oublié"—written in alexandrines, the 12-syllable line traditional to French verse—will afford an opportunity for comparison.

etc.) the norm of the line depends mutually on a counting of stresses and syllables both, and on a more or less regular alternation between the stressed and unstressed syllables. Wallace Stevens' "Sunday Morning" is the most beautiful modern example I know.

In Free Verse the norm as definable in terms of syllable- or stress-counting is absent. In the background of some free verse, traditional meters may seem to linger, but more often they can be regarded as a remembered set of expectations to which the free verse is deliberately running counter, usually in the direction of speech. The free-verse line is treated by some as a unit of time, or of thought, or of breath, or as a variation on stress-verse (Accentuals); but exceptions to all these ways of managing the line exist in practice. The very nature of free verse allows us to say with confidence only that the norm will be established, if at all, more or less anew in each poem, and that its success will depend greatly on the ear of the poet. For this reason it is probably the most difficult of all the meters to write in, and perhaps the most challenging. Good modern examples: some of W. C. Williams, some of Stevens, some recent Louis Simpson. Notice, for instance, the different principles of lining (that is, the division into lines) at work in Stevens' "Disillusionment of Ten O'Clock" and Williams' "To Elsie." Over and over Williams gains a temporary effect of ambiguity and surprise by his divisions of lines, taking advantage of our conventional tendency to delay, however slightly, at the end of a line, as if the phrase were complete: "and young slatterns bathed/ in filth." Stevens, as he plays variations on the color combinations the night-gowns of his poem are not going to be decorated with, also plays slight variations on the apparent lengths of the lines, though the "time" of each line is probably intended to remain approximately the same: here the syntactical parallels call attention to the rhythmic parallels, or vice versa.

One of the attractions of Accentuals and Syllabics is that they free the contemporary poet from what so many have complained of as the tyranny of the iamb, without at the same time reducing him to the desperate expedient of chaos, toward which some free verse tends. On the other hand, most poetry today continues to be written in the traditional Accentual-Syllabic meters, perhaps because it seems possible to register more precisely on so well-defined a base any meaningful departures from it.

The iamb (light-HEAVY; ᴗ/), which has since the Renaissance remained the most natural and flexible foot in English, will seem more tyrannical if the principles of variation in Accentual-Syllabics are not understood. For the monotony of perpetually reiterated rhythmical pattern is unbearable. Some variation, since the syllables of the language are of different duration (or quantity), is of course unavoidable: for this reason no two lines, though measured as identical iambic pentameters, for instance, will sound exactly alike. But variations beyond this, and beyond the placing of pauses at different points from line to line, are also desirable, and it is possible to codify the practice of centuries in this respect. The so-called "permissive" variations, then, are these:

1. The iamb is reversed, especially in the first foot of a line. (/ᴗ for ᴗ/) One of the rare instances of a reversed final foot occurs, incidentally, in "Sunday Morning."

2. Two weakly stressed syllables replace the single weakly stressed syllable of the iamb (or the reversed iamb), especially where elision seems possible. (ᴗᴗ/ for ᴗ/; or /ᴗᴗ for /ᴗ) There is precedent for many of the "poetical" elisions in our speech habits with some single words and combinations of words. Examples of potential elision: *being, riot* (y-glide); *ruinous, followers, shadowy* (w-glide); *murmuring, reason* (semi-vowels).[3]

3. An extra weakly stressed syllable—sometimes two or more—is added at the end of a line (feminine ending) or after a heavy pause in the middle. (Similar to 2.)

4. What John Crowe Ransom calls an "ionic" or double foot replaces two successive iambs. (ᴗᴗ// or //ᴗᴗ for ᴗ/ᴗ/) "When to the ses*sions of sweet si*lent thought . . ."

[3] Elision was formerly shown by the now superfluous apostrophe in words like *o'er*, as in Keats' "To Autumn."

5. The first weakly stressed syllable or, very rarely, a weakly stressed syllable elsewhere is dropped, especially in Chaucer and recent verse. "Ginglen in a whistling wind as clere"

Some would add to the three characteristics of poetry we have attempted to describe a fourth, that poetry is somehow involved with the making of images. And it is true that images—from simple sense-data to the elaborate figures of speech of the seventeenth-century poets like Donne—are much more frequent in most verse than in most prose, although it is possible to find passages of prose in which, for instance, figures of speech abound, and poems which, strictly speaking, are almost devoid of them. Perhaps we may say that the objects and events mentioned in such a poem as Williams' "Landscape with the Fall of Icarus"—the farmer, for example—serve in themselves as images almost as the more rhetorically open metaphors of other poems do: as Williams himself put it—"No ideas but in things." The *things,* then, of a poem, like figures of speech, may come to seem illustrative, or by their very choice and order (like the effects of montage in films) may communicate perception, or may strike us as moral analogues (like the animals in beast-fables) for human experience. It has seemed to many, Aristotle and Coleridge among them, that the image-making faculty, the ability to associate and perceive relations, especially between apparently unlike things, as in the formation of most images, which are usually comparative, forms an essential part of the poet's nature. All that we are saying, perhaps, is that the presence of openly expressed figures of speech does not seem a necessary part of a given poem's style. At the same time it may be plausible to suggest not only of the poem, but of the novel, the short story, and the play as well—in short, of all creative forms of written expression—that as a whole and in each of its parts it will be, in one sense or another, an image.

The poet gains his own understanding of the character of poetry most profoundly and intimately, of course, through writing poems, and there is little doubt that that understanding will always be partly intuitive and, so long as his attitude toward his craft remains healthy, constantly changing. Poets may or may not write good critical essays; in any case, their critical sense can be inferred from their poems. The stages of revision through which most poems pass reflect this critical sense of the poet, and a study of the manuscript pages of Keats, Housman, and Yeats—to mention only a few, some of whose worksheets have been studied in books like Phyllis Bartlett's *Poems in Process* (Oxford University Press, 1951) or critical anthologies such as Cleanth Brooks' and Robert Penn Warren's *Understanding Poetry* (Holt, Rinehart & Winston, 1960)—can prove indirectly instructive to others, as can the accounts poets have given of the composition of a poem, ranging from Poe through Valéry down to contemporaries like Stephen Spender, Randall Jarrell, Karl Shapiro, and W. D. Snodgrass. The first version, for instance, of the second stanza of Keats' autumn ode began:

> Who hath not seen thee? for thy haunts are many
> Sometimes whoever seeks for thee may find

Here apparently the necessity for rhyming the last word of the first line dictated the improvement in the finished poem,[4] but it is interesting to observe, for those who find it a profitable study, the great variety of critical factors which affect the revisions poets make. Even in the choice of subject matter, the starting point of the poem, it is not only the poet's interests of the moment and whatever deep-seated obsessions or preoccupations he may suffer from or rejoice in which may be revealed, but his critical understanding of his art itself.

If the fault of much amateur poetry is its failure to define, or focus, or even to recognize what its subject is, it follows that this failing may come from an inadequate understanding of what poetry itself is or may be. Such vagueness of definition suggests that the

---

[4] For a fuller analysis of Keats' revisions, see M. R. Ridley, *Keats' Craftsmanship* (University of Nebraska Press, 1963).

poet (as implicit critic) conceives of poetry as dealing with the supernal, perhaps, for which the vague is too often mistaken. To court experience for the subject matter it provides is another common form of "critical" error. The life of anyone is subject matter enough: Emily Dickinson wrote poems; Colonel Higginson, whose life was far more exciting, wrote verse. The experience out of which the failed poem rises may be compelling (to the poet), his feeling strong: this is not enough. The words, the images, the rhythms will float in a sort of vacuum; one or more of these may even be truly handsome, but until they cohere about a center, the richest details are only the starting point and not the poem. As Valéry's testimony regarding the composition of *Le Cimitière marin* shows, the experience of a naked rhythm can be, for a poem, as significant a beginning as the death (as Poe would have it) of a beautiful young woman. Nor is poetry concerned, as some in the past have felt, only with the beautiful or the true—in its subject matter. Once it is a finished poem it may be both beautiful and true, aesthetically speaking. But the mistake in Poe's recommending as the most promising subject the death of a beautiful young woman is in shifting the attention away from the form of the poem (which includes its subject matter) to the mere subject itself, which is fairly detachable. The life of an ugly old man is as plausible a subject.

But if any subject will serve, it nevertheless remains true that the treatment, the form that will eventually result from a verbal mastering of the subject, is conditioned by the choice of subject and is companionably obedient, if not subservient, to it. Decorum is the standard critical term for this principle. A serious poem in the trisyllabic meters usually reserved for light verse must work very hard to achieve that sense of congruency and harmony among all its parts which this principle would exact of the poem. But any question of decorum involves a question of tone as well, and it is a modern tendency to modify, to mix, to qualify, to be inclusive—that is, to prefer, even for many serious subjects, an ironic tone. Especially with a subject which invites sentiment such a tone may prevent the treatment from going soft and at the same time, by intruding a harsh realistic note, make the inevitable sentiment acceptable. Ransom's "Dead Boy" is a classic modern instance. "A pig with a pasty face" is a hard saying at the funeral of a dead child, but the context softens it, just as this toughens the context; not that the various incongruities blend into a soft-tough blur, but they remain distinct and are in themselves better defined by the contrasts among them, since they exist in and are governed by a total order. The principle of decorum must consequently be interpreted broadly enough to include what actually happens in poetry that pleases, and thus will have to include not only the satisfying of whatever tonal expectations the subject arouses as one possibility but, as another, their reversal or modification. Incongruity may then, by this token, be decorous. In fact, a convincing reversal of expectation often contributes to our sense that a poem is fresh and original.

The subject of a poem is not the most important thing about it, certainly. Auden's "Musée des Beaux Arts" and Williams' "Landscape with the Fall of Icarus" start with exactly the same subject, Brueghel's famous painting. But through a different selection of detail, through a different tonal handling, through different choices of rhythm, diction, and form, the real subject of each, its total meaning, proves in the long run to be very different. No paraphrase of a poem's meaning, we have been told repeatedly and truly, is the poem. Robert Frost defined poetry as that which was untranslatable, and this is true enough as far as it goes, for there is always something in a poem which cannot be reduced either to the plain sense of a prose paraphrase or carried over into the verse of another language. Valéry suggests that the distinction between poetry and prose is analogous to that between dancing and walking: the one is a gratuitous act, having no end but itself; the other useful, going somewhere. Although music may be pure sound and pure rhythm, poetry, however relative the value of its subject, can hardly become so as long as the subject remains, and it inevitably does remain. Some poems, perhaps especially such Renaissance songs as

Peele's for Bathsabe, approach this condition of purity and no doubt owe their survival to their "music" rather than to any sense they may, without much meaning to, make.

But most poetry most of the time is dealing with the real world, with human experience, though with tantalizing indirectness at times. And since in the real world the acts of men have value, some of this value adheres to them when they become the subject of poetry. Thus it is possible to say that the subject of one poem is trivial compared to the subject of another; both poems may be good poems, but it seems that the greater the subject, the more meaningful for us in terms of human life, the greater the poem will be, all else being equal. Since the unique perception with which each person is presumably endowed, his special way of looking at things, is a necessary factor in every poem, the poet's character, even in the most objective-seeming poem, becomes a part of the subject as it strives toward form. It is in some such sense as this that the old saying, "The style is the man," becomes relevant. This is not to say that if the man is good the poem will be good, though if the man is dull the poem is likely to be so too. The poet who would write more interesting poems, with richer and finer perceptions, had better become a more interesting person, capable of finer and richer perceptions. Language alone will not do the trick, though naturally without language all is lost.

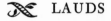

MUSÉE DES BEAUX ARTS

About suffering they were never wrong,
The Old Masters: how well they understood
Its human position; how it takes place
While someone else is eating or opening a window or just walking
    dully along;
How, when the aged are reverently, passionately waiting
For the miraculous birth, there always must be
Children who did not specially want it to happen, skating
On a pond at the edge of the wood:
They never forgot
That even the dreadful martyrdom must run its course
Anyhow in a corner, some untidy spot
Where the dogs go on with their doggy life and the torturer's horse
Scratches its innocent behind on a tree.

In Breughel's *Icarus*, for instance: how everything turns away
Quite leisurely from the disaster; the ploughman may
Have heard the splash, the forsaken cry,
But for him it was not an important failure; the sun shone
As it had to on the white legs disappearing into the green
Water; and the expensive delicate ship that must have seen
Something amazing, a boy falling out of the sky,
Had somewhere to get to and sailed calmly on.

                        —*W. H. Auden*

LAUDS

        Among the leaves the small birds sing;
        The crow of the cock commands awaking:
        In solitude, for company.

Bright shines the sun on creatures mortal;
Men of their neighbors become sensible:
In solitude, for company.

The crow of the cock commands awaking;
Already the mass-bell goes dong-ding:
In solitude, for company.

Men of their neighbors become sensible;
God bless the Realm, God bless the People:
In solitude, for company.

Already the mass-bell goes dong-ding;
The dripping mill-wheel is again turning:
In solitude, for company.

God bless the Realm, God bless the People;
God bless the green world temporal:
In solitude, for company.

The dripping mill-wheel is again turning;
Among the leaves the small birds sing:
In solitude, for company.

—*W. H. Auden*

THE GODDESS

When eyeless fish meet her on
her way upward, they gently
turn together in the dark
brooks.   But naked and searching
as a wind, she will allow
no hindrance, none, and bursts up

through potholes and narrow flues
seeking an outlet. Unslowed
by fire, rock, water or clay,
she after a time reaches
the soft abundant soil, which
still does not dissipate her

force—for look! sinewy thyme
reeking in the sunlight; rats
breeding, breeding in their nests;
and the soldier by a park
bench with his greatcoat collar
up, waiting all evening for

a woman, any woman
whose dress is tight across her
ass as bark in moonlight.
Proserpina! it is we,
vulnerable, quivering,
who stay you to abundance.

—*Thom Gunn*

TO ISHTAR

Is it less than your brilliance, Ishtar,
How the snowfield smarts in the fresh sun,
And the bells of its melting ring, and we blink
At the light flexing in trickles?

It is the Spring's disgrace
That already, before the prone arbutus
Will risk its whiteness, you have come down
To the first gate and darkened.

Forgive us, who cannot conceive you
Elsewhere and maiden, but love you only
Fallen among us in rut and furrow,
  In the shade of amassing leaves,

Or scrawny in plucked harvest,
Your losses having fattened the world
Till crownless, starless, you stoop and enter
  The low door of Irkalla.

There too, in the year's dungeon
Where love takes you, even our itch
For defilement cannot find you out,
  Your death being so perfect.

It is all we can do to witness
The waste motions of empty trees,
The joyless tittering duff, the grass-mats
  Blanched and scurfy with ice,

And in the desert heat
Of vision force from rotten sticks
Those pure and inconceivable blooms
  Which, rising, you bear beyond us.

                              —*Richard Wilbur*

✕ MISSING DATES

Slowly the poison the whole blood stream fills.
It is not the effort nor the failure tires.
The waste remains, the waste remains and kills.

It is not your system or clear sight that mills
Down small to the consequence a life requires;
Slowly the poison the whole blood stream fills.

They bled an old dog dry yet the exchange rills
Of young dog blood gave but a month's desires;
The waste remains, the waste remains and kills.

It is the Chinese tombs and the slag hills
Usurp the soil, and not the soil retires.
Slowly the poison the whole blood stream fills.

Not to have fire is to be a skin that shrills.
The complete fire is death.   From partial fires
The waste remains, the waste remains and kills.

It is the poems you have lost, the ills
From missing dates, at which the heart expires.
Slowly the poison the whole blood stream fills.
The waste remains, the waste remains and kills.

—*William Empson*

✖ TO ELSIE

The pure products of America
go crazy—
mountain folk from Kentucky

or the ribbed north end of
Jersey
with its isolate lakes and

valleys, its deaf-mutes, thieves
old names
and promiscuity between

devil-may-care men who have taken
to railroading
out of sheer lust of adventure—

and young slatterns bathed
in filth
from Monday to Saturday

to be tricked out that night
with gauds
from imaginations which have no

peasant traditions to give them
character
but flutter and flaunt

sheer rags—succumbing without
emotion
save numbed terror

under some hedge of choke-cherry
or viburnum—
which they cannot express—

Unless it be that marriage
perhaps
with a dash of Indian blood

will throw up a girl so desolate
so hemmed round
with disease or murder

that she'll be rescued by an
agent—
reared by the state and

sent out at fifteen to work in
some hard pressed
house in the suburbs—

some doctor's family, some Elsie—
voluptuous water
expressing with broken

brain the truth about us—
her great
ungainly hips and flopping breasts

addressed to cheap
jewelry
and rich young men with fine eyes

as if the earth under our feet
were
an excrement of some sky

and we degraded prisoners
destined
to hunger until we eat filth

while the imagination strains
after deer
going by fields of goldenrod in

the stifling heat of September
Somehow
it seems to destroy us

It is only in isolate flecks that
something
is given off

No one
to witness
and adjust, no one to drive the car

—*William Carlos Williams*

✂ LANDSCAPE WITH THE FALL OF ICARUS

According to Brueghel
when Icarus fell
it was spring

a farmer was ploughing
his field
the whole pageantry

of the year was
awake tingling
near

the edge of the sea
concerned
with itself

sweating in the sun
that melted
the wings' wax

unsignificantly
off the coast
there was

a splash quite unnoticed
this was
Icarus drowning

—William Carlos Williams

✖ AFTER THE TRIAL

Hearing the judges' well-considered sentence,
The prisoner saw long plateaus of guilt,
And thought of all the dismal furnished rooms
The past assembled, the eyes of parents
Staring through walls as though forever
To condemn and wound his innocence.

And if I raise my voice, protest my innocence,
The judges won't revoke their sentence.
I could stand screaming in this box forever,
Leaving them deaf to everything but guilt;
All the machinery of law devised by parents
Could not be stopped though fire swept the rooms.

Whenever my thoughts move to all those rooms
I sat alone in, capable of innocence,
I know now I was not alone, that parents
Always were there to speak the hideous sentence:
"You are our son; be good; we know your guilt;
We stare through walls and see your thoughts forever."

Sometimes I wished to go away forever;
I dreamt of strangers and of stranger rooms
Where every corner held the light of guilt.
Why do the judges stare? I saw no innocence
In them when they pronounced the sentence;
I heard instead the believing voice of parents.

I can remember evenings when my parents,
Settling my future happily forever,
Would frown before they spoke the sentence:
"Someday the time will come to leave these rooms
Where, under our watchful eyes, you have been innocent;
Remember us before you seize the world of guilt."

Their eyes burn. How can I deny my guilt
When I am guilty in the sight of parents?
I cannot think that even they were innocent.
At least I shall not have to wait forever
To be escorted to the silent rooms
Where darkness promises a final sentence.

We walk forever to the doors of guilt,
Pursued by our own sentences and eyes of parents,
Never to enter innocent and quiet rooms.

—Weldon Kees

✵ THE WINE MENAGERIE

Invariably when wine redeems the sight,
Narrowing the mustard scansions of the eyes,
A leopard ranging always in the brow
Asserts a vision in the slumbering gaze.

Then glozening decanters that reflect the street
Wear me in crescents on their bellies. Slow
Applause flows into liquid cynosures:
—I am conscripted to their shadows' glow.

Against the imitation onyx wainscoting
(Painted emulsion of snow, eggs, yarn, coal, manure)
Regard the forceps of the smile that takes her.
Percussive sweat is spreading to his hair. Mallets,
Her eyes, unmake an instant of the world. . .

What is it in this heap the serpent pries—
Whose skin, facsimile of time, unskeins
Octagon, sapphire transepts round the eyes;

—From whom some whispered carillon assures
Speed to the arrow into feathered skies?

Sharp to the window-pane guile drags a face,
And as the alcove of her jealousy recedes
An urchin who has left the snow
Nudges a cannister across the bar
While August meadows somewhere clasp his brow.

Each chamber, transept, coins some squint,
Remorseless line, minting their separate wills—
Poor streaked bodies wreathing up and out,
Unwitting the stigma that each turn repeals:
Between black tusks the roses shine!

New thresholds, new anatomies! Wine talons
Build freedom up about me and distill
This competence—to travel in a tear
Sparkling alone, within another's will.

Until my blood dreams a receptive smile
Wherein new purities are snared; where chimes
Before some flame of gaunt repose a shell
Tolled once, perhaps, by every tongue in hell.
—Anguished, the wit that cries out of me:

"Alas,—these frozen billows of your skill!
Invent new dominoes of love and bile. . .
Ruddy, the tooth implicit of the world
Has followed you. Though in the end you know
And count some dim inheritance of sand,
How much yet meets the treason of the snow.

"Rise from the dates and crumbs. And walk away,
Stepping over Holofernes' shins—
Beyond the wall, whose severed head floats by
With Baptist John's. Their whispering begins.

"—And fold your exile on your back again;
Petrushka's valentine pivots on its pin."

                                    —*Hart Crane*

✎ SUNDAY MORNING

I

Complacencies of the peignoir, and late
Coffee and oranges in a sunny chair,
And the green freedom of a cockatoo
Upon a rug mingle to dissipate
The holy hush of ancient sacrifice.
She dreams a little, and she feels the dark
Encroachment of that old catastrophe,
As a calm darkens among water-lights.
The pungent oranges and bright, green wings
Seem things in some procession of the dead,
Winding across wide water, without sound.
The day is like wide water, without sound,
Stilled for the passing of her dreaming feet
Over the seas, to silent Palestine,
Dominion of the blood and sepulchre.

II

Why should she give her bounty to the dead?
What is divinity if it can come
Only in silent shadows and in dreams?
Shall she not find in comforts of the sun,
In pungent fruit and bright, green wings, or else
In any balm or beauty of the earth,
Things to be cherished like the thought of heaven?
Divinity must live within herself:
Passions of rain, or moods in falling snow;
Grievings in loneliness, or unsubdued
Elations when the forest blooms; gusty
Emotions on wet roads on autumn nights;
All pleasures and all pains, remembering
The boughs of summer and the winter branch.
These are the measures destined for her soul.

III

Jove in the clouds had his inhuman birth.
No mother suckled him, no sweet land gave
Large-mannered motions to his mythy mind.
He moved among us, as a muttering king,
Magnificent, would move among his hinds,
Until our blood, commingling, virginal,
With heaven, brought such requital to desire
The very hinds discerned it, in a star.
Shall our blood fail? Or shall it come to be
The blood of paradise? And shall the earth
Seem all of paradise that we shall know?
The sky will be much friendlier then than now,
A part of labor and a part of pain,
And next in glory to enduring love,
Not this dividing and indifferent blue.

IV

She says, "I am content when wakened birds,
Before they fly, test the reality
Of misty fields, by their sweet questionings;
But when the birds are gone, and their warm fields
Return no more, where, then, is paradise?"
There is not any haunt of prophecy,
Nor any old chimera of the grave,
Neither the golden underground, nor isle
Melodious, where spirits gat them home,
Nor visionary south, nor cloudy palm
Remote on heaven's hill, that has endured
As April's green endures; or will endure
Like her remembrance of awakened birds,
Or her desire for June and evening, tipped
By the consummation of the swallow's wings.

V

She says, "But in contentment I still feel
The need of some imperishable bliss."

Death is the mother of beauty; hence from her,
Alone, shall come fulfilment to our dreams
And our desires. Although she strews the leaves
Of sure obliteration on our paths,
The path sick sorrow took, the many paths
Where triumph rang its brassy phrase, or love
Whispered a little out of tenderness,
She makes the willow shiver in the sun
For maidens who were wont to sit and gaze
Upon the grass, relinquished to their feet.
She causes boys to pile new plums and pears
On disregarded plate. The maidens taste
And stray impassioned in the littering leaves.

VI

Is there no change of death in paradise?
Does ripe fruit never fall? Or do the boughs
Hang always heavy in that perfect sky,
Unchanging, yet so like our perishing earth,
With rivers like our own that seek for seas
They never find, the same receding shores
That never touch with inarticulate pang?
Why set the pear upon those river-banks
Or spice the shores with odors of the plum?
Alas, that they should wear our colors there,
The silken weavings of our afternoons,
And pick the strings of our insipid lutes!
Death is the mother of beauty, mystical,
Within whose burning bosom we devise
Our earthly mothers waiting, sleeplessly.

VII

Supple and turbulent, a ring of men
Shall chant in orgy on a summer morn
Their boisterous devotion to the sun,
Not as a god, but as a god might be,
Naked among them, like a savage source.
Their chant shall be a chant of paradise,
Out of their blood, returning to the sky;
And in their chant shall enter, voice by voice,
The windy lake wherein their lord delights,

The trees, like serafin, and echoing hills,
That choir among themselves long afterward.
They shall know well the heavenly fellowship
Of men that perish and of summer morn.
And whence they came and whither they shall go
The dew upon their feet shall manifest.

VIII

She hears, upon that water without sound,
A voice that cries, "The tomb in Palestine
Is not the porch of spirits lingering.
It is the grave of Jesus, where he lay."
We live in an old chaos of the sun,
Or old dependency of day and night,
Or island solitude, unsponsored, free,
Of that wide water, inescapable.
Deer walk upon our mountains, and the quail
Whistle about us their spontaneous cries;
Sweet berries ripen in the wilderness;
And, in the isolation of the sky,
At evening, casual flocks of pigeons make
Ambiguous undulations as they sink,
Downward to darkness, on extended wings.

—Wallace Stevens

DISILLUSIONMENT OF TEN O'CLOCK

The houses are haunted
By white night-gowns.
None are green,
Or purple with green rings,
Or green with yellow rings,
Or yellow with blue rings.
None of them are strange,

With socks of lace
And beaded ceintures.
People are not going
To dream of baboons and periwinkles.
Only, here and there, an old sailor
Drunk and asleep in his boots,
Catches tigers
In red weather.

—*Wallace Stevens*

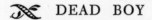 DEAD BOY

The little cousin is dead, by foul subtraction,
A green bough from Virginia's aged tree,
And none of the county kin like the transaction,
Nor some of the world of outer dark, like me.

A boy not beautiful, nor good, nor clever,
A black cloud full of storms too hot for keeping,
A sword beneath his mother's heart—yet never
Woman bewept her babe as this is weeping.

A pig with a pasty face, so I had said,
Squealing for cookies, kinned by poor pretense
With a noble house. But the little man quite dead,
I see the forbears' antique lineaments.

The elder men have strode by the box of death
To the wide flag porch, and muttering low send round
The bruit of the day. O friendly waste of breath!
Their hearts are hurt with a deep dynastic wound.

He was pale and little, the foolish neighbors say;
The first-fruits, saith the Preacher, the Lord hath taken;
But this was the old tree's late branch wrenched away,
Grieving the sapless limbs, the shorn and shaken.

—John Crowe Ransom

TO AUTUMN

I

Season of mists and mellow fruitfulness,
    Close bosom-friend of the maturing sun;
Conspiring with him how to load and bless
    With fruit the vines that round the thatch-eves run;
To bend with apples the moss'd cottage-trees,
    And fill all fruit with ripeness to the core;
        To swell the gourd, and plump the hazel shells
    With a sweet kernel; to set budding more,
And still more, later flowers for the bees,
Until they think warm days will never cease,
        For Summer has o'er-brimm'd their clammy cells.

II

Who hath not seen thee oft amid thy store?
    Sometimes whoever seeks abroad may find
Thee sitting careless on a granary floor,
    Thy hair soft-lifted by the winnowing wind;
Or on a half-reap'd furrow sound asleep,
    Drows'd with the fume of poppies, while thy hook
        Spares the next swath and all its twined flowers:
And sometimes like a gleaner thou dost keep
    Steady thy laden head across a brook;
    Or by a cyder-press, with patient look,
        Thou watchest the last oozings hours by hours.

III

Where are the songs of Spring?   Ay, where are they?
   Think not of them, thou hast thy music too,—
While barred clouds bloom the soft-dying day,
   And touch the stubble-plains with rosy hue;
Then in a wailful choir the small gnats mourn
   Among the river sallows, borne aloft
     Or sinking as the light wind lives or dies;
And full-grown lambs loud bleat from hilly bourn;
   Hedge-crickets sing; and now with treble soft
   The red-breast whistles from a garden-croft;
     And gathering swallows twitter in the skies.

—John Keats

✕ JE N'AI PAS OUBLIÉ

Je n'ai pas oublié, voisine de la ville,
Notre blanche maison, petite, mais tranquille;
Sa Pomone de plâtre et sa vieille Vénus
Dans un bosquet chétif cachant leurs membres nus.
Et le soleil, le soir, ruisselant et superbe,
Qui derrière la vitre où se brisait sa gerbe,
Semblait, grand œil ouvert dans le ciel curieux,
Contempler nos diners longs et silencieux,
Répandant largement ses beaux reflets de cierge
Sur la nappe frugale et les rideaux de serge.

—Charles Baudelaire

BATHSABE'S SONG

Hot sun, cool fire, tempered with sweet air,
Black shade, fair nurse, shadow my white hair:
Shine, sun; burn, fire; breathe, air, and ease me;
Black shade, fair nurse, shroud me and please me:
Shadow, my sweet nurse, keep me from burning,
Make not my glad cause, cause for mourning,
    Let not my beauty's fire
    Inflame unstaid desire,
    Nor pierce any bright eye
    That wandereth lightly.

                    —George Peele

FINE KNACKS FOR LADIES

Fine knacks for ladies, cheap, choice, brave and new!
Good pennyworths! but money cannot move.
I keep a fair but for the fair to view;
A beggar may be liberal of love.
Though all my wares be trash, the heart is true.

Great gifts are guiles and look for gifts again;
My trifles come as treasures from my mind.
It is a precious jewel to be plain;
Sometimes in shell the Orient's pearls we find.
Of others take a sheaf, of me a grain.

Within this pack pins, points, laces, and gloves,
And divers toys fitting a country fair.
But in my heart, where duty serves and loves,
Turtles and twins, court's brood, a heavenly pair.
Happy the heart that thinks of no removes!

—John Dowland

The Novelist as Meddler

GEORGE P. ELLIOTT

The word "novel" has been used to describe almost every sort of long fiction. The *Odyssey*, an epic poem, is sometimes called the first novel. *Tristram Shandy*, a satiric autobiography with no plot whatever, is called a novel, and so is *Alice in Wonderland*. But "novel" has also been used more strictly a good deal of the time, to describe the sort of long prose fiction which has been dominant in western literature for over two centuries. In this essay "novel" means this one species and not the larger genus.

Not many novels are formally pure, in this restricted use of the term "novel." None of the three books listed above is properly a novel, though *Tristram Shandy* is partly one; neither are *Don Quixote*, *The Castle*, and *Moby Dick*. T. S. Eliot and André Gide have said that as pure, as "novelistic" a novelist as ever wrote is Georges Simenon. Perhaps they are right; if so, the lack of strength in his pure novels only suggests the necessity to adulterate fiction, as gold or silver must be adulterated, with some baser alloys to make them strong. Flaubert and James are commonly referred to as formal masters of the novel; an inspection of *Madame Bovary* and *Portrait of a Lady* would disclose the extent to which these books are strengthened with alloys of romance and satire. *War and Peace, Bleak House, The Red and the Black, Huckleberry Finn, The Brothers Karamazov, Remembrance of Things Past, Tom Jones*: all these celebrated books are commonly called novels, and all are by any formal criterion manifestly imperfect. In other

words, the novel is odd in this: great representatives of the form
are impure and imperfect.

The novel, the realistic species of long prose fiction, is differen-
tiated from realistic drama by far more than the form in which it
is printed. James' advice to the novelist to disappear into his material, which he must *render, present, dramatize*, pushes the novel
toward drama and away from essay; yet a true novel is not just a
realistic play with stage directions spelled out and speakers described rather more fully than is conventional with printed plays.
A novel presents the characters' hidden life with an extensiveness,
intimacy, and analytic subtlety which drama forbids, and it is a
story controlled by a narrative voice.

Here is a formal definition of the (realistic) novel.

In the novel, (1) objects, behavior, and social customs resemble
those existing in some actual society at some actual time, and moti-
vation is probable, which is to say that the characters are mostly in
the middle range of experience without being altogether consistent and if their behavior is extremely irrational it is presented in
the light of convention as criminal or mad; (2) the principle for
selecting and arranging the parts derives primarily from concern
to reveal and to explore the pattern of relations, both hidden and
open, of characters with one another, with social institutions, with
ideas, with the natural world, or each with himself and his own
beliefs; and (3) the reader's relation to the imagined characters
is appreciably modified by the attitude of the narrator (who may
or may not also be the author) toward the reader, toward the moral
and social values of the world he is describing, and toward the
characters as imagined persons, including the narrator's earlier self
if that self is one of the characters.

The content of the novel, as here defined, is intercourse among
a few credible characters and between them and the reader, who
knows them by their public actions, their intimate words, and their
unrecognized impulses. But this is also the area of moral concern.
Both in fiction and in life, an attitude toward the behavior and
motive of individuals related in and to a natural and social world

almost necessarily becomes moral as it becomes engaged. The scientific attitude toward behavior and motive is that of detached observation; Balzac, Flaubert, and Zola all announced their intention of assuming this disengaged stance, but in fact neither they nor any other novelist worth reading ever did so consistently. The aesthetic attitude of pure interest is much more congenial to a writer than the scientific one, the novel being, after all, a form of art. "Let us become epicures of experience, valuing it according to its refinement and intensity." Gide is the practicing apologist of this attitude. It is possible to read his *Strait Is the Gate* and *Lafcadio's Adventures* in such a way as to value Alissa's spiritual agony above Lafcadio's zeal for gratuitous malice only because imagining her agony is a more refined and intense pleasure than imagining his malice. Pleasure of this kind is of course a part of the enjoyment afforded by even as non-aesthetic, propagandistic a novel as *Uncle Tom's Cabin*. But Gide's theoretical amorality is in fact extremely rare in fiction; it is also possible to read his finest novel, *Strait is the Gate*, as a work of moral commitment. The very process of writing a novel and imagining characters engages the spirit, and this engagement almost necessarily assumes a moral quality. Even Gide the aesthete trembles on the verge of *ought;* his position can be imagined as this: "To purify experience to its finest and then to explore it, either actually or imaginatively, is my (the?) highest good." In sum, it is possible for a novelist to take the position of purely aesthetic engagement with matters which are the heart of moral concern, but it is rare for him to do so and the results at best are lacking in strength.

Meanwhile, perfect or imperfect, great or small, whatever the moral stance, novels and part-novels all face certain problems in common. Formally, the most important of these is point of view. The ideal held up by James the theorist and by his critical descendants is of an invisible, inaudible author; preferably there should be no narrator; if he is there he must meddle with the characters and their world only ironically, that is, in such a way as to reveal his own character; to author and reader, a narrator should be only another personage in the story. But since almost all substantial novelists do in fact meddle (including James the novelist) and since such meddling is apt to be not just formal but also moral in nature, this essay will concern itself both with ways in which author-meddling does not damage a novel but instead leaves it pretty much unscathed and also with ways by which such meddling can be turned to a novel's advantage, and then at the end with the one sort of meddling for which there is no forgiveness.

A harmless sort of intrusion is for the author to turn from the story to expound his theories on some subject or other directly to the reader. His justification for doing this is that you should understand the true nature of old maids, the gods, social upheaval, storytelling, whatever, in order to appreciate the significance of his characters' acts and thoughts. But what ordinarily happens is that you listen for a while to what the author as a private person has to say, and then you go back into the world of the novel with your own opinions on the subject intact and with your connection with the characters untouched; for as a man of opinions a novelist is no better than his neighbor.

> In devotion woman is sublimely superior to man. It is the only superiority she cares to have acknowledged, the only quality which she pardons man for letting her excel him in.

I doubt it; but this disagreement does not interfere with my understanding of Eugénie Grandet, of whom it is said, or with my affection for Balzac, who said it. Tolstoy's long quarrel with the French historians, in *War and Peace*, and his elaborate theory of history have so little to do with what is valuable in the novel that a disagreeing reader takes to skipping those sections. The most to be learned from those chapters is the hardly surprising knowledge that a novelist, who is primarily concerned with individuals, finds the way of an historian, who is primarily concerned with social movements, exasperating and uncongenial. Meanwhile, however, the long asides do not damage the novel proper, because they are presented openly and separately and because an understanding of the characters' behavior does not depend upon them. One can find Tolstoy's notions about how to write a history of the Napoleonic invasion of Rusia silly and yet find, while reading the novel proper, that every action and thought of every important character during his account of that invasion rings absolutely true. For the worth of the novel, the truth of this ring is what matters.

So long as an author is saying *This is what I think,* all goes well enough; when he begins to say *This is what you ought to think,* the reader is likely to resist. Even so, if this preaching is open and is separable from the novel proper, it will do no essential harm.

> That is the whole history of the search for happiness, whether it be your own or somebody else's that you want to win. It ends, and it always ends, in the ghastly sense of the bottomless nothingness into which you will inevitably fall if you strain any further.

I feel Lawrence pushing me with his rhetoric to accept this as true not only for the character who is dimly supposed to be thinking it, but for the world at large. I not only doubt the truth of this opinion, I also balk at being pushed. Even so, my pleasure in *The Fox* remains unimpaired, and my regard for Lawrence continues only slightly impaired.

When a novelist's comments on experience strike you as true and good, your pleasure is increased.

> There are in the music of the violin—if one does not see the instrument itself, and so cannot relate what one hears to its form, which modifies the fullness of the sound—accents which are so closely akin to those of certain contralto voices, that one has the illusion that a singer has taken her place amid the orchestra. One raises one's eyes; one sees only the wooden case, magical as a Chinese box; but, at moments, one is still tricked by the deceiving appeal of the Siren; at times, too, one believes that one is listening to a captive spirit, struggling in the darkness of its masterful box, a box quivering with enchantment, like a devil immersed in a stoup of holy water; sometimes, again, it is in the air, at large, like a pure and supernatural creature that reveals to the ear, as it passes, its invisible message.

This passage has little or nothing to do with any of the characters in Proust's novel, except as it is one of the opinions of Marcel the narrator, who in such respects is Proust himself. But it and a thousand others of its kind constitute much of the excellence of the book. It has a legitimate if slight tonal function in the section in which it occurs, "Swann in Love"; but its main virtue is to give elegant expression to something true, something with which one cannot disagree and for which one could not possibly have found better words.

To a novelist with the urge to tell the reader what something of the world is like, the best, hopeless advice is: Be subtle, be wise.

A description of surroundings is likely to be closer to the heart of a novel than is a general comment on life, because the circumstances in which a character acts modify what he does and our understanding of him. The operative principle here is plain enough: the amount and intensity of the description of anything should be proportionate to the importance of that thing in revealing character but should not be determined by the author's personal interest in the thing described.

Descriptions of nature are notoriously long-winded and are commonly skipped—for example, those in the romances of Scott and Cooper. Descriptions of hunting and fishing sometimes go on longer than necessary, even the famous set-pieces of Tolstoy in *War and Peace* and of Hemingway in many of his fictions. Readers who like these sports for their own sake find the passages delightful, but those who are indifferent to these sports find the descriptions excessive for presenting character—though they are not very damaging to the novel since they are abridgeable by the impatient reader. Surely the authors dwelt upon these scenes at such length mostly because they themselves loved those sports. But here is a description of nature, from Mary Webb's *Precious Bane*, which is wholly justified.

> When I look out of my window and see the plain and the big sky with clouds standing up on the mountains, I call to mind the thick, blotting woods of Sarn, and the crying of the mere when the ice was on it, and the way the water would come into the cupboard under the stairs when it rose at the time of the snow melting.

There was but little sky to see there, saving that which was reflected in the mere; but the sky that is in the mere is not the proper heavens. You see it in a glass darkly, and the long shadows of rushes go thin and sharp across the sliding stars, and even the sun and moon might be put out down there, for, times, the moon would get lost in lily leaves, and times, a heron might stand before the sun.

It is a novel of country people who see the world alive with mysterious connections, as the narrator in this description does; and none of the novel's descriptions goes on too long.

Closer yet to the heart of fiction are descriptions of man-made things, for the artifacts a character has made or has chosen to exist among affect him, reveal him. Here, the usual advice is to let concrete things speak for themselves, and Flaubert is the model. Emma goes with Léon to the house of the wet-nurse who is taking care of her baby.

The ground-floor bedroom—the only bedroom in the house—had a wide uncurtained bed standing against its rear wall; the window wall (one pane was mended with a bit of wrapping paper) was taken up by the kneading-trough. In the corner behind the door was a raised slab for washing, and under it stood a row of heavy boots with shiny hobnails and a bottle of oil with a feather in its mouth. A Mathieu Laensberg almanac lay on the dusty mantelpiece among gun flints, candle ends and bits of tinder. And as a final bit of clutter there was a figure of Fame blowing her trumpets —a picture probably cut out of a perfume advertisement and now fastened to the wall with six shoe tacks.

The author imposes on the reader no attitude toward this room and the items in it he has chosen to describe; "a final bit of clutter" does not exceed the bounds of reasonable observation. Two sentences later, Léon's attitude is given: "it seemed to him a strange sight, this elegant lady in her nankeen gown here among all this squalor." Indeed, this is about as meticulously hands-off as a novelist can be. But here is a pasage from *Our Mutual Friend* which operates on another principle entirely.

Mr. and Mrs. Veneering were bran-new people in a bran-new house in a bran-new quarter of London. Everything about the

Veneerings was spick and span new. All their furniture was new, all their friends were new, all their servants were new, their plate was new, their carriage was new, their harness was new, their horses were new, their pictures were new, they themselves were new, they were as newlymarried as was lawfully compatible with their having a bran-new baby, and if they had set up a great-grandfather, he would have come home in matting from the Pantechnicon, without a scratch upon him, French-polished to the crown of his head.

For, in the Veneering establishment, from the hall-chairs with the new coat of arms, to the grand pianoforte with the new action, and upstairs again to the new fire-escape, all things were in a state of high varnish and polish. And what was observable in the furniture, was observable in the Veneerings—the surface smelt a little too much of the workshop and was a trifle sticky.

This description is not so concrete as Flaubert's, but surely it is fictionally valuable to learn a little about this house in such a way as to learn far more about what its owners are like; and Dickens' openly satiric view of the Veneerings is surely no less legitimate than Flaubert's professedly objective but, in the whole novel, covertly satiric view of the world of *Madame Bovary*. And here is a passage from *The Ambassadors*. Strether is visiting Miss Gostrey's place in Paris.

Her compact and crowded little chambers, almost dusky, as they at first struck him, with accumulations, represented a supreme general adjustment to opportunities and conditions. Wherever he looked he saw an old ivory or an old brocade, and he scarce knew where to sit for fear of a misappliance. The life of the occupant struck him, of a sudden, as more charged with possession even than Chad's or than Miss Barrace's; wide as his glimpse had lately become of the empire of "things", what was before him still enlarged it; the lust of the eyes and the pride of life had indeed thus their temple. It was the innermost nook of the shrine—as brown as a pirate's cave. In the brownness were glints of gold; patches of purple were in the gloom; objects, all, that caught, through the muslin, with their high rarity, the light of the low windows. Nothing was clear about them but that they were precious, and they brushed his ignorance with their contempt as a flower, in a liberty taken with him, might have been whisked under his nose. But after a full look at his hostess he knew, none the less, what most concerned him. The circle in which they stood together was warm with life, and every question between them would live there as nowhere else.

This is literary impressionism: there is not a concrete image in the passage; yet, by suggesting the effect the room makes on Strether, James succeeds in creating in the reader's mind a sense of the room, its owner, and its viewer. And though James' own attitude toward the room is as scrupulously absent as was Flaubert's toward the wet-nurse's room, one is in no doubt of James' aesthetic love of it.

In *Laocoön*, Lessing suggests that, in a competition between a visual and a verbal representation of a thing, the visual must win. If he is right, as he probably is even for people with strong image-making faculties, the usual advice about the best way to describe things in a novel needs qualifying. It is no more valuable to let the things in the room speak for themselves as Flaubert does than it is to give the impression of a room as James does or to give both that and also the narrator's opinion of the room and its inhabitants as Dickens does. Words can carry a thing-in-itself not at all and an image of the thing vividly but imperfectly; but they can, marvelously if less vividly, carry someone's impression of it and relation to it.

Because a point of view is literally, geographically fixed, there is a kind of assumption that the metaphorical "point of view" of fiction should be fixed too. To a writer who feels bound to maintain one consistent point of view and to keep the same distance from events and people, all sorts of special benefits come from his restricting himself to one clearly defined consciousness, which ordinarily means using *I*. The most obvious benefit of *I* is the increase of credibility: "I was there, I saw it." That the body of *Wuthering Heights* is narrated by Nelly Dean, the respectable housekeeper, to Lockwood, the respectable lawyer, gives the book a credibility and solidity it could not possibly have had if told in the free manner of a Gothic horror story. Another benefit of *I* is that certain of the actual author's narrative or stylistic peculiarities can be put to use by being so disposed as to reflect upon and reveal the character of *I*. Conrad's fondness for generalizing was never put to better use than when it became part of Marlow's character as he tells *Heart of Darkness*, nor James' famous ambiguity than as it opened depths in the story within a story of *The Turn of the Screw*.

But it is only theoretically that lack of consistency in point of view matters very much. Critical prescriptions are to be reached inductively: if many good novels violate a formal prescription, then that prescription must be modified or discarded; and many do violate the one about consistent point of view. *The Possessed* is told by an *I* most of the time, but when it is inconvenient for the *I* to be present at a scene, he simply disappears from the book and the scene is told by Dostoevsky from the unspecified point of view conventional in narratives of all sorts; nor does the book suffer from it. And in *Crime and Punishment*—which is surely one of the greatest novels—Dostoevsky begins one chapter:

> It would be difficult to describe the exact reasons which gave Mrs. Marmeladov the idea of the absurd funeral meal.

For the rest of the paragraph, Dostoevsky speculates on her possible motives. But during the course of the chapter he gets more and more involved with her—presenting her, to be sure, by external description and by objective reporting of what she says—until early in the next chapter he is close enough to say:

> Mrs. Marmeladov remained standing in the same place, as though thunderstruck. She could not understand how Mr. Luzhin could have disavowed her father's hospitality, for by now she believed in it blindly.

Only a narrow theory would object to such a shift in how much the novelist should allow himself to reveal of what is going on in a character's mind. Fielding is sometimes reproved for his intrusions and shifts.

> [Jones] returned the fellow his empty pistol, advised him to think of honester means of relieving his distress, and gave him a couple

of guineas for the immediate support of his wife and his family; adding, 'he wished he had more for his sake, for the hundred pound that had been mentioned was not his own.'

Our readers will probably be divided in their opinions concerning this action; some may applaud it perhaps as an act of extraordinary humanity, while those of a more saturnine temper will consider it as a want of regard to that justice which every man owes his country. Partridge certainly saw it in that light; for he testified much dissatisfaction on the occasion, quoted an old proverb, and said, he should not wonder if the rogue attacked them again before they reached London.

The highwayman was full of expressions of thankfulness and gratitude. He actually dropped tears, or pretended so to do.

Here Fielding moves from a rather distant reporting of action, to an author-comment which would break any illusion, back to an even cooler reporting. But the shift is open, the author's voice is clear, and the story and characters have vigor enough to survive the comments of writer and reader alike. *Here is the way to look at my characters*: this is bad only if the author's way of looking is stupid and the characters but half-alive. So, at least, the power, delight, and formal satisfactoriness of *Tom Jones* suggest.

The theory that the Dostoevsky-Fielding-Balzac method is so inferior to the Conrad-Joyce-Flaubert method as to render their novels inferior as works of art makes one huge assumption: that the reader of a novel should not feel himself in the hands of an artificer or storyteller and that the novelist's true art is to create an illusory actuality, appearing to have no art. But this assumption goes too far. It is the equivalent of that theatrical assumption that the audience can be looking through a fourth wall into an actual room. Just as a spectator never really forgets that he is in a theater watching actors, so the reader of a novel does not really forget he is being told a story. When the narrator is open about his role as storyteller, as most have been in every sort of fiction, the reader happily allows him all sorts of liberties of point of view: everyone recognizes the artifice and enjoys it. Only when consistency is promised must inconsistency disturb.

As for fixity of remove—the steady distance which "point of

view" metaphorically promises—it is made nothing by the example of the best, Tolstoy. He moves at will from the most panoramic aloofness above a battlefield to an account of the inmost feelings of a man at the moment before his death, and he moves anywhere between when and as it pleases him; and it is hard to imagine this lordly freedom troubling a reader for any reason but a narrow literary theory or his own private and uninteresting pathology. There is a great peace in delivering oneself into the hands of a writer who *knows*: "Tell us what you know, any way you will."

In fiction the point of view that matters most, and is least like the geographical one, is the author's set of values, what he considers important, especially morally; for this gets at the heart of the novel, the characters' being and doing. The subject is so important, and so tricky, that I am looking at it under two aspects: first, the relation of the author's values to the reader, and then the author's relation to the characters he is creating.

Before going on, I must spell out an assumption: that everyone concerned with a novel, reader, writer, and character, has a set of attitudes, preferences, judgments, or values about human conduct, and that, whether these values are conscious or unconscious, articulated with logical coherence or only manifest in sometimes contradictory acts, they must finally be considered—if the word "moral" is to mean anything—moral values. This is no more than an ad hoc definition, much too loose to satisfy any ethical philosopher. Its justification in this essay is to insist that everyone says, or at least implies, "good" or "bad" when he looks at human conduct or when he himself acts: the hyperconscious aesthete for whom the high good is savoring refined experience; the self-indulgent reader who seems to ask no more than that a novel remove him from moral concern but who is also asking for the author and the story to assure him, at least temporarily, that self-indulgence and sloth are all right; even Faulkner's feeble-minded Ike Snopes, whose great good is to love, though he knows that the world thinks he should not love, a cow. These are extreme cases. Typically, people accept the code of conduct of their society, class, religion, province, whatever, without much distinguishing between convention and morality. It is a considerable part of the novelist's art both to let the reader understand the code of the imagined world and also to define the characters as they conform to, modify, rebel against, ignore, affirm, use this code.

The novelist's understanding of the imagined society's code of manners and values is essential to the reader's understanding of the characters, but the novelist's own code need not be and seldom is identical with the imagined code. Even where there is a substantial agreement, as with Jane Austen, the excellent novelist yet has a moral vision which much of the time perceives in the characters, including the narrator if there is one, a disparity between official reason and private motive, between society's requirements and the heart's need, that delights the reader and rings true to what he knows. One may say that a novelist will be interested in manners and convention, if only because he needs them to portray his people, and that his code of moral values may greatly differ from that code of manners but cannot utterly deny it. Any sort of writer who, like a mystic, says that social mores are of no importance or who, like a nihilist, says that all actual societies deserve destruction will have little interest in writing novels. Tolstoy the radical prophet necessarily rejected the works of Tolstoy the novelist. To this extent a true novelist is conservative: he says that the society he is writing about is worth at least our attention, for within it and of it are people worth noticing, worthy of our concern. The coherence of a novel depends in part upon the coherence of its characters and of their society. No doubt the society which every novel presents could or should be improved; meanwhile, something has been presented worthy of improvement. Nobody who can be considered an adequate reader of fiction requires that the code of conduct in the novel's world be the "right" code, if only because a part of what a novel can do is to bring news of strange parts, news of people with unfamiliar customs or with different attitudes toward familiar customs. Similarly no reader asks that the novelist's own moral code be the "right" one; for those who think they know exactly what the right code is and how to apply it to a given occasion are happier with sermons than with a form so relative, so much a network of relationships and opinions, as the novel.

Nevertheless, since the narrator, whether the novelist himself or a character, is in fact going to have his own personal and moral opinions about the characters, his expression of them openly need not interfere with the reader but may very well please and help him. Both Dickens the novelist and David Copperfield the narrator dislike and disapprove of Uriah Heep, and any reasonable reader so fully shares this attitude that the expression of it adds to his pleasure. But in *Bleak House* Esther Summerson's view of herself is not likely to be identical with a reader's view of her; her humility is too conscious and she is too keen to report the praise of others for her to be accepted at her own evaluation, or, for that matter, at that of the other characters; and in this very disparity Dickens' own estimation of her reveals itself—to the reader's pleasure—as being not identical with any of those in the book. When the expressed view of a character is neither acceptable in itself nor dramatically acceptable as being a character's but is eccentrically the author's own, trouble may enter in but it need not be very serious. Fielding's excessive affection for and approval of Sophia in *Tom Jones* need interfere only slightly with a reader's somewhat reserved fondness for her; and Richardson's almost commercial equating of virtue and virginity in *Pamela* impairs the book but does not prevent one from seeing Pamela's holding out for marriage as a matter of some moral interest and complexity. In both these cases, the authors have created characters and situations of sufficient vitality to flourish apart from their creators' opinions of them. Bad trouble comes when the characters lack this vitality— in which case the author's opinion of them will not help or hurt much anyway. Worst of all is for the characters and actions to exist chiefly to demonstrate the author's views—whether Dostoevsky's anemic saints or Gênet's evil-be-thou-my-good satanists or Katherine Mansfield's only-to-be-pitied victims. For in such cases the author's opinions come to be what matters, not the characters, and the reader has experience of polemic in the guise of fiction.

The relation of reader to writer is like that of two acquaintances talking about a mutual friend (in this case a character in a novel). The writer may express his opinions and the reader may share those opinions or allow himself to be persuaded by them; but finally the reader wants to make up his own mind on the evidence of the character's actions and thoughts. The trouble is, he can't. The analogy to the friends and their mutual acquaintance breaks down, because all the reader can know of the character is what the writer tells, shows, arranges, and comments on. The reader may think he is free to make his own connection with a character but in fact he is controlled.

Flaubert's ambition in *Madame Bovary* was to do nothing but present the evidence. However, what reader is (or should be) allowed to admire Homais? Every novelist, even if he does not overtly develop his personal and moral opinions as such, has those opinions and they will manifest themselves whether he intends them to or not. "In a corner of every notary's heart lie the moldy remains of a poet," Flaubert opines like any Balzac and then ducks back into the story out of sight. But whether it shows itself overtly, the author's moral judgment will—must—inform the very structure of action and delineation of character. That Emma Bovary should kill herself at the end of the book is right and inevitable in every way, including that of reflecting the author's moral views; but that the details of her dying are reported so extensively and with such vividness mainly reflects Flaubert's punishing cruelty, just as the hideous blind man's improbable appearance outside Emma's window at the moment of her death singing a love-ditty reflects very little more than Flaubert's weakness for romantic irony.

If a novelist is wise enough, he need manifest his moral views only in the actions and contours of his characters and in little cues along the way; if he is not wise enough for that, at least he will do no harm by telling the reader his opinions openly so the reader can estimate how much the novelist's opinions are affecting the presentation of characters and his response to them.

The reader prefers not to trouble himself over the writer's attitude to the character, though he will keep an eye on the narrator when the story is told in the first person. When he agrees with the writer, as he agrees with Dickens about Uriah Heep, or when the writer is so powerful and wise as to give the ultimate illusion "life is really like that," as Tolstoy often does, then the reader happily pays attention only to the characters and actions.

But the novelist can never afford to neglect the reader. He must never forget that his connection with a character does not exist for its own sake only but exists partly to create the reader's connection with the character. Sometimes the writer's unspoken connection with a character helps control the way a reader is connected with that character: to read *War and Peace* is to love Natasha, to grieve at her fall, and to rejoice when André forgives her, as Tolstoy surely did. But usually, the novelist's assurance being less than immortal, he must be prudent and study strategies.

In this the most intimate and crucial of novelistic relationships—the writer creating character—there is, finally, the necessity on the novelist not to meddle. He may like the character as a person, and say so; he may disapprove and say so; he may develop all sorts of general theories about the type of person the character is or the social institutions he belongs to; he may be close to the character sometimes and far off at others; he may do all he can to control and direct the reader's response to the character when the character's acts or thoughts are not the instant focus of attention. But at the moment of action, of speaking, of thinking, of choice, he must not interfere; for if at that moment anything whatever gets between the character and the reader, nothing good will be created. Dickens notoriously could not let a dying child alone. Here is the death of Jo in *Bleak House*.

"It's turned wery dark, sir. Is there any light a-comin?"

"It is coming fast, Jo."

Fast. The cart is shaken all to pieces, and the rugged road is very near its end.

"Jo, my poor fellow!"

"I hear you, sir, in the dark, but I'm a-gropin—a-gropin—let me catch hold of your hand."

"Jo, can you say what I say?"

"I'll say anythink as you say, sir, for I knows it's good."

"OUR FATHER."

" 'Our Father!'—yes, that's very good, sir."

"WHICH ART IN HEAVEN."

" 'Art in Heaven'—is the light a-comin, sir?"

"It is close at hand. HALLOWED BE THY NAME!"

" 'Hallowed be—thy—' "

The light is come upon the dark benighted way. Dead!

Dead, your Majesty. Dead, my lords and gentlemen. Dead, Right Reverends and Wrong Reverends of every order. Dead, men and women, born with Heavenly compassion in your hearts. And dying thus around us every day.

Plato loved Socrates, Boswell loved Dr. Johnson, in *Heart of Darkness* Marlow had strong and complicated feelings about Kurtz; yet the deaths of those three subjects affect us far more than Jo's does because their telling is clean. Tolstoy himself sometimes falters even in his greatest fictions. At the moment of the death of Ivan Ilych, Tolstoy does not just report what was going on in the character's mind but makes his wish Ivan's.

"And the pain?" he asked himself. "What has become of it? Where are you, pain?"

He turned his attention to it.

"Yes, here it is. Well, what of it? Let the pain be."

"And death . . . where is it?"

He sought his former accustomed fear of death and did not find it. "Where is it? What death?" There was no fear because there was no death.

In place of death there was light.

"So that's what it is!" he suddenly exclaimed aloud. "What joy!"

The reader knows he is no longer seeing Ivan's experience plain and responding to that, as he feels he has been doing up to this passage of the story; he also sees this as Tolstoy's wish and must shove Tolstoy aside in order to get cleanly to Ivan.

Here, ultimately, technical advice to a novelist becomes moral advice to any man. Grant others their otherness. "Justice," says Socrates in *The Republic*, "means minding one's own business and not meddling with other men's concerns"—which concern, for a novelist, is the intercourse of reader and character. At the moment of greatest intimacy, of creation, do not judge, or you will be judged for having judged. Like a god, grant your creatures their free will. Like a father, give your children their independence. Like a friend, love them and leave them alone.

⚬ ANNA KARENINA
Leo Tolstoy

In the hunting scene from ANNA KARENINA, *Tolstoy suggests to the reader something of the magic quality which the morning hunt has for Levin. The servants are sleeping as though bewitched, Levin is directed by an old woman in a doorway, he finds what he seeks, and he displays his prowess before an admirer. All this is done within the realistic conventions, with Tolstoy darting from detail to detail with such energy and such vividness that everything seems to the reader natural and wonderful, as the world is seeming to Levin. Indeed, so natural, so sympathetic with nature, is Levin's feeling, that Tolstoy dares, for the reader's sake, to violate a convention of realism and enter the consciousness of the dog Laska. As with a lesser human character introduced along the way in the story, the novelist does not enter Laska's mind far nor does he represent her as thinking any thoughts that could not reasonably be conjectured as fitting. It is just that, without self-consciousness or the slightest affectation, the author asks the reader to enter for a few moments into an experience which is for the main character magical and to do this by entering imaginatively into the mind of the natural creature most sympathetic to him. When the chapter is isolated from the rest of the book as it is here, the reader is alerted and notices the unconventional leap in point of view; but in the whole novel, what happens in this chapter accords so perfectly with Levin's character and his love of nature that the reader does not even notice that the writer has done technically what in another writer might seem merely cute, or if the reader does notice it he does not say "How clever" but "How wonderful," and all is consonant.*

PART VI, CHAPTER XII

Waking at daybreak Levin tried to rouse his companions. Vasenka was lying face downwards, one stockinged leg outstretched, and sleeping so soundly that he could not wake him. Oblonsky sleepily declined to budge so early. Even Laska, who had slept curled round in the hay, got up reluctantly, and lazily stretched and settled one hind leg and then the other. Levin put on his boots and stockings, took his gun, cautiously opened the creaking door of the barn, and went out into the open air. The coachmen were asleep beside the vehicles, the horses were dozing. Only one was lazily eating oats, scattering and blowing them about in the trough. The outside world was still grey.

'Why are you up so early, my dear?' the old woman of the hut asked from the doorway, addressing him in a friendly tone as a good acquaintance of long standing.

'I'm off shooting, Granny. Can I get to the marsh this way?'

'Straight along at the back; past our threshing-floors, my dear, and then by the hemp-patches. You'll find the footpath.'

Treading carefully with her bare, sunburnt feet, the old woman conducted him to the threshing-floor and moved back the fence for him.

'Go straight on and you'll come upon the marsh. Our lads took the horses that way last night.'

Laska bounded gaily ahead along the footpath. Levin followed with a light, brisk step, continually glancing up at the sky. He was anxious to get to the marsh before sunrise. But the sun would not wait. The moon, which had been bright when he first came out, now only gleamed like quicksilver. The pink flush of dawn, which one could not help seeing before, now had to be sought to be discerned at all. What had been vague smudges in the distant countryside were now quite distinct. They were shocks of rye. The dew, not visible till the sun was up, on the tall fragrant hemp which had already shed its pollen, drenched Levin's legs and his blouse even above the belt. In the translucent stillness of the morning the minutest sounds were audible. A bee flew past Levin's ear like the whizz of a bullet. He looked close, and saw another, and then a third. They all came from behind the wattle-fence of an apiary, and disappeared over the hemp-field in the direction of the marsh. The path led straight to the marsh, which was recognizable by the vapours rising from it, thicker in one place and thinner in another, so that the reeds and willow-bushes swayed like little islands in the mist. At the edge of the marsh by the road the peasant boys and men, who had pastured their horses in the night, were lying under their coats, having fallen asleep at daybreak. Near by three hobbled horses were moving about, one of them clattering its chain. Laska trotted beside her master, beseeching to be allowed to run forward, and looking around. Passing the sleeping peasants and reaching the first bog, Levin examined his percussion caps and let the dog go. One of the horses, a sleek, chestnut three-year-old, shied at the sight of Laska, switched its tail and snorted. The other horses were also startled, and splashed through the water with their hobbled feet, making a sucking sound as they drew their hooves out of the thick, clayey mud and began floundering their way out of the marsh. Laska stopped, looking derisively at the horses and inquiringly at Levin. Levin patted her, and gave a whistle to tell her she might begin.

Joyful and intent, Laska started through the bog, which gave beneath her feet.

Running into the marsh, Laska at once detected all over the place, mingled with the familiar smells of roots, marsh grass, slime, and the extraneous odour of horse dung, the scent of birds—of that strong-smelling bird that always excited her more than any other. Here and there among the moss and swamp-sage this scent was very strong, but it was impossible to be sure in which direction it grew stronger or fainter. To find this out it was necessary to get farther to the lee of the wind. Scarcely aware of her legs under her, Laska bounded on with a stiff gallop, so that at each bound she could stop short, going to the right, away from the morning breeze blowing from the east, and turned to face the wind. Sniffing in the air with dilated nostrils, she knew at once that not their scent only but they themselves were here before her, and not only one but a great many of them. Laska slackened her pace. They were here, but precisely where she could not yet decide. To find the exact spot, she began circling round, when suddenly her master's voice drew her off. 'Laska! Here!' he called, pointing to the other side. She stood still, asking him if it would not be better to let her go on as she had begun. But he repeated his command in an angry voice, pointing to a tufty place under water, where there could not be anything. She obeyed, pretending to search, and to please him went over the whole place and then returned to the first spot, and was at once on the scent again. Now, when he was not hindering her, she knew what to do, and without looking where she was stepping, stumbling impatiently over hummocks and falling into water, but righting herself with her strong, supple legs, she began the circle that was to make everything clear. *Their* scent came to her more and more pungently, more and more distinctly, until all at once it became quite plain that one of them was here, on the other side of this tuft of reeds, five paces in front of her. She stopped and her whole body grew rigid. Her short legs prevented her from seeing ahead, but by the scent she was certain it was there, not five paces off. More and more conscious of its presence, she stood still, in the joy of anticipation. Her tail was stretched straight and tense, only the very tip twitching. Her mouth was slightly open, her ears pricked. One ear had got folded back when she was running. She breathed heavily but warily, and still more warily looked round, more with her eyes than her head, to her master. He was coming along, with his familiar face but ever terrible eyes, stumbling over the hummocks and talking to her an unusually long time. She thought he came slowly but in reality he was running.

From Laska's peculiar posture—her mouth half open and her body crouched down as if dragging her hind legs along the ground—Levin knew she was pointing at snipe, and with an inward prayer for success, especially with his first bird, he ran towards her. When he came up close to her and looked beyond, he saw from his height what she had perceived with her nose. In a little space between two hummocks he caught sight of a snipe. It had turned its head and was listening. Then lightly preening and folding its wings, it disappeared round a corner with an awkward jerk of its tail.

'Go, Laska, go!' shouted Levin, giving her a shove from behind.

'But I can't go,' thought Laska. 'Where am I to go? I can scent them from here, but if I move I shan't know where they are or what they are.' But now he pushed her with his knee, and in an excited whisper said, 'Go, Laska, good dog, go!'

'All right, if that's what he wants, but I can't answer for myself now,' thought Laska, and rushed forward at full tilt between the hummocks. She was no longer on the scent, but only saw and heard, without understanding anything.

Ten paces from her former place a snipe rose with a guttural cry, its wings making the hollow sound peculiar to snipe. And immediately following the report it fell heavily on its white breast in the wet bog. Another rose behind Levin, without waiting to be put up by the dog. By the time Levin had turned towards it, it was already some way off. But his shot caught it. It flew on about twenty feet, rose sharply, and then, turning over and over like a ball, dropped heavily to the ground, on a dry spot.

'This looks like business!' thought Levin, stowing the warm fat snipe into his game-bag. 'Eh, Laska, what do you think?'

When Levin had reloaded his gun and moved on, the sun, though still invisible behind the clouds, had already risen. The moon had lost all her splendor, and gleamed pale in the sky like a small cloud. There was no longer a single star to be seen. The sedge, silvery with dew before, now glistened like gold. The patches of rust were now amber. The bluish grass had turned a yellowy-green. Marsh-birds bustled about in the bushes that sparkled with dew and cast long shadows beside the brook. A hawk woke up and settled on a haycock, turning its head from side to side and surveying the marsh with an air of discontent. Crows were flying about the field, and a barefooted boy was already driving the horses towards an old man, who had raised himself from under his coat and was scratching different parts of his body. The smoke from the gun stretched white as milk over the green grass.

One of the boys ran up to Levin.

'There were wild ducks here yesterday!' he shouted, following Levin at a distance.

And Levin knew a double pleasure in killing three more snipe, one after another, in sight of the boy, who expressed his approval.

❈ THE RED BADGE OF COURAGE

Stephen Crane

In the chapter from RED BADGE OF COURAGE, *Crane is dealing with as intimate an experience in the life of his main character (the youth) as one can imagine. The author is scrupulously absent, except for his voice. With this voice, however, he maintains a steady and cool distance from everything: the external appearance of the youth, events in the forest, the youth's feelings and thoughts. All are seen in the light of observing intelligence. "He began to pity himself acutely." We are not asked to immerse ourselves vicariously in his pity, but to see it for what it is and to feel with him in his misery, not to feel the misery itself. All this is done in the realistic mode of fiction. Crane thought of his fictional method as "naturalistic," of his people as parts of Nature; but in fact, as in most very good passages of realistic storytelling, there is here an indispensable element of romance. That the youth should come upon a patch of forest that seemed to him like a church and that in this natural church there should be the corpse of a soldier— these are probable enough, granted the circumstances. But that he should happen upon the church and the reproachful corpse just at this moment represents more than the temporary power of his own imagination to charge a part of the forest and a corpse with special significance. It also comes from Crane's own fabulous imagination, which (whatever his theories) could not but fill the actual with the marvelous.*

CHAPTER VII

The youth cringed as if discovered in a crime. By heavens, they had won after all! The imbecile line had remained and become victors. He could hear cheering.

He lifted himself upon his toes and looked in the direction of the fight. A yellow fog lay wallowing on the treetops. From beneath it came the clatter of musketry. Hoarse cries told of an advance.

He turned away amazed and angry. He felt that he had been wronged.

He had fled, he told himself, because annihilation approached. He had done a good part in saving himself, who was a little piece of the army. He had considered the time, he said, to be one in which it was the duty of every little piece to rescue itself if possible. Later the officers could fit the little pieces together again and make a battle front. If none of the little pieces together were wise enough to save themselves from the flurry of death at such a time, why, then, where would be the army? It was all plain that he had proceeded according to very correct and commendable rules. His actions had been sagacious things. They had been full of strategy. They were the work of a master's legs.

Thoughts of his comrades came to him. The brittle blue line had withstood the blows and won. He grew bitter over it. It seemed that the blind ignorance and stupidity of those little pieces had betrayed him. He had been overturned and crushed by their lack of sense in holding the position, when intelligent deliberation would have convinced them that it was impossible. He, the enlightened man who looks afar in the dark, had fled because of his superior perceptions and knowledge. He felt a great anger against his comrades. He knew it could be proved that they had been fools.

He wondered what they would remark when later he appeared in camp. His mind heard howls of derision. Their density would not enable them to understand his sharper point of view.

He began to pity himself acutely. He was ill used. He was trodden beneath the feet of an iron injustice. He had proceeded with wisdom and from the most righteous motives under heaven's blue only to be frustrated by hateful circumstances.

A dull, animal-like rebellion against his fellows, war in the abstract, and fate grew within him. He shambled along with bowed head, his brain in a tumult of agony and despair. When he looked lowering up, quivering at each sound, his eyes had the expression of those of a criminal who thinks his guilt and his punishment great, and knows that he can find no words; (who, through his suffering, thinks that he peers into the core of things and sees that the judgement of man is thistledown in wind.)

He went from the fields into a thick wood, as if resolved to bury himself. He wished to get out of hearing of the crackling shots which were to him like voices.

The ground was cluttered with vines and bushes, and the trees grew close, and spread out like bouquets. He was obliged to force his way with much noise. The creepers, catching against his legs, cried out harshly as their sprays were torn from the barks of trees. The swishing saplings tried to make known his presence to the world. He could not conciliate the forest. As he made his way, it was always calling out protestations. When he separated embraces of trees and vines the disturbed foliages waved their arms and turned their face leaves toward him. He dreaded lest these noisy motions and cries should bring men to look at him. So he went far, seeking dark and intricate places.

After a time the sound of musketry grew faint and the cannon boomed in the distance. The sun, suddenly apparent, blazed among the trees. The insects were making rhythmical noises. They seemed to be grinding their teeth in unison. A woodpecker stuck his impudent head around the side of a tree. A bird flew on lighthearted wing.

Off was the rumble of death. It seemed now that Nature had no ears.

This landscape gave him assurance. A fair field holding life. It was the religion of peace. It would die if its timid eyes were compelled to see blood. He conceived Nature to be a woman with a deep aversion to tragedy.

He threw a pine cone at a jovial squirrel, and he ran with chattering fear. High in a treetop he stopped, and poling his head cautiously from behind a branch, looked down with an air of trepidation.

The youth felt triumphant at this exhibition. There was the law, he said. Nature had given him a sign. The squirrel, immediately upon recognizing the danger, had taken to his legs without ado. He did not stand stolidly baring his furry belly to the missile, and die with an upward glance at the sympathetic heavens. On the contrary, he had fled as fast as his legs could carry him; and he was but an ordinary squirrel, too—doubtless no philosopher of his race. The youth wended, feeling that Nature was of his mind. She re-enforced his argument with proofs that lived where the sun shone.

Once he found himself almost into a swamp. He was obliged to walk upon bog tufts, and watch his feet to keep from the oily mire. Pausing at one time to look about him he saw, out at some black water, a small animal pounce in and emerge directly with a gleaming fish.

The youth went again into the deep thickets. The brushed branches made a noise that drowned the sounds of cannon. He walked on, going from obscurity into promises of a greater obscurity.

At length he reached a place where the high, arching boughs made a chapel. He softly pushed the green doors aside and entered. Pine needles were a gentle brown carpet. There was a religious half-light.

Near the threshold he stopped, horror-stricken at the sight of a thing.

He was being looked at by a dead man, who was seated with his back against a columnlike tree. The corpse was dressed in a uniform that once had been blue, but was now faded to a melancholy shade of green. The eyes, staring at the youth, had changed to the dull hue to be seen on the side of a dead fish. The mouth was open. Its red had changed to an appalling yellow. Over the gray skin of the face ran little ants. One was trundling some sort of a bundle along the upper lip.

The youth gave a shriek as he confronted the thing. He was for moments turned to stone before it. He remained staring into the liquid-looking eyes. The dead man and the living man exchanged a long look. Then the youth cautiously put one hand behind him and brought it against a tree. Leaning upon this he retreated, step by step, with his face still toward the thing. He feared that if he turned his back the body might spring up and stealthily pursue him.

The branches, pushing against him, threatened to throw him over upon it. His unguided feet, too, caught aggravatingly in brambles; and with it all he received a subtle suggestion to touch the corpse. As he thought of his hand upon it he shuddered profoundly.

At last he burst the bonds which had fastened him to the spot and fled, unheeding the underbrush. He was pursued by a sight of the black ants swarming greedily upon the gray face and venturing horribly near to the eyes.

After a time he paused, and, breathless and panting, listened. He imagined some strange voice would come from the dead throat and squawk after him in horrible menaces.

The trees about the portal of the chapel moved soughingly in a soft wind. A sad silence was upon the little guarding edifice.

❦ MIDDLEMARCH

George Eliot

In the chapter from MIDDLEMARCH, *George Eliot looks at her heroine at a romantic moment when the reader's sympathies cannot but be engaged: an idealistic and charming young bride is discovering that her husband is less than she had thought he was. Instead of settling for our easy pity, the author assumes it in the reader and then looks at the situation with all her intelligence. Eliot is there as the authorial I speaking to the reader about the character as one intelligent person speaks to another. She looks at Dorothea in several ways: as a type, as a character in a story, as a particular person. And she is always scrupulous in informing the reader about how she is looking at Dorothea at any particular moment. Moreover, Eliot is so easy in her role as an author speaking to a reader that she is free to expand for a time about larger matters as they occur to her. The last three sentences of the sixth paragraph are of the highest and noblest rhetoric, justified here not for any of the usual formal reasons of fiction but as establishing the author's supreme authority. When a writer speaks of life with such intelligence, we will attend eagerly to what she says about her characters; our understanding of them will come through her analysis as much as from their represented actions. Moreover, later in the chapter when she gives the characters' words and actions, she keeps us at a certain remove from them, by the stiffness of their discourse; her ironic comments on them are not interruptions in a dialogue between people we are intimate with emotionally; the characters are looked at from a certain distance and are kept at that distance.*

CHAPTER XX

A child forsaken, waking suddenly
Whose gaze afeard on all things round doth rove,
And seeth only that it cannot see
      The meeting eyes of love.

Two hours later, Dorothea was seated in an inner room or boudoir of a handsome apartment in the Via Sistina.

I am sorry to add that she was sobbing bitterly, with such aban-
donment to this relief of an oppressed heart as a woman habitu-
ally controlled by pride on her own account and thoughtfulness
for others will sometimes allow herself when she feels securely
alone. And Mr. Casaubon was certain to remain away for some
time at the Vatican.

Yet Dorothea had no distinctly shapen grievance that she could
state even to herself; and in the midst of her confused thought and
passion, the mental act that was struggling forth into clearness
was a self-accusing cry that her feeling of desolation was the fault
of her own spiritual poverty. She had married the man of her
choice, and with the advantage over most girls that she had con-
templated her marriage chiefly as the beginning of new duties:
from the very first she had thought of Mr. Casaubon as having
a mind so much above her own, that he must often be claimed by
studies which she could not entirely share; moreover, after the
brief narrow experience of her girlhood she was beholding Rome,
the city of visible history, where the past of a whole hemisphere
seems moving in funeral procession with strange ancestral images
and trophies gathered from afar.

But this stupendous fragmentariness heightened the dream-like
strangeness of her bridal life. Dorothea had now been five weeks
in Rome, and in the kindly mornings when autumn and winter
seemed to go hand in hand like a happy aged couple one of whom
would presently survive in chiller loneliness, she had driven about
at first with Mr. Casaubon, but of late chiefly with Tantripp and
their experienced courier. She had been led through the best
galleries, had been taken to the chief points of view, had been
shown the grandest ruins and the most glorious churches, and she
had ended by oftenest choosing to drive out to the Campagna
where she could feel alone with the earth and sky, away from the
oppressive masquerade of ages, in which her own life too seemed
to become a masque with enigmatical costumes.

To those who have looked at Rome with the quickening power
of a knowledge which breathes a growing soul into all historic

shapes, and traces out the suppressed transitions which unite all contrasts, Rome may still be the spiritual center and interpreter of the world. But let them conceive one more historical contrast: the gigantic broken revelations of that Imperial and Papal city thrust abruptly on the notions of a girl who had been brought up in English and Swiss Puritanism, fed on meagre Protestant histories and on art chiefly of the hand-screen sort; a girl whose ardent nature turned all her small allowance of knowledge into principles, fusing her actions into their mould, and whose quick emotions gave the most abstract things the quality of a pleasure or a pain; a girl who had lately become a wife, and from the enthusiastic acceptance of untried duty found herself plunged in tumultuous preoccupation with her personal lot. The weight of unintelligible Rome might lie easily on bright nymphs to whom it formed a background for the brilliant picnic of Anglo-foreign society; but Dorothea had no such defence against deep impressions. Ruins and basilicas, palaces and colossi, set in the midst of a sordid present, where all that was living and warm-blooded seemed sunk in the deep degeneracy of a superstition divorced from reverence; the dimmer but yet eager Titanic life gazing and struggling on walls and ceilings; the long vistas of white forms whose marble eyes seemed to hold the monotonous light of an alien world: all this vast wreck of ambitious ideals, sensuous and spiritual, mixed confusedly with the signs of breathing forgetfulness and degradation, at first jarred her as with an electric shock and then urged themselves on her with that ache belonging to a glut of confused ideas which check the flow of emotion. Forms both pale and glowing took possession of her young sense, and fixed themselves in her memory even when she was not thinking of them, preparing strange associations which remained through her after-years. Our moods are apt to bring with them images which succeed each other like the magic-lantern pictures of a doze; and in certain states of dull forlornness Dorothea all her life continued to see the vastness of St. Peter's, the huge bronze canopy, the excited intention in the attitudes and garments of the prophets and evangelists in the mosaics above, and the red drapery which was being hung for Christmas spreading itself everywhere like a disease of the retina.

Not that this inward amazement of Dorothea's was anything very exceptional: many souls in their young nudity are tumbled out among incongruities and left to "find their feet" among them, while their elders go about their business. Nor can I suppose that when Mrs. Casaubon is discovered in a fit of weeping six weeks after her wedding, the situation will be regarded as tragic. Some discouragement, some faintness of heart at the new real future which replaces the imaginary, is not unusual, and we do not expect people to be deeply moved by what is not unusual. That element of tragedy which lies in the very fact of frequency, has not yet wrought itself into the coarse emotion of mankind; and perhaps our frames could hardly bear much of it. If we had a keen vision and feeling of all ordinary human life, it would be like hearing the grass grow and the squirrel's heart beat, and we should die of that roar which lies on the other side of silence. As it is, the quickest of us walk about well wedded with stupidity.

However, Dorothea was crying, and if she had been required to state the cause, she could only have done so in some such general words as I have already used: to have been driven to be more particular would have been like trying to give a history of the lights and shadows; for that new real future which was replacing the imaginary drew its material from the endless minutiae by which her view of Mr. Casaubon and her wifely relation, now that she was married to him, was gradually changing with the secret motion of a watch-hand from what it had been in her maiden dream. It was too early yet for her fully to recognize or at least admit the change, still more for her to have readjusted that devotedness which was so necessary a part of her mental life that she was almost sure sooner or later to recover it. Permanent rebellion, the disorder of a life without some loving reverent resolve, was not possible to her; but she was now in an interval when the very force of her nature heightened its confusion. In this way, the early months of marriage often are times of critical tumult—whether that of a shrimp-pool or of deeper waters—which afterwards subsides into cheerful peace.

But was not Mr. Casaubon just as learned as before? Had his forms of expression changed, or his sentiments become less laudable? O waywardness of womanhood! did his chronology fail him, or his ability to state not only a theory but the names of those who held it; or his provision for giving the heads of any subject on demand? And was not Rome the place in all the world to give free play to such accomplishments? Besides, had not Dorothea's enthusiasm especially dwelt on the prospect of relieving the weight and perhaps the sadness with which great tasks lie on him who has to achieve them?—And that such weight pressed on Mr. Casaubon was only plainer than before.

All these are crushing questions; but whatever else remained the same, the light had changed, and you cannot find the pearly dawn at noonday. The fact is unalterable, that a fellow-mortal with whose nature you are acquainted solely through the brief entrances and exits of a few imaginative weeks called courtship, may, when seen in the continuity of married companionship, be disclosed as something better or worse than what you have preconceived, but will certainly not appear altogether the same. And it would be astonishing to find how soon the change is felt if we had no kindred changes to compare with it. To share lodgings with a brilliant dinner-companion, or to see your favourite politician in the Ministry, may bring about changes quite as rapid: in these cases too we begin by knowing little and believing much, and we sometimes end by inverting the quantities.

Still, such comparisons might mislead, for no man was more incapable of flashy make-believe than Mr. Casaubon; he was as genuine a character as any ruminant animal, and he had not actively assisted in creating any illusions about himself. How was it that in the weeks since her marriage, Dorothea had not distinctly observed but felt with a stifling depression, that the large vistas and wide fresh air which she had dreamed of finding in her husband's mind were replaced by anterooms and winding passages which seemed to lead nowhither? I suppose it was that in courtship everything is regarded as provisional and preliminary, and the smallest sample of virtue or accomplishment is taken to guarantee delightful stores which the broad leisure of marriage will reveal. But the door-sill of marriage once crossed, expectation is concentrated on the present. Having once embarked on your marital voyage, it is impossible not to be aware that you make no way and that the sea is not within sight—that, in fact, you are exploring an enclosed basin.

In their conversation before marriage, Mr. Casaubon had often dwelt on some explanation or questionable detail of which Dorothea did not see the bearing; but such imperfect coherence seemed due to the brokenness of their intercourse, and, supported by her faith in their future, she had listened with fervid patience to a recitation of possible arguments to be brought against Mr. Casaubon's entirely new view of the Philistine god Dagon and other fish-deities, thinking that hereafter she should see this subject which touched him so nearly from the same high ground whence doubtless it had become so important to him. Again, the matter-of-course statement and tone of dismissal with which he treated what to her were the most stirring thoughts, was easily accounted for as belonging to the sense of haste and preoccupation in which she herself shared during their engagement. But now, since they had been in Rome, with all the depths of her emotion roused to tumultuous activity, and with life made a new problem by new elements she had been becoming more and more aware, with a certain terror, that her mind was continually sliding into inward fits of anger and repulsion, or else into forlorn weariness. How far the judicious Hooker or any other hero of erudition would have been the same at Mr. Casaubon's time of life, she had no means of knowing, so that he could not have the advantage of comparison; but her husband's way of commenting on the strangely impressive objects around them had begun to affect her with a sort of mental shiver: he had perhaps the best intention of acquitting himself worthily, but only of acquitting himself. What was fresh to her mind was worn out to his; and such capacity of thought and feeling as had ever been stimulated in him by the general life of mankind had long shrunk to a sort of dried preparation, a lifeless embalmment of knowledge.

When he said, "Does this interest you, Dorothea? Shall we stay a little longer? I am ready to stay if you wish it,"—it seemed to her as if going or staying were alike dreary. Or "Should you like to go to the Farnesina, Dorothea? It contains celebrated frescoes designed or painted by Raphael, which most persons think it worth while to visit."

"But do you care about them?" was always Dorothea's question.

"They are, I believe, highly esteemed. Some of them represent the fable of Cupid and Psyche, which is probably the romantic invention of a literary period, and cannot, I think, be reckoned as a genuine mythical product. But if you like these wall-paintings we can easily drive thither; and you will then, I think, have seen the chief works of Raphael, any of which it were a pity to omit in a visit to Rome. He is the painter who has been held to combine the most complete grace of form with sublimity of expression. Such at least I have gathered to be the opinion of conoscenti."

This kind of answer given in a measured official tone, as of a clergyman reading according to the rubric, did not help to justify the glories of the Eternal City, or to give her the hope that if she knew more about them the world would be joyously illuminated for her. There is hardly any contact more depressing to a young ardent creature than that of a mind in which years full of knowledge seem to have issued in a blank absence of interest or sympathy.

On other subjects indeed Mr. Casaubon showed tenacity of occupation and an eagerness which are usually regarded as the effect of enthusiasm, and Dorothea was anxious to follow this spontaneous direction of his thoughts, instead of being made to feel that she dragged him away from it. But she was gradually ceasing to expect with her former delightful confidence that she should see any wide opening where she followed him. Poor Mr. Casaubon himself was lost among closets and winding stairs, and in an agitated dimness about the Cabeiri, or in an exposure of other mythologists' ill-considered parallels, easily lost sight of any purpose which had prompted him to these labours. With his taper stuck before him he forgot the absence of windows, and in bitter manuscript remarks on other men's notions about the solar deities, he had become indifferent to the sunlight.

These characteristics, fixed and unchangeable as bone in Mr. Casaubon, might have remained longer unfelt by Dorothea if she had been encouraged to pour forth her girlish and womanly feeling —if he would have held her hands between his and listened with the delight of tenderness and understanding to all the little histories which made up her experience, and would have given her the same sort of intimacy in return, so that the past life of each could be included in their mutual knowledge and affection—or if she could have fed her affection with those childlike caresses which are the bent of every sweet woman, who had begun by showering kisses on the hard pate of her bald doll, creating a happy soul within that woodenness from the wealth of her own love. That was Dorothea's bent. With all her yearning to know what was afar from her and to be widely benignant, she had ardour enough for what was near, to have kissed Mr. Casaubon's coat-sleeve, or to have caressed his shoe-latchet, if he would have made any other sign of acceptance than pronouncing her, with his unfailing propriety, to be of a most affectionate and truly feminine nature, indicating at the same time by politely reaching a chair for her that he regarded these manifestations as rather crude and startling. Having made his clerical toilette with due care in the morning, he was prepared only for those amenities of life which were suited to the well-adjusted stiff cravat of the period, and to a mind weighted with unpublished matter.

And by a sad contradiction Dorothea's ideas and resolves seemed like melting ice floating and lost in the warm flood of which they had been but another form. She was humiliated to find herself a mere victim of feeling, as if she could know nothing except through that medium: all her strength was scattered in fits of agitation, of struggle, of despondency, and then again in visions of more complete renunciation, transforming all hard conditions into duty. Poor Dorothea! She was certainly troublesome—to herself chiefly; but this morning for the first time she had been troublesome to Mr. Casaubon.

She had begun, while they were taking coffee, with a determination to shake off what she inwardly called her selfishness, and turned a face all cheerful attention to her husband when he said, "My dear Dorothea, we must now think of all that is yet left undone, as a preliminary to our departure. I would fain have returned home earlier that we might have been at Lowick for the Christmas; but my inquiries here have been protracted beyond their anticipated period. I trust, however, that the time here has not been passed unpleasantly to you. Among the sights of Europe, that of Rome has ever been held one of the most striking and in some respects edifying. I well remember that I considered it an epoch in my life when I visited it for the first time; after the fall of Napoleon, an event which opened the Continent to travellers. Indeed I think it is one among several cities to which an extreme hyperbole has been applied—'See Rome and die'; but in your case I would propose an emendation and say, 'See Rome as a bride, and live thenceforth as a happy wife'."

Mr. Casaubon pronounced this little speech with the most conscientious intention, blinking a little and swaying his head up and down, and concluding with a smile. He had not found marriage a rapturous state, but he had no idea of being anything else than a irreproachable husband, who would make a charming young woman as happy as she deserved to be.

"I hope you are thoroughly satisfied with our stay—I mean, with the result so far as your studies are concerned," said Dorothea, trying to keep her mind fixed on what most affected her husband.

"Yes," said Mr. Casaubon, with that peculiar pitch of voice which makes the word half a negative. "I have been led farther than I had foreseen, and various subjects for annotation have presented themselves which, though I have no direct need of them, I could not pretermit. The task, notwithstanding the assistance of my amanuensis, has been a somewhat laborious one, but your society has happily prevented me from that too continuous prosecution of thought beyond the hours of study which has been the snare of my solitary life."

"I am very glad that my presence has made any difference to you," said Dorothea, who had a vivid memory of evenings in which she had supposed that Mr. Casaubon's mind had gone too deep during the day to be able to get to the surface again. I fear there was a little temper in her reply. "I hope when we get to Lowick, I shall be more useful to you, and be able to enter a little more into what interests you."

"Doubtless, my dear," said Mr. Casaubon, with a slight bow. "The notes I have here made will want sifting, and you can, if you please, extract them under my direction."

"And all your notes," said Dorothea, whose heart had already burned within her on this subject, so that now she could not help speaking with her tongue. "All those rows of volumes—will you not now do what you used to speak of?—will you not make up your mind what part of them you will use, and begin to write the book which will make your vast knowledge useful to the world? I will write to your dictation, or I will copy and extract what you tell me: I can be of no other use." Dorothea, in a most unaccountable, darkly-feminine manner, ended with a slight sob and eyes full of tears.

The excessive feeling manifested would alone have been highly disturbing to Mr. Casaubon, but there were other reasons why Dorothea's words were among the most cutting and irritating to him that she could have been impelled to use. She was as blind to his inward troubles as he to hers: she had not yet learned those hidden conflicts in her husband which claim our pity. She had not yet listened patiently to his heart-beats, but only felt that her own was beating violently. In Mr. Casaubon's ear, Dorothea's voice gave loud emphatic iteration to those muffled suggestions of consciousness which it was possible to explain as mere fancy, the

illusion of exaggerated sensitiveness: always when such suggestions are unmistakably repeated from without, they are resisted
as cruel and unjust. We are angered even by the full acceptance of
our humiliating confessions—how much more by hearing in hard
distinct syllables from the lips of a near observer, those confused
murmurs which we try to call morbid, and strive against as if they
were the oncoming of numbness! And this cruel outward accuser
was there in the shape of a wife—nay, of a young bride, who, instead of observing his abundant pen-scratches and amplitude of
paper with the uncritical awe of an elegant-minded canary-bird,
seemed to present herself as a spy watching everything with a
malign power of inference. Here, towards this particular point of
the compass, Mr. Casaubon had a sensitiveness to match Dorothea's, and an equal quickness to imagine more than the fact. He
had formerly observed with approbation her capacity for worship-
ping the right object; he now foresaw with sudden terror that this
capacity might be replaced by presumption, this worship by the
most exasperating of all criticism—that which sees vaguely a great
many fine ends, and has not the least notion what it costs to reach
them.

For the first time since Dorothea had known him, Mr. Casaubon's
face had a quick angry flush upon it.

"My love," he said, with irritation reined in by propriety, "you
may rely upon me for knowing the times and the seasons, adapted
to the different stages of a work which is not to be measured by
the facile conjectures of ignorant onlookers. It had been easy for
me to gain a temporary effect by a mirage of baseless opinion;
but it is ever the trial of the scrupulous explorer to be saluted with
the impatient scorn of chatterers who attempt only the smallest
achievements, being indeed equipped for no other. And it were
well if all such could be admonished to discriminate judgments
of which the true subject-matter lies entirely beyond their reach,
from those of which the elements may be compassed by a narrow
and superficial survey."

This speech was delivered with an energy and readiness quite unusual with Mr. Casaubon. It was not indeed entirely an improvisation, but had taken shape in inward colloquy, and rushed out like the round grains from a fruit when sudden heat cracks it. Dorothea was not only his wife: she was a personification of that shallow world which surrounds the ill-appreciated or desponding author.

Dorothea was indignant in her turn. Had she not been repressing everything in herself except the desire to enter into some fellowship with her husband's chief interests?

"My judgment *was* a very superficial one—such as I am capable of forming," she answered, with a prompt resentment, that needed no rehearsal. "You showed me the rows of note-books—you have often spoken of them—you have often said that they wanted digesting. But I never heard you speak of the writing that is to be published. Those were very simple facts, and my judgment went no farther. I only begged you to let me be of some good to you."

Dorothea rose to leave the table and Mr. Casaubon made no reply, taking up a letter which lay beside him as if to reperuse it. Both were shocked at their mutual situation—that each should have betrayed anger toward the other. If they had been at home, settled at Lowick in ordinary life among neighbours, the clash would have been less embarrassing: but on a wedding journey, the express object of which is to isolate two people on the ground that they are all the world to each other, the sense of disagreement is, to say the least, confounding and stultifying. To have changed your longitude extensively, and placed yourselves in a moral solitude in order to have small explosions, to find conversation difficult and to hand a glass of water without looking, can hardly be regarded as satisfactory fulfilment even to the toughest minds. To Dorothea's inexperienced sensitiveness, it seemed like a catastrophe, changing all prospects; and to Mr. Casaubon it was a new pain, he never having been on a wedding journey before, or found himself in that close union which was more of a subjection than he had been able to imagine, since this charming young bride not only obliged him to much consideration on her behalf (which he had sedulously given), but turned out to be capable of agitating him cruelly just where he most needed soothing. Instead of getting a soft fence against the cold, shadowy, unapplausive audience of life, had he only given it a more substantial presence?

Neither of them felt it possible to speak again at present. To have reversed a previous arrangement and declined to go out would have been a show of persistent anger which Dorothea's conscience shrank from, seeing that she already began to feel herself guilty. However just her indignation might be, her ideal was not to claim justice, but to give tenderness. So when the carriage came to the door, she drove with Mr. Casaubon to the Vatican, walked with him through the stony avenue of inscriptions, and when she parted with him at the entrance to the Library, went on through the Museum out of mere listlessness as to what was around her. She had not spirit to turn round and say that she would drive anywhere. It was when Mr. Casaubon was quitting her that Naumann had first seen her, and he had entered the long gallery of sculpture at the same time with her; but here Naumann had to await Ladislaw with whom he was to settle a bet of champagne about an enigmatical medieval-looking figure there. After they had examined the figure, and had walked on finishing their dispute, they had parted, Ladislaw lingering behind while Naumann had gone into the Hall of Statues where he again saw Dorothea, and saw her in that brooding abstraction which made her pose remarkable. She did not really see the streak of sunlight on the floor more than she saw the statues: she was inwardly seeing the light of years to come in her own home and over the English fields and elms and hedge-bordered highroads; and feeling that the way in which they might be filled with joyful devotedness was not so clear to her as it had been. But in Dorothea's mind there was a current into which all thought and feeling were apt sooner or later to flow—the reaching forward of the whole consciousness towards the fullest truth, the least partial good. There was clearly something better than anger and despondency.

On Writing a Play

LIONEL ABEL

How should "one" write a play? This question can, of course, be answered, while the much more personal and pertinent question: how should "you" write a play? probably cannot. If the play-writing is to be done by "one," it will have to be of a very different sort from such playwriting as may be done by "you." Matisse once said of Max Weber that he could make almost any kind of picture, but could not make a Max Weber. "One" can be told how to write a play. But the play will have been written by "one." Can "you" be told how to write the play which is to be genuinely "yours"?

So it is difficult for me to tell you how a play should be written by you. For if you are indeed "you" why should you listen to me? Only you can find out what it is needful for you to know. In fact, if you read my piece you may even suspect yourself of wanting to write some other kind of play than the one you would like to write. But since you may read me anyway, I must tell you something. What?

Thomas Lovell Beddoes said that a successful play in verse would have to be written by a "bold, trampling" man. Oddly enough, the fine poet and dramatist whom Lytton Strachey called the "last Elizabethan," in a fit of madness, hysteria, or self-hatred hacked off one of his own "bold, trampling" legs. In fact, Beddoes did not restore the verse play to the nineteenth-century stage. But he was right in his prescription. The playwright who is to contribute to the theater should be both bold and trampling.

Wise, perhaps, but in a very contrary sense, Franz Kafka wrote: "The only way is wavering." Of course, he was not thinking of the theater, to which he did not contribute; his one written play—I think it is called *The Keeper of the Crypt*—is rather boring on the stage; so is Kafka's novel *The Trial* in Gide's play version and in Orson Welles' film version of it. No, the way of the playwright must be Beddoes', not Kafka's.

It is probably impossible for "one" to waver—it takes a "you" to waver; I think it also takes a "you" to trample; such trampling as is done by "one" seems to me about as painless as the pies flung in the Sennett comedies. So if you are going to write your play you ought to be audacious.

Can I say anything else? What I can do is give you an abstract recipe for your play; it will have to be abstract because I cannot tell you your play's ingredients; these you will have to determine for yourself; and the choice of the ingredients will surely alter the value of any purely formal hints about how you are to get on with your work. . .

All you can do on the stage is to conduct a character or characters from fortune to misfortune, from misfortune to fortune; you can emphasize or minimize the difference between fortune and misfortune, but you can hardly make these identical without causing the audience to lose interest in your work. *Plus ça change, plus c'est la même chose* is not a theatrical principle. And were it a really true principle, we would probably never go to the theater at all. There is, of course, the permanent, and there is, of course, the changing. Possibly the most interesting conceivable change, though one can hardly speak of this without illogic, would be change within the permanent itself. According to Professor Kitto, this is what takes place in possibly the greatest tragedy ever written, *The Oresteia* of Aeschylus. In that work, as Professor Kitto interprets it, Zeus, who represents the permanent, changes, and represents the permanent differently at the end of the play than he did when the play began.[1]

But whatever you do with the plot of your play, all that happens in it should be onstage, and to the greatest degree possible. Perhaps not everything can be, but it is desirable for whatever is important in a play to be on stage, taking into account, of course, the physical limits of a theatrical presentation, and also the cultural taste of the time. I think this is a universal law holding for no matter what theatrical work.

What is meant by the on-stage principle? The best explanation, I think, would be by illustration. Take the opening scene of *Othello*. Iago gets Roderigo, the suitor Desdemona has turned down, to wake Desdemona's father, Brabantio, and inform him that his daughter is at that very moment "making the beast with the double back" with Othello. The problems of the main characters are thus set forth with extraordinary swiftness in a dramatic way and without the need of any kind of exposition, or rather, the exposition—for there is some—is given naturally by the characters, who have other interests than the author's exposition in mind. Another instance. In the great scene in Aeschylus' *Oresteia* when Clytemnestra kills her husband, Agamemnon, although we do not actually see the bloody scene—Greek taste was against the direct representation of violent or bloody acts—yet Aeschylus, despite this Greek canon, was able, by a marvel of dramaturgy, to put the act of murder satisfactorily on-stage. Inside the palace of Agamemnon, Clytemnestra and Aegisthus are hacking the king to death; outside the palace Cassandra describes to the chorus and the audience what is taking place even as it occurs; then she describes what her own death will be, and to the amazement of the chorus, instead of trying to escape, enters the palace to be slain. In this scene Aeschylus succeeded in satisfying the general dramatic principle that everything should be on-stage, and also the

[1] The change in Zeus is expressed, of course, through the varying fortunes and misfortunes of the human protagonists.

Greek norm which required that particularly violent acts be kept off-stage as much as possible.

Our taste is not like that of the Greeks, and we are capable of watching murder and even rape performed before us. But it would be wrong to think of the on-stage principle as covering only the most violent actions; where these are concerned there is surely some justification for placing a curtain between the spectator and the event. Everything else being equal, whatever can be seen should be on-stage. But sometimes it is necessary, or more tasteful, to keep some action off the stage. But wherever no basic taboo is involved, no outrage, beyond our possibility of endurance, everything that happens should be presented directly to the spectator.

The on-stage principle means something more than that what is seen on the stage is likely to be believed; often this is not the case. More importantly the principle I am arguing for asserts that what is already believed, when seen, will interest. We are often shown actions on the stage—sometimes by the very best playwrights—which we have no particular interest in continuing to observe for more than a moment. Do we actually want to see Hamlet dueling with Laertes? We have no interest in the swordsmanship of either character; we have no appreciation of the skill of one or the other, so I should say we do not really want to watch them fighting. The swordsmanship of Hamlet and of Laertes are not on-stage, only their rapiers are. Hence their duel should be limited in time. It is very different when Cyrano is fighting. We know something of his swordsmanship, which has already been made an important part of his character. Moreover, while Cyrano duels, he composes a ballad, and the last line of each stanza is, "At the last line I hit." And at the last line of the *envoi*, he does indeed hit his antagonist. This is the most interesting duel I have ever seen on the stage, the reason being that it is so supremely on-stage.

So whatever the action of your play is, the significant events in it must be, in conformity with taste, of course, to the greatest possible degree on-stage. But what is an action? Or to put it more precisely, what is the only possible action in any drama? This question has already been answered. It is the movement of some character or characters from fortune to misfortune, or conversely. The question now arises: should not such movement have some general or ideological meaning, quite apart from the utterly abstract principle that there is change in the universe and that the human individual is always situated somewhere between fortune and misfortune? Now what gives general meaning to a dramatic action? This can only be the dramatic theme which has excited the playwright to order the action of his play. It is the theme of a play that makes its action important, the action of the play which makes its theme interesting. What then is a theme? I do not know if there is any generalization wide enough to cover the whole range of themes for dramatic works. The theme, for instance, may be merely the playwright's mood of lyrical exaltation. If he can find an action to give interest to his theme, he will produce a true play. But a theme may also be something more objective, like the state of society at a given moment, like the power of the powerful, or, contradicting this, and perhaps more interesting to us moderns, the power of the oppressed. A theme, then, may be subjective or objective. In any case, it should be of some importance, if only to the playwright himself; otherwise why should he write about it? I must add that in the modern theater it is rather good for a theme to have some topicality or local interest. This need not limit the resonance of the work, and may make for its being more directly grasped by the spectator. And certainly the action should do more than illustrate the theme, or argue for it, or try to prove it. In the last instance, the action tends to become an argument, and may reduce the theme to the status of a thesis; thus we have the thesis play, under which category are works not to be despised, but, I think, not one single masterpiece.

The action of a play can be simple, even if the dramatist is aiming at subtlety. But every particular form of art has its own special form of subtlety. There is the subtlety of the finely drawn line; there can be a comparable and equal subtlety in the drawing of a very broad line. A play is more like a broad line than like a fine one, though one play's broad line may be drawn with finesse. The subtlety of a play? I should say this lies in the relation of its action to what the play is about, rather than in any ambiguity in the simple action. Consider, for example, Samuel Beckett's fine play *All That Fall.* Its conclusion is, in my opinion, unsatisfactory, mainly because the playwright tried to complicate the action at the end of the play and thereby blurred its meaning. What is the action of *All That Fall?* Mrs. Rooney, a "lady in her seventies," struggles to get to the railroad station; she wants to be present when her blind husband, returning from a trip, arrives. We suffer with her as she trudges along, hitches a ride; we experience her haps and mishaps. She gets to the station. We wait with her for the train to come. Now the train arrives late. Why was it delayed? It seems a child was thrown out the window of the train; moreover it was Mr. Rooney, the blind husband, who threw the child out the window. Now the theme of the play is old age; of course, in throwing a child from the window of a train, Mr. Rooney was expressing, and very strongly, the hatred of the old for the young. So his deed relates to and expresses the play's theme. But, on the other hand, since the action of the play almost throughout has been Mrs. Rooney's vicissitudes on the way to the station, and since these vicissitudes have taken up almost the whole duration of the play, we cannot, in the few moments in which the murder of a child is revealed to us, connect the incident with the many incidents of Mrs. Rooney's journey. Suddenly what her husband has done becomes more interesting than anything she has done, but at the same time it is far more abstract—for it occurred offstage. Actually, the revelation of the murder of the child serves to make us lose interest in Mrs. Rooney and in her adventure; thus it weakens the action, instead of strengthening it, and gives a very unsatisfactory climax to what might otherwise have been a perfect work. The kind of thing Beckett has done here would be possible, permissible in a story or in a short novel; but in his play it is invalid, that is to say, it defeats its intended purpose: the murder of the child does not really dramatize any hatred the old may feel for the young; it remains a mere fact, and never takes on true dramatic value. We never suffered with Mr. Rooney before he threw the child out of the window, the way we did with Mrs. Rooney on her journey to the station.

I said that the real subtlety of a play lies in the relation between the theme and the action, and of course I must give examples to illustrate what I have in mind. First, I will take a modern, though not a contemporary, play, Shaw's *Man and Superman*. The theme of this play is the need to be hardheaded, even cruel, ruthlessly fact-minded in order to make society a place fit to live in. Or to express the idea more precisely: we need to get rid of every trace and vestige of romanticism, in sex, in morals, in politics, in philosophy, and in religion. Now what is the action of the play? It is the entrapment of John Tanner, theoretically committed to the program of renovation Shaw wants, by Ann Whitefield, who, without any intellectual interests, simply wants to marry him and have children by him. Now John Tanner does not want to be trapped into marrying anyone. But this desire is a romantic vestige in his character, and there is little doubt that it is because of some romantic trait in him that he is capable of taking his program of hardheadedness so seriously, so enthusiastically. According to his program he should want to be trapped by Ann and made to marry her; but if he felt that way he would not have been capable of feeling so seriously about his program for others. Ann, carrying out her utterly non-intellectual program of getting married to John Tanner, forces him to accept his own program in the most personal and direct way: the husband of Ann will never be romantic about anything. What is so immensely subtle in this play is that the theme, stated in many remarkable speeches, by Ann's victim, John Tanner, is also stated with the much greater vividness of uncompromising intent by Ann herself, who has no interest in any ideas but only in getting married. The action dramatizes John Tanner's personal defeat, but the very same action dramatizes the truth of his ideas, which express the play's theme.

Another instance, this time from Shakespeare: the action of

Anthony and Cleopatra is, I should say, Antony's transformation into a woman or a womanish man; this is inevitable once Cleopatra's charm for him has become absolute. Here is the real event in the play which the particular incidents serve to advance or express. There is a speech in which the play's action is stated in a very clear symbolism: Cleopatra tells her attendants:

> That time? O times!
> I laugh'd him out of patience; and that night
> I laugh'd him into patience; and next morn
> Ere the ninth hour I drunk him to his bed,
> Then put my tires and mantles on him, whilst
> I wore his sword Philippan.

What actually happens in the play? Antony puts on morally and militarily Cleopatra's tires and mantles; she takes his sword Philippan, determining him to fight at sea when his military advisers and common sense dictate that he fight on land; she also gets him to break off the naval engagement and try to escape, when, once committed to battle, he should have continued fighting. Now Shakespeare clearly wanted his audience to adore Antony for having allowed Cleopatra to make him womanish. Enobarbus, Antony's hardheaded military adviser, is so disgusted with Antony for basing his decisions on Cleopatra's whims and thereby incurring defeat that he goes over to Antony's enemy Octavius; whereupon Antony, hearing of his desertion, sends word to Enobarbus of his, Antony's, forgiveness. And Enobarbus kills himself. Certainly Shakespeare must have calculated that members of any audience, watching *Antony and Cleopatra,* would not think of themselves as more hardheaded than Enobarbus. If this man would yield to the magic of Antony's magnanimity and womanishness, how could they not? As a further subtlety Shakespeare put the fullest statement of Cleopatra's power of sex and enchantment in the mouth of Enobarbus who delivers the famous speech:

> The barge she sat in, like a burnish'd throne,
> Burn'd on the water.

The action of *Antony and Cleopatra* is the transformation of Antony into a woman, or a womanish man; but what is the theme of the play? It is the power of the erotic: the mysterious, mystical power of the erotic, represented at first by Cleopatra, the eastern queen, who captivates the noblest male and military figure of the Roman world. And it is interesting to compare the relation of theme to action in this play with the relation of theme to action in Shaw's masterpiece. In both plays the protagonist is defeated by a woman. In Shaw's play the defeated hero is forced to accept fully the consequences of his own true view of life; in Shakespeare's play the defeated hero is forced to accept the one true magic of which he, the Roman male, by becoming womanish, is finally the noblest representative. And in both plays by the subtle interrelationship of theme and action an effect is achieved scarcely to be found outside of a very few—and these are the greatest— tragedies: the effect I would call one of the successful defeat. Is there anything more subtle in the theater?

If it is the theme of a play which makes its action important, what determines the importance of its theme? I am tempted to say the theme's truth, its validity, but this judgment simply will not do; the theme of a play may not be statable in such a way that it can be judged true or false. The theme may express nothing more than a mood, an excitement, an exaltation, a despair, and not the kind of judgment which can be examined, proved, or disproved. There is a sense, too, in which the importance of the theme is tested by the play itself, by whether it makes the play important. However, there are themes which can be clearly stated. And the truth or falsity of such themes may determine the validity of the play as a whole.

Let me make this point more clearly: Take two of Jean Genet's plays, *The Maids* and *The Blacks*. The themes of both plays, stated as ideas, are strangely antithetical. The theme of the earlier play, *The Maids*, when stated, will be seen to be a false idea; and as a consequence, I think, the action of the play is false, too; the characters also are false. To be sure, Genet has a liking for the false. But if he liked only that, he would not be the playwright he is. The theme of *The Blacks,* on the other hand, is a true and significant one; and, as a result, the action, while it, too, can be termed false in the sense that it is limited to the putting on of a show, does have some real and significant consequence off-stage; moreover, one we accept. And the characters, while not highly complex or interesting dramatic figures, strike us as authentic; they ring true and are meant to ring true. Claire and Solange in *The Maids* do not.

Both plays treat relations between masters and servants, master and slave, if you like. But the idea expressed by Genet in *The Maids* is that whoever has been servile can never achieve freedom or equality; the servants in *The Maids,* according to Genet, can never be on an equal footing with the "Madame" of that play. Now while this idea does express a certain feeling all persons in a position of social inferiority must have experienced at some time or other, as an idea it is false; the slave can indeed liberate himself, the servant become the master, the maids can become equal to Madame. In both *The Maids* and *The Blacks* Genet is treating in very different ways the notion expressed by Hegel that the master, recognized by the slave, does not recognize the slave. Thus in *The Maids* the two servants want most of all to get Madame, their mistress, to recognize them. And they are so intent on being recognized they are even willing for Madame to discover how they are trying to kill her. In fact, they do not really believe that by killing Madame they will be able to force her to recognize them. As a result, their action is a fake action. Finally, one of the maids puts on Madame's clothes and drinks the poison they have prepared for her.

A much truer idea, also stated very powerfully in Hegel, is that one of the great moments of history, possibly the greatest, comes when the master is forced to recognize the slave. This is a revolutionary, a culminating moment. The preparation for this moment is dramatized by Genet in *The Blacks*. In this play the Blacks are preparing themselves to force real recognition of themselves by their white masters. And we see a rehearsal of that recognition, not the real thing, in the second part of the play in which the white Queen, the white General, the white Bishop, the white Minister of State, played by Negroes wearing white masks, are killed in a mock action by the Blacks. It may be said the action is essentially a fake action. True enough, there always has to be fake action in some sense in Genet's theater, but the fake action here is a genuine preparation for what may be a true action. The idea of the play is socially and philosophically positive, whereas the idea of *The Maids* is negative, defeatist, and, I think, false. Interestingly enough, it is said that Genet was disappointed when he saw *The Blacks* performed because of the social positiveness—what I have called the truth—in that work. However, a work once done, the opinion of it by its author hardly counts. It is because of the positiveness and truth and bigness, in a philosophic sense, of the idea in *The Blacks*—I am using the word "idea" here as interchangeable with "theme"—that the play had such resonance in this country, where a civil rights revolution is going on.

There are theme and action, but it is the character who joins the theme to the action in a play. A character can be important if the theme is important, interesting if the action is; he can also make the theme more important, the action more interesting, than either would be without his interest, his importance. In other words, the quality of the character will add to, subtract from, or simply support the quality of the theme, of the action. Is character then merely a relation between the action and the theme of a play? Is not character also what philosophers call a "term" as opposed to a mere "relation"? I do not want to venture more than a little into metaphysics, but I am inclined to a relational or, if you like, Platonic view, rather than one which emphasizes discreet entities of any sort, particularly in drama. After all, why should the human world be so different from the world described by physicists? The molecule is a relationship among atoms, the atom a relationship among some thirty-four so-called entities, which may themselves be relationships among we do not know what. Psychologically and morally when we think seriously about anyone we think of his or her relations with others. For us to think about an individual who is unrelated to any other individual we have to suppose him related to God. We must always have at least two people in mind in order to think seriously about one person.

What do we mean, though, by a "great" character? Do we mean that those characters we call "great" owe their greatness to the theme and the action of the play they are in? But then there are plays without clear themes, without adequate action in which there are characters we call "great." For instance, Tartuffe is greater than the theme of the play Molière placed him in; and Hamlet is greater and more interesting than the action of Shakespeare's play about him. Now these two characters are among the greatest in all dramatic literature, and their interest and importance cannot be derived from the interest and importance of the themes and actions of the plays they appear in. In fact, so interesting is Hamlet that he makes action in the play about him almost unnecessary, though not quite, to be sure. The play is faulty. So important is it that someone like Tartuffe exists that the theme of the play he is in is absorbed almost totally into his character. Moreover, it is Tartuffe who makes the action interesting. So there is the great character, not great because of the great importance of the theme, not interesting because of the interest of the action. In some way, characters are "terms," too, not just relations.

Are there great characters only in faulty plays? Certainly there is something about the character of a character which makes him not want to be merely a relation between the theme and the action of the play in which he is placed. There is something revolutionary in character, in revolt against the very laws of drama. The more true characters there are in a play, the harder it is to give that play a real unity. Nevertheless, let us not be misled by modern taste too far in our admiration for the character of character. I do not believe that the theater can ever become entirely a place for characters and character-worship, as Carlyle thought life could be a theater for heroes and hero-worship. Besides, we admire characters for the situation, fortunate or unfortunate, in which they are placed by chance, as well as for their own traits. And we admire characters also for what they represent even as we admire them for personal inclinations of one sort or another. In any case, dramatic character cannot exist in the absence of dramatic theme or dramatic action. A character can exist with only one of these and without the other, also at the expense of the other; but a character cannot exist independently of both theme and action. Here the playwright may have to make a choice. Which does he prefer, the great character in the faulty play or the perfect play in which there is nobody greater than the play itself?

There are plays, though, in which the great character is great in accordance with the needs of the action and the theme, and in his or her greatness fulfills the play's requirements. Such a character is Hedda Gabler. As a matter of fact, in Ibsen's play not only Hedda herself but the other main characters serve to connect action and theme. However, of all the characters only Hedda can be called great in her own right. What is the action of the play? The destruction of Lovborg's manuscript—hence of Lovborg. Now Lovborg is the only person in the play who seems to have escaped the brutal conformism of bourgeois life—and the play's theme is the lack of adventure and inspiration in this life. Lovborg has escaped its constriction through disregard for academic success and the emotional support of Thea who loves him—though she is married to someone else. Hedda, who does not love her husband, does not want to inspire, except to his destruction, anyone who is not her husband. So her perfect victim is Lovborg, who has escaped from what she cannot escape. The remarkable thing about Hedda, if we think of her as a character in a play, is that every facet of her personality—and she is marvelously rich in traits—serves to connect the burning of Lovborg's manuscript with the whole play's accusation of that world in which this manuscript is the only indication of genuine life. But Tesman, who is content to be mediocre, and Judge Brack, who wants to escape conformism through unacknowledged affairs with other men's wives, also connect action and theme. In fact, the most extraordinary thing about *Hedda Gabler* is that every character is functional to the highest degree. But Hedda is more than functional. She is the woman Europe and America have seen for the last seventy-five years since she appeared on Ibsen's stage. Hedda with her boredom, her cowardice, her desire for power, her greater interest in women than in men, her yearning for and fear of adventure, her hatred of anyone who can have adventure, is of course still with us. But in Ibsen's play all these traits of her character connect the playwright's judgment of bourgeois society with the intrigue which leads to Lovborg's and Hedda's destruction. There is no play, or novel, for that matter, which outlines as precisely as does Ibsen's what is lacking in middle-class life and society. But Hedda Gabler is the perfect expression through her action of what the middle class is wanting in.

Your play will have an action, a theme, and characters. And your play will, of course, be written in dialogue. Now, what is dialogue?

Risky though it be to disagree with Greek thought, I will make bold to assert that dialogue is the very soul of the play, and not its plot or its action, as Aristotle held. For dialogue is the living element of the play, the medium in which the truth of the characters, the interest of action, the importance of the theme, the ability of the character or characters to join theme to action are determined. Dialogue is not expressed only by people on the stage; before the curtain goes up, it is already present, it haunts the audience. People in the theater will not be silenced by silence, only by speech on the stage itself. Whose speech? The speech of the characters, to be sure, and true dialogue must advance the action, express the theme, and be the true utterance of those characters who mediate between the action and the theme. But dialogue is even more than these things. It is also the voice, or different voices, of the playwright himself; and beyond that it is the voice of the civilization or culture of which he is a member and in support of which in some ultimate sense he has conceived his action, theme, and characters. The dialogue in the French plays of the seventeenth century was for the most part in alexandrines, never spoken in real life. In Elizabethan England, people even in court did not talk blank verse; on the stage they did.

Dialogue, what is said on the stage, is also what the characters, given their circumstances, ought to say, and not just what they might be likely to say; so there is an idealizing element in dialogue. Othello, to stop the fighting, says: "Put up your bright swords or the dew will rust them." This, which Othello does say, is also so perfectly what he ought to have said that we cannot fail to be touched by it. Of course, Othello was able to speak in Shakespeare's blank verse. That measure or any alternative verse measure can no longer be the medium in which a character in a given predicament says not only what he wants to say but also what he ought to say under the circumstances. Because of historical development of our language, the medium of verse can, I think, no longer reveal to the playwright the perfect expression of his characters—what they ought to say. Because poetry seems an ideal expression, we tend to think, but I believe wrongly, that the idealizing element in dialogue is somehow dependent on verse form. This is not the case, as the plays of Ibsen, Chekhov, and Shaw illustrate abundantly. When in *Major Barbara* the Salvation Army commander, having received a sum of money from Andrew Undershaft, exclaims, "Thank God," the millionaire replies, "Why not thank me?" the retort is what Undershaft, given his character and position, ought to say, just as much so as the line of Othello I cited. Certainly dialogue must never lose this idealizing element, as it so often does in extremely naturalistic or realistic theater pieces. The idealizing element is a constant in the theater, not a variable. But the modes of idealizing are variable, and historically determined. The poet who wants to write a play in verse perhaps thinks it would be wonderful to make everyone speak poetry. My answer to this is that he has perhaps a superficial view of poetry in mind, making it dependent on verse form. There was no greater master of verse in English poetry than Milton, but there is not one speech in the one play he wrote, *Samson Agonistes*, equal in poetic and dramatic force to Samson's simple utterance in the Bible just before he pulls the pillars of the temple down on himself and on the Philistines: "Now for my two eyes, Lord." This is what Samson ought to have said. He says this in the Bible, and not in Milton's verse.

In the theater the true character of a civilization, what it has been, what it is, and what it is likely to become are all revealed, and revealed in the speech of the characters. For the right way of saying the right thing is fateful. So it is not that good plays in verse cannot be written any more. Perhaps they can. In such plays, though, the destiny of our language, the destiny of our sense of appropriateness, of our feeling for the right word in the right context cannot be expressed any more. Since the Elizabethans the verse form has not been creative of true dialogue.

Theme, action, character, and dialogue in a true play form a living whole. If I have not completely dissociated these elements in the play's structure this is because they are not really elements. Separated and discreet, they become unreal and abstract. They are concrete and real only in actual plays. I have tried to do thus far something essentially contradictory: to separate what I consider to be inseparable, and to treat in isolation what I believe cannot exist as isolated, cannot be real as isolated, but only as organically joined together. As I said at the start, it is not really possible to tell you how the play you want to write should be written.

✖ ALL THAT FALL, a radio play
Samuel Beckett

(A SELECTION)

*Rural sounds. Sheep, bird, cow, cock, severally, then together.
Silence.*

*Mrs. Rooney advances along country road towards railway station.
Sound of her dragging feet.*

*Music faint from house by way. "Death and the Maiden." The
steps slow down, stop.*

MRS. ROONEY: Poor woman. All alone in that ruinous old house.

Music louder. Silence but for music playing.

*The steps resume. Music dies. Mrs. Rooney murmurs melody.
Her murmur dies.*

*Sound of approaching cartwheels. The cart stops. The steps
slow down, stop.*

MRS. ROONEY: Is that you, Christy?

CHRISTY: It is, Ma'am.

MRS. ROONEY: I thought the hinny was familiar. How is your poor
wife?

CHRISTY: No better, Ma'am.

MRS. ROONEY: Your daughter then?

CHRISTY: No worse, Ma'am.

Silence.

MRS. ROONEY: Why do you halt? (*Pause.*) But why do I halt?

Silence.

CHRISTY: Nice day for the races, Ma'am.

MRS. ROONEY: No doubt it is. (*Pause.*) But will it hold up? (*Pause. With emotion.*) Will it hold up?

Silence.

CHRISTY: I suppose you wouldn't—

MRS. ROONEY: Hist! (*Pause.*) Surely to goodness that cannot be the up mail I hear already?

Silence. The hinny neighs. Silence.

CHRISTY: Damn the mail.

MRS. ROONEY: Oh thank God for that! I could have sworn I heard it, thundering up the track in the far distance. (*Pause.*) So hinnies whinny. Well, it is not surprising.

CHRISTY: I suppose you wouldn't be in need of a small load of dung?

MRS. ROONEY: Dung? What class of dung?

CHRISTY: Stydung.

MRS. ROONEY: Stydung . . . I like your frankness, Christy. (*Pause.*) I'll ask the master. (*Pause.*) Christy.

CHRISTY: Yes, Ma'am.

MRS. ROONEY: Do you find anything . . . bizarre about my way of speaking? (*Pause.*) No, I mean the words. (*Pause. More to herself.*) I use none but the simplest words, I hope, and yet I sometimes find my way of speaking very . . . bizarre. (*Pause.*) Mercy! What was that?

CHRISTY: Never mind her, Ma'am, she's very fresh in herself to-day.

Silence.

MRS. ROONEY: Dung? What would we want with dung, at our time of life? (*Pause.*) Why are you on your feet down on the road? Why do you not climb up on the crest of our manure and let yourself be carried along? Is it that you have no head for heights?

Silence.

CHRISTY (*to the hinny*): Yep! (*Pause. Louder.*) Yep wiyya to hell owwa that!

Silence.

MRS. ROONEY: She does not move a muscle. (*Pause.*) I too should be getting along, if I do not wish to arrive late at the station. (*Pause.*) But a moment ago she neighed and pawed the ground. And now she refuses to advance. Give her a good welt on the rump. (*Sound of welt. Pause.*) Harder! (*Sound of welt. Pause.*) Well! If someone were to do that for me I should not dally. (*Pause.*) How she gazes at me to be sure, with her great moist cleg-tormented eyes! Perhaps if I were to move on, down the road, out of her field of vision . . . (*Sound of welt.*) No, no, enough! Take her by the snaffle and pull her eyes away from me. Oh this is awful! (*She moves on. Sound of her dragging feet.*) What have I done to deserve all this, what, what? (*Dragging feet.*) So long ago . . . No! No! (*Dragging feet. Quotes.*) "Sigh out a something something tale of things, Done long ago and ill done." (*She halts.*) How can I go on, I cannot. Oh let me just flop down flat on the road like a big fat jelly out of a bowl and never move again! A great big slop thick with grit and dust and flies, they would have to scoop me up with a shovel. (*Pause.*) Heavens, there is that up mail again, what will become of me! (*The dragging steps resume.*) Oh I am just a hysterical old hag I know, destroyed with sorrow and pining and gentility and church-going and fat and rheumatism and childlessness. (*Pause. Brokenly.*) Minnie! Little Minnie! (*Pause.*) Love, that is all I asked, a little love, daily, twice daily, fifty years of twice daily love like a Paris horsebutcher's regular, what normal woman wants affection? A peck on the jaw at morning, near the ear, and another at evening, peck, peck, till you grow whiskers on you. There is that lovely laburnum again.

Dragging feet. Sound of bicycle-bell. It is old Mr. Tyler coming up behind her on his bicycle, on his way to the station. Squeak of brakes. He slows down and rides abreast of her.

MR. TYLER: Mrs. Rooney! Pardon me if I do not doff my cap, I'd fall off. Divine day for the meeting.

MRS. ROONEY: Oh, Mr. Tyler, you startled the life out of me stealing up behind me like that like a deer-stalker! Oh!

MR. TYLER (*playfully*): I rang my bell, Mrs. Rooney, the moment I sighted you I started tinkling my bell, now don't you deny it.

MRS. ROONEY: Your bell is one thing, Mr. Tyler, and you are another. What news of your daughter?

MR. TYLER: Fair, fair. They removed everything, you know, the whole . . . er . . . bag of tricks. Now I am grandchildless.

Dragging feet.

MRS. ROONEY: Gracious how you wobble! Dismount, for mercy's sake, or ride on.

MR. TYLER: Perhaps if I were to lay my hand lightly on your shoulder, Mrs. Rooney, how would that be? (*Pause.*) Would you permit that?

MRS. ROONEY: No, Mr. Rooney, Mr. Tyler I mean, I am tired of light old hands on my shoulders and other senseless places, sick and tired of them. Heavens, here comes Connolly's van! (*She halts. Sound of motor-van. It approaches, passes with thunderous rattle, recedes.*) Are you all right, Mr. Tyler? (*Pause.*) Where is he? (*Pause.*) Ah there you are! (*The dragging steps resume.*) That was a narrow squeak.

MR. TYLER: I alit in the nick of time.

MRS. ROONEY: It is suicide to be abroad. But what is it to be at home, Mr. Tyler, what is it to be at home? A lingering dissolution. Now we are white with dust from head to foot. I beg your pardon?

MR. TYLER: Nothing, Mrs. Rooney, nothing, I was merely cursing, under my breath, and the wet Saturday afternoon of my conception. My back tire has gone down again. I pumped it hard as iron before I set out. And now I am on the rim.

MRS. ROONEY: Oh what a shame!

MR. TYLER: Now if it were the front I should not so much mind. But the back. The back! The chain! The oil! The grease! The hub! The brakes! The gear! No! It is too much!

Dragging feet.

MRS. ROONEY: Let us halt a moment and this vile dust fall back upon the viler worms.

Silence. Rural sounds.

MR. TYLER: What a sky! What light! Ah in spite of it all it is a blessed thing to be alive in such weather, and out of hospital.

MRS. ROONEY: Alive?

MR. TYLER: Well half alive shall we say?

MRS. ROONEY: Speak for yourself, Mr. Tyler. I am not half alive nor anything approaching it. (*Pause.*) What are we standing here for? This dust will not settle in our time. And when it does some great roaring machine will come and whirl it all skyhigh again.

MR. TYLER: Well, shall we be getting along in that case?

MRS. ROONEY: No.

MR. TYLER: Come, Mrs. Rooney—

MRS. ROONEY: Go, Mr. Tyler, go on and leave me, listening to the cooing of the ringdoves. (*Cooing.*) If you see my poor blind Dan tell him I was on my way to meet him when it all came over me again, like a flood. Say to him, Your poor wife, she told me to tell you it all came flooding over her again and . . . (*the voice breaks*) . . . she simply went back home . . . straight back home . . .

MR. TYLER: Come, Mrs. Rooney, come, the mail has not yet gone up, just take my free arm and we'll be there with time and to spare.

MRS. ROONEY (*sobbing*): What? What's all this now? (*Calmer.*) Can't you see I'm in trouble? (*With anger.*) Have you no respect for misery? (*Sobbing.*) Minnie! Little Minnie!

MR. TYLER: Come, Mrs. Rooney, come, the mail has not yet gone up, just take my free arm and we'll be there with time and to spare.

MRS. ROONEY (*brokenly.*): In her forties now she'd be, I don't know, fifty, girding up her lovely little loins, getting ready for the change . . .

MR. TYLER: Come, Mrs. Rooney, come, the mail—

MRS. ROONEY (*exploding*): Will you get along with you, Mr. Rooney, Mr. Tyler I mean, will you get along with you now and cease molesting me? What kind of a country is this where a woman can't weep her heart out on the highways and by-ways without being tormented by retired bill brokers! (*Mr. Tyler prepares to mount his bicycle.*) Heavens, you're not going to ride her flat! (*Mr. Tyler mounts.*) You'll tear your tube to ribbons! (*Mr. Tyler rides off. Receding sound of bumping bicycle. Silence. Cooing.*) Venus birds! Billing in the woods all the long summer long. (*Pause.*) Oh cursed corset! If I could let it out, without indecent exposure. Mr. Tyler! Mr. Tyler! Come back and unlace me behind the hedges. (*She laughs wildly, ceases.*) What's wrong with me, what's wrong with me, never tranquil, seething out of my dirty old pelt, out of my skull, oh to be in atoms, in atoms! (*Frenziedly.*) ATOMS! (*Silence. Cooing. Faintly.*) Jesus! (*Pause.*) Jesus!

Sound of car coming up behind her. It slows down and draws up beside her, engine running. It is Mr. Slocum, the Clerk of the Racecourse.

MR. SLOCUM: Is anything wrong, Mrs. Rooney: You are bent all double. Have you a pain in the stomach?

Silence. Mrs. Rooney laughs wildly. Finally.

MRS. ROONEY: Well, if it isn't my old admirer, the Clerk of the Course, in his limousine.

MR. SLOCUM: May I offer you a lift, Mrs. Rooney? Are you going in my direction?

MRS. ROONEY: I am, Mr. Slocum, we all are. (*Pause.*) How is your poor mother?

MR. SLOCUM: Thank you, she is fairly comfortable. We manage to keep her out of pain. That is the great thing, Mrs. Rooney, is it not?

MRS. ROONEY: Yes, indeed, Mr. Slocum, that is the great thing, I don't know how you do it. (*Pause. She slaps her cheek violently.*) Ah these wasps!

MR. SLOCUM (*coolly*): May I then offer you a seat, Madam?

MRS. ROONEY (*with exaggerated enthusiasm*): Oh that would be heavenly, Mr. Slocum, just simply heavenly. (*Dubiously.*) But would I ever get in, you look very high off the ground to-day, these new balloon tires, I presume. (*Sound of door opening and Mrs. Rooney trying to get in.*) Does this roof never come off? No? (*Efforts of Mrs. Rooney.*) No . . . I'll never do it . . . you'll have to get down, Mr. Slocum, and help me from the rear. (*Pause.*) What was that? (*Pause. Aggrieved.*) This is all your suggestion, Mr. Slocum, not mine. Drive on, Sir, drive on.

MR. SLOCUM (*switching off the engine*): I'm coming, Mrs. Rooney, I'm coming, give me time, I'm as stiff as yourself.

Sound of Mr. Slocum extracting himself from driver's seat.

MRS. ROONEY: Stiff! Well I like that! And me heaving all over back and front. (*To herself*). The dry old reprobate!

MR. SLOCUM (*in position behind her*): Now, Mrs. Rooney, how shall we do this?

MRS. ROONEY: As if I were a bale, Mr. Slocum, don't be afraid. (*Pause. Sounds of effort.*) That's the way! (*Effort.*) Lower! (*Effort.*) Wait! (*Pause.*) Suppose I do get up, will I ever get down?

MR. SLOCUM (*breathing hard*): You'll get down, Mrs. Rooney, you'll get down. We may not get you up, but I warrant you we'll get you down.

He resumes his efforts. Sound of these.

MRS. ROONEY: Oh! . . . Lower . . . Don't be afraid! . . . We're past the age when . . . There! . . . Now! . . . Get your shoulder under it. . . . Oh! . . . (*Giggles*) Oh glory! . . . Up! UP. . . Ah! . . . I'm in! (*Panting of Mr. Slocum. He slams the door. In a scream.*) My frock! You've nipped my frock! (*Mr. Slocum opens the door. Mrs. Rooney frees her frock. Mr. Slocum slams the door. His violent unintelligible muttering as he walks round to the other door. Tearfully.*) My nice frock! Look what you've done to my nice frock! (*Mr. Slocum gets into his seat, slams driver's door, presses starter. The engine does not start. He releases starter.*) What will Dan say when he sees me?

MR. SLOCUM: Has he then recovered his sight?

MRS. ROONEY: No, I mean when he knows, what will he say when he feels the hole? (*Mr. Slocum presses starter. As before. Silence.*) What are you doing, Mr. Slocum?

MR. SLOCUM: Gazing straight before me, Mrs. Rooney, through the windscreen, into the void.

MRS. ROONEY: Start her up I beseech you, and let us be off. This is awful!

MR. SLOCUM (*dreamily*): All morning she went like a dream and now she is dead. That is what you get for a good deed. (*Pause. Hopefully.*) Perhaps if I were to choke her. (*He does so, presses the starter. The engine roars. Roaring to make himself heard.*) She was getting too much air!

He throttles down, grinds in his first gear, moves off, changes up in a grinding of gears.

MRS. ROONEY (*in anguish*): Mind the hen! (*Scream of brakes. Squawk of hen.*) Oh mother, you have squashed her, drive on, drive on! (*The car accelerates. Pause.*) What a death! One minute picking happy at dung, on the road, in the sun, with now and then a dust bath, and then—bang! all her troubles over. (*Pause.*) All the laying and the hatching. (*Pause.*) Just one great squawk and then . . . peace. (*Pause.*) They would have slit her weasand in any case. (*Pause.*) Here we are, let me down. (*The car slows down, stops, engine running. Mr. Slocum blows his horn. Pause. Louder. Pause.*) What are you up to now, Mr. Slocum? We are at a standstill, all danger is past and you blow your horn. Now if instead of blowing it now you had blown it at the unfortunate—

Horn violently. Tommy the porter appears at top of station steps.

MR. SLOCUM (*calling*): Will you come down, Tommy, and help this lady out, she's stuck. (*Tommy descends the steps.*) Open the door, Tommy, and ease her out.

Tommy opens the door.

TOMMY: Certainly, Sir. Nice day for the races, Sir. What would you fancy for—

MRS. ROONEY: Don't mind me. Don't take any notice of me. I do not exist. The fact is well known.

MR. SLOCUM: Do as you're asked, Tommy, for the love of God.

TOMMY: Yessir. Now, Mrs. Rooney. (*He starts pulling her out.*)

MRS. ROONEY: Wait, Tommy, wait now, don't bustle me, just let me wheel round and get my feet to the ground. (*Her efforts to achieve this.*) Now.

TOMMY (*pulling her out*): Mind your feather, Ma'am. (*Sounds of effort.*) Easy now, easy.

MRS. ROONEY: Wait, for God's sake, you'll have me beheaded.

TOMMY: Crouch down, Mrs. Rooney, crouch down, and get your head in the open.

MRS. ROONEY: Crouch down! At my time of life! This is lunacy!

TOMMY: Press her down, Sir. (*Sounds of combined efforts.*)

MRS. ROONEY: Merde!

TOMMY: Now! She's coming! Straighten up, Ma'am! There! (*Mr. Slocum slams the door.*)

MRS. ROONEY: Am I out?

The voice of Mr. Barrell, the stationmaster, raised in anger.

MR. BARRELL: Tommy! Tommy! Where the hell is he?

Mr. Slocum grinds in his gear.

TOMMY (*hurriedly*): You wouldn't have something for the Ladies Plate, Sir, I was given Flash Harry.

MR. SLOCUM (*Scornfully*): Flash Harry! That carthorse!

MR. BARRELL (*at top of steps, roaring*): Tommy! Blast your bleeding bloody—(*He sees Mrs. Rooney.*) Oh, Mrs. Rooney . . .
(*Mr. Slocum drives away in a grinding of gears.*) Who's that
crucifying his gearbox, Tommy?

TOMMY: Old Cissy Slocum.

MRS. ROONEY: Cissy Slocum! That's a nice way to refer to your
betters. Cissy Slocum! And you an orphan!

MR. BARRELL (*angrily to Tommy*): What are you doing stravaging
down here on the public road? This is no place for you at all!
Nip up there on the platform now and whip out the truck!
Won't the twelve-thirty be on top of us before we can turn
around?

TOMMY (*bitterly*): And that's the thanks you get for a Christian
act.

MR. BARRELL (*violently*): Get on with you now before I report
you! (*Slow feet of Tommy climbing steps.*) Do you want me
to come down to you with the shovel? (*The feet quicken,
recede, cease.*) Ah, God forgive me, it's a hard life. (*Pause.*)
Well, Mrs. Rooney, it's nice to see you up and about again.
You were laid up there a long time.

MRS. ROONEY: Not long enough, Mr. Barrell. (*Pause.*) Would I
were still in bed, Mr. Barrell. (*Pause.*) Would I were lying
stretched out in my comfortable bed, Mr. Barrell, just wasting
slowly painlessly away, keeping up my strength with arrow-
root and calves-foot jelly, till in the end you wouldn't see me
under the blankets any more than a board. (*Pause.*) Oh no
coughing or spitting or bleeding or vomiting, just drifting
gently down into the higher life, and remembering, remembering . . . (*the voice breaks*) . . . all the silly unhappiness . . .
as though . . . it had never happened . . . what did I do with
that handkerchief? (*Sound of handkerchief loudly applied.*)
How long have you been master of this station now, Mr.
Barrell?

MR. BARRELL: Don't ask me, Mrs. Rooney, don't ask me.

MRS. ROONEY: You stepped into your father's shoes, I believe, when
he took them off.

MR. BARRELL: Poor Pappy! (*Reverent pause.*) He didn't live long to enjoy his ease.

MRS. ROONEY: I remember him clearly. A small ferrety purple-faced widower, deaf as a doornail, very testy and snappy. (*Pause.*) I suppose you'll be retiring soon yourself, Mr. Barrell, and growing your roses. (*Pause.*) Did I understand you to say the twelve-thirty would soon be upon us?

MR. BARRELL: Those were my words.

MRS. ROONEY: But according to my watch, which is more or less right—or was—by the eight o'clock news, the time is now coming up to twelve ... (*pause as she consults her watch*) ... thirty-six. (*Pause.*) And yet upon the other hand the up mail has not yet gone through. (*Pause.*) Or has it sped by unbeknown to me? (*Pause.*) For there was a moment there, I remember now, I was so plunged in sorrow I wouldn't have heard a steam roller go over me. (*Pause. Mr. Barrell turns to go.*) Don't go, Mr. Barrell! (*Mr. Barrell goes. Loud.*) Mr. Barrell! (*Pause. Louder.*) Mr. Barrell!

Mr. Barrell comes back.

MR. BARRELL (*testily*): What is it, Mrs. Rooney, I have my work to do.

Silence. Sound of wind.

MRS. ROONEY: The wind is getting up. (*Pause. Wind.*) The best of the day is over. (*Pause. Wind. Dreamily.*) Soon the rain will begin to fall and go on falling, all afternoon. (*Mr. Barrell goes.*) Then at evening the clouds will part, the setting sun will shine an instant, then sink, behind the hills. (*She realizes Mr. Barrell has gone.*) Mr. Barrell! Mr. Barrell! (*Silence.*) I estrange them all. They come towards me, uninvited, bygones, bygones, full of kindness, anxious to help ... (*the voice breaks*) ... genuinely pleased ... to see me again ... looking so well ... (*Handkerchief.*) A few simple words ... from my heart ... and I am all alone ... once more ... (*Handkerchief. Vehemently.*) I should not be out at all! I should never leave the grounds! (*Pause.*) Oh there is that Fitt woman, I wonder will she bow to me. (*Sound of Miss Fitt approaching, humming a hymn. She starts climbing the steps.*) Miss Fitt! (*Miss*

Fitt halts, stops humming.) Am I then invisible, Miss Fitt? Is this cretonne so becoming to me that I merge into the masonry? (*Miss Fitt descends a step.*) That is right, Miss Fitt, look closely and you will finally distinguish a once female shape.

MISS FITT: Mrs. Rooney! I saw you, but I did not know you.

MRS. ROONEY: Last Sunday we worshipped together. We knelt side by side at the same altar. We drank from the same chalice. Have I so changed since then?

MISS FITT (*shocked*): Oh but in church, Mrs. Rooney, in church I am alone with my Maker. Are not you? (*Pause.*) Why, even the sexton himself, you know, when he takes up the collection, knows it is useless to pause before me. I simply do not see the plate, or bag, whatever it is they use, how could I? (*Pause.*) Why even when all is over and I go out into the sweet fresh air, why even then for the first furlong or so I stumble in a kind of daze as you might say, oblivious to my coreligionists. And they are very kind, I must admit—the vast majority—very kind and understanding. They know me now and take no umbrage. There she goes, they say, there goes the dark Miss Fitt, alone with her Maker, take no notice of her. And they step down off the path to avoid my running into them. (*Pause.*) Ah yes, I am distray, very distray, even on week-days. Ask Mother, if you do not believe me. Hetty, she says, when I start eating my doily instead of the thin bread and butter, Hetty, how can you be so distray? (*Sighs.*) I suppose the truth is I am not there, Mrs. Rooney, just not really there at all. I see, hear, smell and so on, I go through the usual motions, but my heart is not in it, Mrs. Rooney, but heart is in none of it. Left to myself, with no one to check me, I would soon be flown . . . home. (*Pause.*) So if you think I cut you just now, Mrs. Rooney, you do me an injustice. All I saw was a big pale blur, just another big pale blur. (*Pause.*) Is anything amiss, Mrs. Rooney, you do not look normal somehow. So bowed and bent.

MRS. ROONEY (*ruefully*): Maddy Rooney, nee Dunne, the big pale blur. (*Pause.*) You have piercing sight, Miss Fitt, if you only knew it, literally piercing.

Pause.

MISS FITT: Well . . . is there anything I can do, now that I am here?

MRS. ROONEY: If you would help me up the face of this cliff, Miss Fitt, I have little doubt your Maker would requite you, if no one else.

MISS FITT: Now, now, Mrs. Rooney, don't put your teeth in me. Requite! I make these sacrifices for nothing—or not at all. (*Pause. Sound of her descending steps.*) I take it you want to lean on me, Mrs. Rooney.

MRS. ROONEY: I asked Mr. Barrell to give me his arm, just give me his arm. (*Pause.*) He turned on his heel and strode away.

MISS FITT: Is it my arm you want then? (*Pause. Impatiently.*) Is it my arm you want, Mrs. Rooney, or what is it?

MRS. ROONEY (*exploding*): Your arm! Any arm! A helping hand! For five seconds! Christ, what a planet!

MISS FITT: Really . . . Do you know what it is, Mrs. Rooney, I do not think it is wise of you to be going about at all.

MRS. ROONEY (*violently*): Come down here, Miss Fitt, and give me your arm, before I scream down the parish!

Pause. Wind. Sound of Miss Fitt descending last steps.

MISS FITT (*resignedly*): Well, I suppose it is the Protestant thing to do.

MRS. ROONEY: Pismires do it for one another. (*Pause.*) I have seen slugs do it. (*Miss Fitt proffers her arm.*) No, the other side, my dear, if it's all the same to you, I'm left-handed on top of everything else. (*She takes Miss Fitt's right arm.*) Heavens, child, you're just a bag of bones, you need building up. (*Sound of her toiling up steps on Miss Fitt's arm.*) This is worse than the Matterhorn, were you ever up the Matterhorn, Miss Fitt, great honeymoon resort. (*Sound of toiling.*) Why don't they have a hand rail? (*Panting.*) Wait till I get some air. (*Pause.*) Don't let me go. (*Miss Fitt hums her hymn. After a moment Mrs. Rooney joins in with the words.*) . . . the encircling gloo-oom (*Miss Fitt stops humming.*) . . . tum

tum me on. (*Forte.*) The night is dark and I am far from ho-ome, tum tum—

MISS FITT (*hysterically*): Stop it, Mrs. Rooney, stop it, or I'll drop you.

MRS. ROONEY: Wasn't it that they sung on the Lusitania? Or Rock of Ages? Most touching it must have been. Or was it the Titanic?

Attracted by the noise a group, including Mr. Tyler, Mr. Barrell and Tommy, gathers at top of steps.

MR. BARRELL: What the—

Silence.

MR. TYLER: Lovely day for the fixture.

Loud titter from Tommy cut short by Mr. Barrell with back-handed blow in the stomach. Appropriate noise from Tommy.

FEMALE VOICE (*shrill*): Oh look, Dolly, look!

DOLLY: What, Mamma?

FEMALE VOICE: They are stuck! (*Cackling laugh.*) They are stuck!

MRS. ROONEY: Now we are the laughing stock of the twenty-six counties. Or is it thirty-six?

MR. TYLER: That is a nice way to treat your defenceless subordinates, Mr. Barrell, hitting them without warning in the pit of the stomach.

MISS FITT: Has anybody seen my mother?

MR. BARRELL: Who is that?

TOMMY: The dark Miss Fitt.

MR. BARRELL: Where is her face?

MRS. ROONEY: Now, deary, I am ready if you are. (*They toil up remaining steps.*) Stand back, you cads!

Shuffle of feet.

FEMALE VOICE: Mind yourself, Dolly!

MRS. ROONEY: Thank you, Miss Fitt, thank you, that will do, just prop me up against the wall like a roll of tarpaulin and that will be all, for the moment. (*Pause.*) I am sorry for all this ramdam, Miss Fitt, had I known you were looking for your mother I should not have importuned you, I know what it is.

MR. TYLER (*in marvelling aside*): Ramdam!

FEMALE VOICE: Come, Dolly darling, let us take up our stand before the first-class smokers. Give me your hand and hold me tight, one can be sucked under.

MR. TYLER: You have lost your mother, Miss Fitt?

MISS FITT: Good morning, Mr. Tyler.

MR. TYLER: Good morning, Miss Fitt.

MR. BARRELL: Good morning, Miss Fitt.

MISS FITT: Good morning, Mr. Barrell.

MR. TYLER: You have lost your mother, Miss Fitt?

MISS FITT: She said she would be on the last train.

MRS. ROONEY: Do not imagine, because I am silent, that I am not present, and alive, to all that is going on.

MR. TYLER (*to Miss Fitt*): When you say the last train—

MRS. ROONEY: Do not flatter yourselves for one moment, because I hold aloof, that my sufferings have ceased. No. The entire scene, the hills, the plain, the racecourse with its miles and miles of white rails and three red stands, the pretty little wayside station, even you yourselves, yes, I mean it, and over all the clouding blue, I see it all, I stand here and see it all with eyes . . . (*the voice breaks.*) . . . through eyes . . . oh, if you had my eyes . . . you would understand . . . the things they have seen . . . and not looked away . . . this is nothing . . . nothing, . . . what did I do with that handkerchief?

Pause.

MR. TYLER (*to Miss Fitt*): When you say the last train—(*Mrs. Rooney blows her nose violently and long*)—when you say the last train, Miss Fitt, I take it you mean the twelve-thirty.

MISS FITT: What else could I mean, Mr. Tyler, what else could I conceivably mean?

MR. TYLER: Then you have no cause for anxiety Miss Fitt, for the twelve-thirty has not yet arrived. Look. (*Miss Fitt looks.*) No, up the line. (*Miss Fitt looks.*) (*Patiently.*) No, Miss Fitt, follow the direction of my index. (*Miss Fitt looks.*) There. You see now. The signal. At the bawdy hour of nine. (*In rueful afterthought.*) Or three alas! (*Mr. Barrell stifles a guffaw.*) Thank you, Mr. Barrell.

MISS FITT: But the time is now getting on for—

MR. TYLER (*patiently*): We all know, Miss Fitt, we all know only too well what the time is now getting on for, and yet the cruel fact remains that the twelve-thirty has not yet arrived.

MISS FITT: Not an accident, I trust! (*Pause.*) Do not tell me she has left the track! (*Pause.*) Oh darling mother! With the fresh sole for lunch!

Loud titter from Tommy, checked as before by Mr. Barrell.

MR. BARRELL: That's enough old guff out of you. Nip up to the box now and see has Mr. Case anything for me.

Tommy goes.

MRS. ROONEY (*sadly.*): Poor Dan!

MISS FITT (*in anguish*): What terrible thing has happened?

MR. TYLER: Now now, Miss Fitt, do not—

MRS. ROONEY (*with vehement sadness*): Poor Dan!

MR. TYLER: Now now, Miss Fitt, do not give way . . . to despair, all will come right . . . in the end. (*Aside to Mr. Barrell.*) What is the situation, Mr. Barrell? Not a collision surely?

MRS. ROONEY (*enthusiastically*): A collision! Oh that would be wonderful!

MISS FITT (*horrified*): A collision. I knew it!

MR. TYLER: Come, Miss Fitt, let us move a little up the platform.

MRS. ROONEY: Yes, let us all do that. (*Pause.*) No? (*Pause.*) You have changed your mind? (*Pause.*) I quite agree, we are better here, in the shadow of the waiting room.

MR. BARRELL: Excuse me a moment.

MRS. ROONEY: Before you slink away, Mr. Barrell, please, a statement of some kind, I insist. Even the slowest train on this brief line is not ten minutes and more behind its scheduled time without good cause, one imagines. (*Pause.*) We all know your station is the best kept of the entire network, but there are times when that is not enough, just not enough. (*Pause.*) Now, Mr. Barrell, leave off chewing your whiskers, we are waiting to hear from you—we the unfortunate ticket-holders' nearest if not dearest.

Pause.

MR. TYLER (*reasonably*): I do think we are owed some kind of explanation, Mr. Barrell, if only to set our minds at rest.

MR. BARRELL: I know nothing. All I know is there has been a hitch. All traffic is retarded.

MRS. ROONEY (*derisively*): Retarded! A hitch! Ah these celibates! Here we are eating our hearts out with anxiety for our loved ones and he calls that a hitch! Those of us like myself with heart and kidney trouble may collapse at any moment and he calls that a hitch! In our ovens the Saturday roast is burning to a shrivel and he calls that—

MR. TYLER: Here comes Tommy, running! I am glad I have been spared to see this.

TOMMY (*excitedly, in the distance*): She's coming. (*Pause. Nearer.*) She's at the level-crossing!

Immediately exaggerated station sounds. Falling signals. Bells. Whistles. Crescendo of train whistle approaching. Sound of train rushing through station.

MRS. ROONEY (*above rush of train*): The up mail! The up mail! (*The up mail recedes, the down train approaches, enters the station, pulls up with great hissing of steam and clashing of couplings. Noise of passengers descending, doors banging, Mr. Barrell shouting "Boghill! Boghill!", etc. Piercingly.*)

Dan! . . . Are you all right? Where is he? . . . Dan! . . . did you see my husband? . . . Dan! . . . (*Noise of station emptying. Guard's whistle. Train departing, receding. Silence.*) He isn't on it! The misery I have endured, to get here, and he isn't on it! . . . Mr. Barrell! . . . Was he not on it? (*Pause.*) Is anything the matter, you look as if you had seen a ghost. (*Pause.*) Tommy! . . . Did you see the master?

TOMMY: He'll be along, Ma'am, Jerry is minding him.

Mr. Rooney suddenly appears on platform, advancing on small boy Jerry's arm. He is blind, thumps the ground with his stick and pants incessantly.

MRS. ROONEY: Oh, Dan! There you are! (*Her dragging feet as she hastens towards him. She reaches him. They halt.*) Where in the world were you?

MR. ROONEY (*coolly*): Maddy.

❧ MAN AND SUPERMAN

George Bernard Shaw

(A SELECTION)

THE STATUE (*impressed*): A very clever point that, Juan: I must think it over. You are really full of ideas. How did you come to think of this one?

DON JUAN: I learnt it by experience. When I was on earth, and made those proposals to ladies which, though universally condemned, have made me so interesting a hero of legend, I was not infrequently met in some such way as this. The lady would say that she would countenance my advances, provided they were honorable. On inquiring what that proviso meant, I found that it meant that I proposed to get possession of her property if she had any, or to undertake her support for life if she had not; that I desired her continual companionship, counsel, and conversation to the end of my days, and would take a most solemn oath to be always enraptured by them: above all, that I would turn my back on all other women for ever for her sake. I did not object to these conditions because they were exorbitant and inhuman: it was their extraordinary irrelevance that prostrated me. I invariably replied with perfect frankness that I had never dreamt of any of these things; that unless the lady's character and intellect were equal or superior to my own, her conversation must degrade and her counsel mislead me; that her constant companionship might, for all I knew, become intolerably tedious to me; that I could not answer for my feelings for a week in advance, much less to the end of my life; that to cut me off from all natural and unconstrained intercourse with half my fellow-creatures would narrow and warp me if I submitted to it, and, if not, would bring me under the curse of clandestinity; that, finally, my proposals to her were wholly unconnected with any of these matters, and were the outcome of a perfectly simple impulse of my manhood towards her womanhood.

ANA: You mean that it was an immoral impulse.

DON JUAN: Nature, my dear lady, is what you call immoral. I blush for it; but I cannot help it. Nature is a pandar, Time is a wrecker, and Death a murderer. I have always preferred to stand up to those facts and build institutions on their recognition. You prefer to propitiate the three devils by proclaiming their chastity, their thrift, and their loving kindness; and to base your institutions on these flatteries. Is it any wonder that the institutions do not work smoothly?

THE STATUE: What used the ladies to say, Juan?

DON JUAN: Oh, come! Confidence for confidence. First tell me what you used to say to the ladies.

THE STATUE: I! Oh, I swore that I would be faithful to the death; that I should die if they refused me; that no woman could ever be to me what she was—

ANA: She! Who?

THE STATUE: Whoever it happened to be at the time, my dear. I had certain things I always said. One of them was that even when I was eighty, one white hair of the woman I loved would make me tremble more than the thickest gold tress from the most beautiful young head. Another was that I could not bear the thought of anyone else being the mother of my children.

DON JUAN (revolted): You old rascal!

THE STATUE (stoutly): Not a bit; for I really believed it with all my soul at the moment. I had a heart: not like you. And it was this sincerity that made me successful.

DON JUAN: Sincerity! To be fool enough to believe a ramping, stamping, thumping lie: that is what you call sincerity! To be so greedy for a woman that you deceive yourself in your eagerness to deceive her: sincerity, you call it!

THE STATUE: Oh, damn your sophistries. I was a man in love, not a lawyer. And the women loved me for it, bless them!

DON JUAN: They made you think so. What will you say when I tell you that though I played the lawyer so callously, they made me think so too? I also had my moments of infatuation in which I gushed nonsense and believed it. Sometimes the desire to give pleasure by saying beautiful things so rose in me on the flood of emotion that I said them recklessly. At other times I argued against myself with a devilish coldness that drew tears. But I found it just as hard to escape when I was cruel as when I was kind. When the lady's instinct was set on me, there was nothing for it but lifelong servitude or flight.

ANA: You dare boast, before me and my father, that every woman found you irresistible.

DON JUAN: Am I boasting? It seems to me that I cut the most pitiable of figures. Besides, I said "When the lady's instinct was set on me." It was not always so; and then, heavens! what transports of virtuous indignation! what overwhelming defiance to the dastardly seducer! what scenes of Imogen and Iachimo!

ANA: I made no scenes. I simply called my father.

DON JUAN: And he came, sword in hand, to vindicate outraged honor and morality by murdering me.

THE STATUE: Murdering! What do you mean? Did I kill you or did you kill me?

DON JUAN: Which of us was the better fencer?

THE STATUE: I was.

DON JUAN: Of course you were. And yet you, the hero of those scandalous adventures you have just been relating to us, you had the effrontery to pose as the avenger of outraged morality and condemn me to death! You would have slain me but for an accident.

THE STATUE: I was expected to, Juan. That is how things were arranged on earth. I was not a social reformer; and I always did what it was customary for a gentleman to do.

DON JUAN: That may account for your attacking me, but not for the revolting hypocrisy of your subsequent proceedings as a statue.

THE STATUE: That all came of my going to heaven.

THE DEVIL: I still fail to see, Señor Don Juan, that these episodes in your earthly career and in that of the Señor Commander in any way discredit my view of life. Here, I repeat, you have all that you sought without anything that you shrank from.

DON JUAN: On the contrary, here I have everything that disappointed me without anything that I have not already tried and found wanting. I tell you that as long as I can conceive something better than myself I cannot be easy unless I am striving to bring it into existence or clearing the way for it. That is the law of my life. That is the working within me of Life's incessant aspiration to higher organization, wider, deeper, intenser self-consciousness, and clearer self-understanding. It was the supremacy of this purpose that reduced love for me to the mere schooling of my faculties, religion for me to a mere excuse for laziness, since it had set up a God who looked at the world and saw that it was good, against the instinct in me that looked through my eyes at the world and saw that it could be improved. I tell you that in the pursuit of my own pleasure, my own health, my own fortune, I have never known happiness. It was not love for Woman that delivered me into her hands: it was fatigue, exhaustion. When I was a child, and bruised my head against a stone, I ran to the nearest woman and cried away my pain against her apron. When I grew up and bruised my soul against the brutalities and stupidities with which I had to strive, I did again just what I had done as a child. I have enjoyed, too, my rests, my recuperations, my breathing times, my very prostrations after strife; but rather would I be dragged through all the circles of the foolish Italian's Inferno than through the pleasures of Europe. That is what has made this place of eternal pleasures so deadly to me. It is the absence of this instinct in you that makes you that strange monster called a Devil. It is the success with which you have diverted the attention of men from their real purpose, which in one degree or another is the same as mine, to yours, that has earned you the name of Tempter. It is the fact that they are doing your will, or rather drifting with your want of will, instead of doing their own, that makes them the uncomfortable, false, restless, artificial, petulant, wretched creatures they are.

THE DEVIL (*mortified*): Señor Don Juan: you are uncivil to my friends.

BIOGRAPHIES OF CONTRIBUTORS

PAUL ENGLE was born in Cedar Rapids, Iowa, in 1908 and began writing poetry while in high school; his book of poems *Worn Earth* won the Yale Series of Younger Poets prize and may have been the first book of poems submitted for a graduate degree in this country (an M.A. at the University of Iowa). He studied for further degrees at both Columbia and Oxford (where he was a Rhodes Scholar), and in 1937 he joined the faculty of the University of Iowa. He is the director of Iowa's program in creative writing and in addition has continued to publish poetry as well as other work including the novel *Always the Land* and the opera libretto *Golden Child;* he has also edited short story and poetry collections and has reviewed and lectured widely. He is married and has two daughters.

R. V. CASSILL was born in Cedar Falls, Iowa, in 1919, attended the State University and served four years in the Army during World War II. He is the author of many short stories and several novels. Since the late Forties his stories have appeared regularly in literary quarterlies and other magazines. Five of them appeared in a collection called *15 x 3* (with stories by Herbert Gold and James B. Hall), and more are scheduled to appear in book form soon. His novels, *Clem Anderson, Pretty Leslie,* and *The President,* have been highly praised. He has taught fiction writing at Columbia University, The New School for Social Research, University of Washington, and, for several years, the Writers' Workshop of the University of Iowa. His text *Writing Fiction* has been widely distributed and adopted for use by several college writing programs.

JEAN TODD FREEMAN was born in Mississippi and graduated from Mount Holyoke in 1951. *Seventeen* published her first story when she was a sophomore and just before graduation she sold a story to the *Ladies' Home Journal,* which then offered her a job. She was with the *Journal* for almost twelve years as a writer, reader of manuscripts, and general editor, becoming associate editor in 1958 and fiction editor in

1962. Since May 1963 she has been free-lancing. She has published not only fiction but also non-fiction and poetry in the *Journal, McCall's, Seventeen,* and *The Saturday Evening Post,* and lives in New York.

BROCK BROWER was born in 1931 in Westfield, New Jersey, and after graduating from Dartmouth, spent a year at Harvard Law School and then went to Oxford as a Rhodes Scholar. He has written short stories, plays, and poetry, as well as a number of articles which have been published in *Esquire, Show, Vogue, Mademoiselle, The New York Times Magazine, Horizon, The Saturday Evening Post,* and others. He has also been the editor of the University of North Carolina Press, assistant editor of *Esquire,* member of the staff at Bread Loaf Writers Conference, and is presently associate editor of *The Transatlantic Review.*

DONALD JUSTICE was born in Miami, Florida, in 1925. He holds degrees from the University of Miami, the University of North Carolina, and the University of Iowa; since 1957 he has taught in the Iowa Writers' Workshop. His first book was *The Summer Anniversaries,* which was the Lamont Poetry Selection for 1959; *A Local Storm* followed in 1963. His criticism has appeared in various journals, and his poetry in such magazines as *Poetry, Paris Review, The New Yorker,* and *Harper's* as well as in numerous anthologies. In the fall of 1964 he will be a Ford Fellow in theater. He is married and the father of one child.

GEORGE P. ELLIOTT was born in Indiana in 1918 and received both a B.A. and an M.A. from the University of California at Berkeley. He has taught English at St. Mary's College, Cornell, Barnard, University of Iowa, University of California at Berkeley, and is currently professor of English at Syracuse. He has published both poetry and fiction, and his books include *Fifteen Modern American Poets, Parktilden Village, Among the Dangs, Fever and Chills, David Knudsen, Types of Prose Fiction,* and *A Piece of Lettuce.*

LIONEL ABEL, born in New York City in 1910, and known for many years as a critic and French translator, became interested in writing for and on the theater in the Fifties. Three of his plays have been produced Off-Broadway, one of them, *Absolom,* winning *The Village Voice's* award for the best Off-Broadway play of 1956. Mr. Abel's theoretical work on drama, *Metatheatre,* was published in March, 1963. A new play of Mr. Abel's is to be produced in Tokyo this winter, and another new play of his is to be done at the American Place Theatre in New York this Fall. Mr. Abel has been lecturer in dramatic arts at Columbia University, has taught aesthetics at Pratt Institute, and is now giving a course in dramatic form at Rutgers University.